Paul Carr was born in 1979 but, thanks to the events described between these covers, he feels at least twenty years older. A former *Guardian* New Media columnist and co-founder of two Internet companies, he knows the world of the Internet moguls both inside and out.

Bringing Nothing to the Party

True Confessions of a New Media Whore

Paul Carr

PHOENIX

A PHOENIX PAPERBACK

First published in Great Britain in 2008
by Weidenfeld & Nicolson
This paperback edition published in 2009
by Phoenix,
an imprint of Orion Books Ltd,
Orion House, 5 Upper St Martin's Lane,
London, WC2H 9EA

An Hachette UK company

1 3 5 7 9 10 8 6 4 2

A CIP catalogue record for this book
is available from the British Library.

ISBN 978-0-7538-2399-6

Typeset by Input Data Services, Ltd
Bridgwater, Somerset

Printed and bound in the UK
by CPI Mackays, Chatham, Kent

The Orion Publishing Group's policy is to use papers
that are natural, renewable and recyclable products and
made from wood grown in sustainable forests. The logging
and manufacturing processes are expected to conform to
the environmental regulations of the country of origin.

www.orionbooks.co.uk

'I have a theory that the truth is never told during the nine-to-five hours'
Hunter S. Thompson

Contents

Prologue

September 2006, and deep in the bowels of the Adam Street private members' club in London a very special group of people is crammed into a private room, supping imported Spanish beer from a free bar.

The value – on paper at least – of the companies owned by those squeezed into this tiny, boiling space would dwarf the debt of a small African nation. Among those present are some of the key players in Europe's Internet industry. The content creators, the entrepreneurs, the inventors, the investors; these are the new media moguls. And tonight they're in their element.

I'm hiding at the back of the room getting slowly drunk with the event's organiser, an entrepreneur who helped raise a ridiculous sum of money for a business networking site that had projected revenues of precisely zero. His mantra, he tells me, is 'revenue is the enemy'. It's not clear what that means, but I have to admit it sounds great.

A microphone is being passed around and we're watching and listening as a succession of young – mostly under forty – men – they're mostly men – rattle off their CVs and their future plans.

'He,' whispers my drinking buddy, pointing the neck of his beer bottle at a short, well-groomed man wearing a yellow checked jacket and bright red trousers, 'was in the *FT* yesterday. Apparently BT are going to buy the company he co-founded for half a billion dollars.'

'Fuck,' I half-whisper back. One habit you soon pick up, hanging out with dot com entrepreneurs, is swearing. 'That's a terrible fit. It's like Friends Reunited* all over again. What the hell are BT going to do with them?'

....

* Bought by ITV for almost £150 million.

1

'Nothing.'

'Nothing?'

'No, the story's bullshit. Totally made up. And they fucking printed it.'

'Fuck.'

'Of course they printed it. They called the investors to check it out, but they refused to comment. So they ran it as a "rumour". And why not? It wouldn't exactly be the most outrageous deal of the year, would it?'

He has a point.

'Do I even want to ask who "leaked" it?' I ask.

My friend smirks and looks down at his beer bottle. He's a notorious gossip monger, and the rumour has his fingerprints all over it – not least because the man in the red trousers is one of his best friends.

Before I can respond – not that I know how to – an enormous cheer goes up. The previous introduction had come from Sean Seton-Rogers of venture capital firm Benchmark; the one before that from Angus Bankes, the technical genius behind Moreover.com, the news aggregation service that was recently sold to Verisign for $30 million ('thirty million and change', the tall American standing behind me stage-whispers to no one in particular). Angus would also – in less than a year – be hugely responsible for my future. But I didn't know that at the time.

These guys are huge players, business celebrities almost. Benchmark were the investors behind eBay; and Bankes, as well as co-founding Moreover, is the former business partner of Nick Denton, founder of Gawker.com – the super-powerful Manhattan media gossip blog whose fearless rabble-rousing and snarky commentary have struck fear into the hearts of America's old media elite and made Denton one of the most influential editors in New York. But right now, no one cares about Benchmark, or Moreover, or even Gawker.

The cheer has been reserved for Alex Tew. Twenty-one years old, baby-faced and clearly loving the adulation, Tew (pronounced 'chew') is the newest, youngest mogul in the room. Even by new media standards, he's dressed casually – baggy jeans, hoodie and horrendously expensive trainers. Trainers which, in less than a year's time, I would throw from the side of a roof-top hot tub into the streets of Soho. But I didn't know that then.

Only twelve months earlier Tew had been sitting in his grotty student flat in Nottingham, on his grotty student bed, trying to find a way to supplement his student loan without actually doing any work. Turning to a fresh page on his notepad, he had written a question. Six words: 'How can I become a millionaire?'

And with that simple question an Internet celebrity was born. After rejecting a number of possible money-spinners Tew came up with the brilliant but simple (natch) idea of setting up a website containing 10,000 tiny squares, each just ten pixels high by ten pixels wide. These pixels – all one million of them – would be sold to advertisers for a dollar each.

Tew gambled that the idea would be quirky enough to get huge media attention, driving traffic to the site and giving advertisers an audience worth paying for. The gamble paid off. The world's media loved the story and The Million Dollar Homepage sold out of pixels in less than six months. So popular was the site that it even became the target of the Russian Mafia, who bombarded it with millions of fake visitors, making it impossible for anyone else to access it. Only if Tew paid a huge ransom would they stop their attacks. Alex stood firm and used a chunk of his new-found wealth to hire a new hosting company that specialised in defending against cyber attacks. The new security measures did the trick and the extra cost was more than covered when Alex fed the story back to the press, bringing more traffic to the site and hundreds of thousands more dollars into the kitty.

In a little shy of twenty-four weeks Alex Tew went from poor student to dollar millionaire – and the crowd tonight loves him for it. Who cares if the shelf life of the business could be measured in months rather than years? Who cares that not one of the site's countless imitators has managed to turn a student scheme into a sustainable business?

The word in the room is that Tew is getting ready to launch his next venture – one he promises will make even more money than the first. I believe him. And so does the crowd.

In the old media world, successful media businesses try to build bigger and bigger newspaper circulation, or to produce long-running TV shows that will go into syndication, or long-running film franchises with career actors and merchandise spin-offs, or to create best-selling, ten-book-deal authors. Stability and longevity is the key, with the long-term cash cows allowing media owners to take risks on new talent and first-time directors and authors.

In this new media world, however, the exact opposite is true. Stability means nothing. Audience attention spans are short and a million Next Big Things are always around the corner. Fads can be created in the morning, be hugely profitable by lunch time and dead in the water by midnight.

Never have wealth and fame been so easy to achieve, and so quick to vanish. Trends change so fast that the best many new media moguls can do is 'get in, get rich, move on'. And no one in this room tonight exemplifies that ideology better than Alex Tew. A true five-minute new media mogul.

Suddenly the microphone is thrust into my hand. 'Paul Carr,' I begin. 'I'm co-founder of a web-to-print publishing company called The Friday Project and I used to write a new media column for the *Guardian* ...'

Fuck it, no one cares. I'm doing okay, making a living, but I'm a book publisher and before that I was a journalist. Old media. Not sexy, not exciting.

'... and given that I'm not trying to raise any money, I'm really just here to get drunk on Alex's tab.'

Big laugh. Excellent. Nothing to see here. Time to get drunk, safe in the knowledge that tomorrow I'll be at my desk, looking for new and interesting websites that we might be able to turn into new and interesting books.

I've been around the people in this room for my entire working life, and count many of them among my good friends. I've written about them in newspapers, and I've published their books. I go to their parties, and share their successes and failures. But I'm not *one of them*. And that's fine by me.

And yet, in the back of my mind, a little bell is ringing. Ring. This guy – this kid – is a dollar millionaire. He's four years younger than me. The Million Dollar Homepage was a bloody good idea – he deserves the success. But I'm a writer – I have a dozen good ideas before lunch – I deserve it, too. Ring. Ring. Ring.

'That's it for tonight, everyone. Finish your drinks and make your way outside.'

Suddenly my friend reappears. 'Drink up. We're going on to the Gardening Club.'

'The Gardening Club? That's a fucking dive.'

And it really is – a tiny, sweaty nightclub tucked away in a corner of Covent Garden, underneath the Rock Garden restaurant. It's a favourite of students and tourists – where the drinks are cheap and the women are available on draught.

My friend looks at me as if I'm an idiot.

'That's the point, you twat. It's student night and all the American students from the LSE* will be there. Fit, smart American girls – and a pound a drink; what's not to love?'

'I've got work tomorrow.'

'Ha. Yeah. Shut up. We're leaving in five minutes.'

I put on my coat and walk out on to the Strand, where maybe half a dozen of the Internet's brightest and best are waiting to make the five-minute walk to a dive bar for £1.00 Vodka Red Bulls and dancing until dawn.

Life doesn't get much better than this, I think.

It's amazing how wrong a person can be.

....

* London School of Economics.

1.0

'Hello World'

My love affair with technology began at an early age. On my seventh birthday, my parents bought me a second-hand ZX Spectrum and, in a foretaste of my life to come, I immediately set about learning how to use it to get attention. It's a sign of how rapidly technology develops that my crappy Spectrum, with its 48k of memory, already had 12k more storage power than the computer that had guided the Apollo 11 moon landing eighteen years earlier.* With power like that, there seemed to be no limit to what I could do.

While my other computer-owning peers would sit for hours while their tape drives squawked away loading 'Manic Miner' or 'Bubble Buster' I was more fascinated by learning to write my own programs. The first of these consisted of just two lines of code† that made the word 'shit' appear again and again on my screen, to the huge amusement of my friends and the irritation of my parents, who obviously had more educational motives for bringing a computer into the house.

From that day on, the possibilities offered by technology to both subvert the norm and get attention had me hooked.

Years later, at secondary school, I convinced my English teacher, Mr Coen, to teach me desktop publishing, ostensibly to work on the official school magazine, but in reality to produce an alternative underground version – complete with less than flattering articles about teachers and fellow pupils and distributed via the publicly accessible shared hard drive that was supposed to be used for

....

* Today you would need 210,000 ZX Spectrums to equal the internal memory of a reasonably decent camera phone.
† 10 PRINT 'shit!'
  20 GOTO 10.

collaborative coursework. That particular stunt got me banned from the school computer room for half a term.

And then, in 1997, I discovered the Internet.

Throughout history, every fame-hungry media dickhead has found his preferred medium for pursuing fame and wealth (in that order). For Tony Parsons – and Hitler, for that matter – it was books. William Randolph Hearst chose newspapers. Don Imus and Howard Stern preferred radio. For Nick Griffin it's inflammatory leaflets. For Tracy Emin it's art. Or at least an approximation of it. With the Internet I had found mine – and it was a doozy.

Of course, every time a new medium is invented there will be people who claim that it's more revolutionary than anything that has come before; that it's going to change the world as we know it; that – to use a wanky phrase beloved of marketers – it represents a 'paradigm shift'.

Sometimes that's undeniably true: Johannes Gutenberg's printing press, for example, turned books from luxury goods beyond the reach of all but the very wealthiest of men into the ultimate mass-market educational tool.* And then there was television – which brought images of the farthest reaches of the world into every living room.

But no matter how revolutionary the medium, there was always the same barrier to entry for anyone hoping to take advantage of it for the pursuit of fame and wealth: distribution.

Thanks to Gutenberg, anyone with a brain and access to a basic printing press could write and print a book, or publish an underground newspaper or pamphlet. Increasingly affordable and lightweight video technology enabled almost anyone to make a film, even if it was just a grainy home video of their dog on a skateboard (awwwww …) or, more usually, a grainy home video of them having sex with their significant other (ewwwww …). Your friendly neighbourhood electronics shop could sell you everything you needed to set up your own pirate radio station … and yet …

....

* In 1424, Cambridge University library owned just over 120 books. So rare and valuable were they that for the cost of a single book you could buy an entire farm. Thanks to mad cow, foot and mouth, blue tongue and bird flu, the same is true today.

... and yet ...

... and yet ...

Getting your book or skateboarding dog porn epic in front of a big audience, getting your radio station heard beyond your immediate neighbourhood, was an expensive business. Prohibitively expensive in fact – to the point where only the very wealthy could afford to reach an audience much beyond their front door.

The same was true for entrepreneurs and inventors. Creating a new product or service was the easy part; finding someone, or somewhere, to sell it meant either trekking up and down the high street convincing shop owners to stock it, or spending a small fortune on setting up your own shop.

And then came the Internet. That rumbling sound you heard was the paradigm shifting.

Suddenly – almost overnight, it seemed – anyone who could get in front of a computer connected to the web could create a website that could be accessed by anyone else with a similar computer, anywhere else in the world. In a blink, the cost of communicating with a single person was exactly the same as reaching the entire world. For almost no money down, we could all be publishers or entrepreneurs and the only criterion for phenomenal success was to create something that lots of people wanted to see, hear, read or buy. The Internet created the ultimate media and marketing meritocracy.

It won't surprise you to learn that, during the mid- to late nineties, I wasn't the only person to have realised this.

In fact, so astonishingly popular did the Internet become in those years that the period became known as 'the Internet Boom'. Barely a nanosecond passed without some hot new website crashing on to the scene, vowing to put its traditional rivals out of business thanks to its bold new business model ('we're going to sell dollar bills with adverts on them for 75 cents!') and a company name that had seemingly been coined by an eighteen-month-old baby ...

Boo!

Yahoo!

Kozmo!

FooDoo!

Awwww, look, baby just created his first Internet brand. Wipe his chin would you, darling?

In the UK all the national newspapers moved online (starting with the *Daily Telegraph*, swiftly followed by the *Guardian* and then all of the others*), offering round-the-clock news reporting and the opportunity for readers to interact with their 'favourite' journalists. Shopping moved online, too, with brands like Amazon and the travel site Expedia vowing to put traditional high street rivals out of business by offering a dizzyingly wide selection of products along with heavy discounts.

1997 saw the arrival of Winamp, the first popular MP3-playing software, bringing high-quality, easy-to-download music to the web for the first time and allowing up-and-coming bands a way to distribute their music at zero cost. By huge coincidence, 1997 is also the year widespread Internet piracy was born. Go figure.

One by one, every other medium – radio, television, even full-length films – became digital, making them available to wider and wider audiences. The fact that no one was making any kind of money out of any of this was totally irrelevant. Media experts (most of whom were building start-ups of their own) were quick to point out that no one made money out of any new medium in the beginning anyway. The mantra was – to borrow from *Field of Dreams* – if we build it, they will pay ... something ... eventually.

We hope.

Please.†

Actually, saying that *no one* was making money from new media was slightly unfair: there was one group of media entrepreneurs that was making tons of money on the web, almost from day one – pornographers. By moving online and taking advantage of the global marketplace, rather than one bound by the cost of distribution and troublesome local laws, even ultra-niche publications like 'busty coffee-drinking housewives who fellate penguins'

---

* Even the *Daily Express* got there in the end, and they've still barely worked out how to be a newspaper.

† Admittedly, earlier revolutions had had snappier mantras. 'The future will be televised!' (except for viewers in Scotland).

became not just viable but potentially hugely profitable.*

As I watched this revolution taking place, what excited me the most wasn't the potential to make huge sums of money with very little outlay or even the troughs full of hardcore pornography that were now at my late teenage fingertips. Although that *was* excellent.

No, what excited me – attention whore that I was – was the possibility of using this new, incredible technology to achieve fame.

Instant, phenomenal fame – on a global scale.

1.1

With each new medium comes a raft of new stars. Stars like 'Stooky Bill'.

In October 1925, Stooky Bill became instantly famous when an image of his decapitated head was chosen by John Logie Baird for the first public demonstration of his new invention – television. Stooky Bill, you understand, was a ventriloquist's dummy. No footage of the demonstration survives today, but, judging from the still photos of the event, Stooky was a natural in front of the camera. Literally the world's first talking head.

Sixty-six years later, in 1991, the Internet equivalent of Stooky Bill turned out to be something even more inanimate, if that's possible: a pot of lukewarm coffee. Located in the Trojan Room of the Computer Science Department of Cambridge University, the coffee pot (name unknown) became the first object to be broadcast live across the Internet, twenty-four hours a day. The motive behind this massive technological innovation? Staff at the university couldn't be bothered to get up from their desks to see if there was any coffee left. Such was the lack of other online programming available at the time

....

* There's an old joke about a kid typing into a search engine 'women sucking off three-legged goats that are on fire' and the search engine asking 'what colour goats are you looking for?' Also it's widely accepted that VCRs became popular so quickly because they allowed horny men to watch pornography in their own homes rather than in grubby adult cinemas. Similarly, it's staggering the number of Internet technologies we now take for granted that were invented by online pornographers to make money: secure credit card payments, streaming video, pop-up adverts, members' only content . . . the list goes on.

that the coffee pot became an instant celebrity, with people logging in all over the world to see if there was any coffee available at the Trojan Room of the Computer Science Department of Cambridge University. Sometimes there was! Other times there wasn't! To achieve that level of success today, the coffee pot broadcast would need a text message-voting element and a behind-the-scenes show on ITV4 with Ant and Dec.

It took five more years – until April 1996 – for someone to realise that there were even sexier things to webcast around the globe than pots of lukewarm coffee. The sexier thing's name was Jennifer Ringley, a red-headed, nineteen-year-old junior at Dickinson College in Pennsylvania. Jennifer's big idea was to rig up a webcam in her dorm room and to point it at … herself … broadcasting her own life, live and uncensored twenty-four hours a day. No matter whether she was studying, sleeping, eating or (with increasing regularity – she *knew* her audience) having sex, it was all shown on camera – uncut, uncensored and without a producer, director or broadcaster between her and her audience.

With such groundbreaking openness, which would soon lead the way to *Big Brother* and reality TV in all its sick and exploitative forms, Jennifer very quickly became even more of a star than Stooky Bill and the coffee pot put together, with up to four million people a day tuning in at the peak of her popularity. Jennifer even crossed over to mainstream television, appearing on *The Late Show with David Letterman* and starring as a fictionalised version of herself in an episode of *Diagnosis Murder*.* Now that's fucking fame on a stick.

Jennicam, as the 'experiment'† was called, lasted until New Year's Eve 2003 when Jenny shut down her camera and disappeared from the radar almost as quickly as she'd appeared on it, amid rumours that her new boyfriend objected to – uh – performing on camera. The speed with which most of the Internet forgot about Jennicam highlights another important lesson of cyber fame: it may be easier

....

* The episode was entitled 'Rear Windows '98', which is actually brilliant. Rejected choices (presumably) include: 'Gone With The Windows', 'Dial M For Microsoft', 'The Internet Connection Wizard of Oz' and 'Photoshop Your Wagon'.

† The word 'experiment' is used on the web in the same way as it is on TV: as a euphemism for 'excuse to show tits in the name of science'.

to achieve than other types of fame but at the same time, more so than any other medium, the flame is fleeting.* The moment you stop stoking the fire ... Pft.

Fade out. Total darkness.

But still, for me in late 1999, nineteen years old and just starting at university, the pull of Internet fame and fortune was too hard to resist. I wanted in. But how?

Less photogenic than Jenny, or even Stooky Bill, and lacking the entrepreneurial nous to build the next Amazon.com, I decided to stick with about the only thing I'd ever been slightly good at: writing words.

Buying every book I could find on web design and working day and night in my first-year digs, I created a site called Zingin.com, which was basically a sweary, sarcastic version of the then all-powerful Yahoo! directory. In those days Yahoo!, founded by Stanford students Jerry Yang and David Filo, was still primarily a directory of useful and entertaining websites, rather than the jack-of-all-features it has since become. The site employed a huge team of human reviewers who trawled the Internet and manually categorised zillions of sites to make them easier for surfers to find. Unfortunately the sheer volume of sites the poor saps had to review meant that Yahoo! site descriptions rarely went into more detail than 'Site offering details of train times for Newcastle, UK'. The Yahoo! description of my own personal website was 'Official site for this UK writer'. It's a wonder I didn't get more traffic.

Zingin.com would be different: instead of trying to review every site on the web, I would just choose the ones I liked, in various categories – shopping, money, family, entertainment ... and so on – and then write proper reviews of them, some stretching up to a hundred words. But the big difference is that the reviews I wrote on Zingin.com would be funny, sarcastic even, and they wouldn't be afraid to swear at you, when the need arose.

The site also featured a weekly round-up of the weirdest corners of the web written by a guy called Tim Ireland who has since gone on to become one of the UK's highest profile online political

....

* Which actually suits Jennifer just fine. Today, she doesn't have so much as a MySpace page.

campaigners. It was Tim who forced Tony Blair to get a publicly accessible email address and who came up with a brilliant scheme to convince elected representatives to start blogging, by encouraging others to create fake blogs in various MPs' names and writing them himself until they agreed to take over.

For all its scatological obsession, the content on Zingin was really pretty tame, particularly by today's weblog standards, but it was funny and snarky enough that it soon built up a healthy audience of a few thousand visitors a day and a subscriber base of over fifty thousand for the daily email newsletter I also sent out, containing all of that day's new reviews.

On the back of this modest success I was able to sell advertising to some of the scores of new ecommerce sites springing up every day, which helped to supplement my student loan rather nicely.

In fact, the success of the site led to an unforeseen problem: how to conceal the source of my new-found disposable income from my university friends? Only a small number of my housemates were privy to the embarrassing secret of what I got up to for hours on end locked in my room – the Internet was not exactly the coolest hobby to have in those days, dot com boom or not. As my income crept up and up and my expenditure became more and more conspicuous – a new mobile phone every couple of months, an increasingly elaborate Scalextric layout snaking around my shared living room and kitchen – I found myself facing increasingly awkward questions from my other friends. Out of desperation I resorted to scaring them off by hinting that it would be better if they didn't pry too closely into where my money came from, lest they somehow become 'involved'. This was quite true, of course: no one wants to be sucked into the murky world of writing knob gags on the Internet for pocket money.

My plan was to use Zingin to get my name known among my Internet peers, and also among publishers and editors, in the hope that I could follow Jennicam's transition to traditional media. And from there? Possibly a book deal, or a gig on a magazine or newspaper. Until the web became more socially acceptable, it would remain very much a stepping stone to something more respectable; something I wasn't embarrassed to tell my friends about.

Miraculously, my plan actually started to work – and even sooner than I'd hoped. At the start of my second term, totally out of the blue, I got an email from Clare Christian, a commissioning editor at the publisher Prentice Hall* who had found Zingin.com while browsing the web for material that could possibly be adapted into books. The reviews on Zingin.com had made her laugh and she wondered if I'd like to write a series of eight Zingin-branded web guide books, based on the eight sections of the site, for her. As it turned out, I would.

I was still recovering from the shock of becoming a soon-to-be-published author when I received a second surprising email – this one from a business partner of comedian-turned-TV impresario Griff Rhys Jones. He wondered whether I might like to be involved in a web-TV project they were working on. A thousand times, yes. This was incredible – I'd built it, they'd come, they'd liked it and now, only a few months after launching Zingin.com, I was going to be paid to write a series of books and develop a web-TV programme. I loved it when a plan came together.

Unfortunately, while I may have craved sudden success, I wasn't very good at the nuts and bolts of delivering on it. One telephone conversation early on in my relationship with Clare Christian stands out as particularly embarrassing when it became apparent that Clare was under the impression that I was a proper grown-up editor with a proper grown-up company and a team of writers, rather than a twenty-year-old chancer working out of his shoebox of a bedroom. On the Internet, they say, nobody knows if you're a dog. The conversation went a bit like this:

Clare: 'We'd like you to write eight books. Do you think your team could handle that?'

Me: 'My ... team?'

Clare: 'Yes, your team of writers. How many sites would you say you guys have in your database?'

Me: 'Database?'

All the big directory sites had vast databases, stored on huge banks of computers, containing all their reviews. When you visited Yahoo! and clicked to a certain category of review, these databases would send a list of relevant sites to another computer, which would

---

* Part of the Pearson Group which also owns Penguin and the *Financial Times*.

slot them all into a nice neat web page to be displayed on your screen. This meant you were always getting the most up-to-date listings. Zingin didn't have a database. Instead, I had to build each page of the site, and each review, by hand and upload them on to the web using my mobile phone connected to a creaking old laptop. When I wanted to add a new review, I had to cut and paste it on to the page before uploading it back to the site.

Clare: 'We'll need the finished manuscripts in a couple of months if that's okay.'

Me: 'That's fine. No problem at all.'

Gulp.

Clare: 'Great! Any other questions?'

Me: 'No. Oh, yes . . .

. . . just one . . .

. . . roughly how many *words* does a book have?'

But idiot or not,* I was still a writer – a proper paid writer, much to the delight of my parents who had high hopes of me becoming a hot-shot lawyer. But I was sure that in time they'd get over the disappointment. I had arrived. I was to be the author of eight books.

Now all I had to do was write the damned things.

After two months chained to a keyboard, mainlining Red Bull, followed by another few months of editing, correcting and approving, the day of publication arrived. I travelled up to London to visit the flagship Borders bookshop to see the books in situ. Clare had phoned me a few weeks earlier with the good news that the bookselling giant had agreed to take thousands of copies of the book. So many, in fact, that they wanted Prentice Hall to print the Borders logo on the cover so that the chain could pretend the series was actually produced in partnership with them. Naturally I was thrilled and couldn't wait to get down to Borders as soon as the books were in stock. Sure enough, on walking into the computer section, there I saw my books: stacked high on the end of every shelf, and covering numerous tables dotted around the shop. Wow! They must really love the books if they were piling them so high around the shop.

It was only months later that I discovered the truth: books are

....

* Idiot.

usually distributed to bookshops on sale or return, with the publisher taking all the risk for how well a particular title sells. The co-branding had been a brilliant wheeze by the sales team at Prentice Hall to limit this risk: once a book cover has been overprinted with a retailer's logo, the retailer can't return it, even if it wants to. By offering Borders a special edition of the book, printed with their logo, Prentice Hall had ensured that the thousands of copies they'd agreed to buy would never be returned. No wonder Borders were piling them high in every corner of the store – they had to shift the whole lot otherwise they'd have to pulp them. Two years later, I was still spotting them in bargain bins: for some reason people didn't want to buy out-of-date web guide books, even for 50p each. But what did I care? Thanks to Borders, I earned my advance before the books were even published and every other copy sold meant a few pence of royalties straight into my pocket.

1.2

With almost two years left of my law degree, and with no intention of doing anything so idiotic as actually attending lectures or studying law, I had plenty of time to come up with my next bid for online fame. The Griff Rhys Jones TV project had stalled after a couple of meetings when everyone involved realised that the idea – to pipe broadband comedy programming into the nation's workplaces under the noses of bosses – was a bit of a non-starter. But I had become quite good friends with Rhys Jones's partner in the project, a comedy writer called Charlie Skelton, and he, Clare and I frequently met to brainstorm possible projects we might work on together. It was during one of these meetings that Clare proposed the idea of starting a comedy magazine – something like *Private Eye*, but for the Internet generation.

My days as a school magazine publisher had taught me that printing magazines and distributing them was a royal pain in the arse and, anyway, if it was to be a magazine for the Internet generation then shouldn't it actually *be* on the Internet? The Zingin.com newsletter had attracted a ton of subscribers and had a distribution cost of basically nothing so why, I suggested, didn't we start a weekly comedy ezine, sent out by email? And, in a nod to Charlie's failed office comedy project, we could target it at bored office workers, sending the email to them on a Friday afternoon to cure the crushing boredom of those final few hours of the working week.

And with that, *The Friday Thing* was born.

To promote our fledgling publication we came up with a brilliant ruse: an online petition to have Friday afternoons declared a national holiday. British people worked harder than any other Europeans (we made up) and so it was only fair that our working week should end at noon on a Friday. We created an official website explaining our demands, registered a web address – letsgetitoff.com (snigger) – and sent a press release to the media. Clearly we had tapped into a seam of strong feeling among the nation's overworked journalists and the campaign was picked up by just about every major newspaper, local radio station and even made it on to the BBC. The campaign went global when *Newsweek* published a feature about the site in its international edition, revealing that the petition had received more than 56,000 signatures in the first week.

Once people had signed the petition, which was to be sent to Tony Blair when it reached 100,000 signatures, they were taken to a second page which told them that – as luck would have it – we were about to launch a hilarious email magazine that would help fill their soon-to-be-free Friday afternoons. With just one extra click they could sign up to the newsletter, completely free of charge. By the time the petition reached its 100,000 signature target in less than a month, more than forty thousand people had subscribed to *The Friday Thing* – all before we'd even published a single issue.

The debut issue of *The Friday Thing* was published in the summer of 2001 and the ezine ran into controversy almost immediately when, a couple of months later, four hijacked planes flew into various American landmarks and fields, sparking what we have come to know as the War on Terror. In the days and weeks after September 11th, it seemed to the three of us at *The Friday Thing* that something was very wrong with the media. George Bush's administration was openly gearing up for war against Afghanistan – a war that, wherever you stood on the issue, would doubtless lead to thousands of innocent lives being lost. And yet huge sections of the press seemed to be too afraid to question any of this, lest they be labelled terrorist sympathisers. And worse than that, no one was making jokes about it all.

Originally, we had intended *The Friday Thing* to be a light-hearted jokey read for bored office workers but, by the end of September 2001, we had dropped any pretence of apolitical niceness and the email had become fiercely satirical and hugely political. Through September and October we lost about 40 per cent of our readers and our mail servers almost crashed with the weight of hate mail. In the end, we created a special email account to filter it all out: terroristsympathisers@thefridaything.co.uk.

Those readers who did stay, though, told their friends about us and *The Friday Thing*'s profile, particularly among journalists and so-called 'opinion formers', grew and grew. At the start of 2002, we decided that our audience was big enough and loyal enough to switch to a paid subscription model – £10 a year for fifty-two issues – to help pay our bills without resorting to advertising. The *Guardian* published a double-page feature on the switch and a huge 20 per cent of our subscribers converted, enough for us to invest in a proper subscription system and actually to think about hiring some new writers. With a proper writing team and money in the bank, *The Friday Thing* continued to grow steadily, thanks in large part to our habit of publishing horrendously inappropriate 'special issues' to mark news events. Our 'The Queen Mother Is Dead' tribute issue hit subscribers' inboxes less than two hours after her death had been announced* and contents included a list, compiled by Charlie, of ten things you didn't know about her late majesty ('No. 8: She once called C. S. Lewis a cunt'). One of my favourite issues, published several years after the Queen Mother one, was also the one that most divided the readers: 'The Seven/Seven Issue',† published

....

* The issue was published so quickly that subscribers assumed we'd written it in advance and put it in a drawer for later. In fact, Charlie and I wrote the whole thing over the phone while watching the coverage of her death.

† The title was supposed to be ironic. The fact that the British press actually adopted the phrase '7/7' to describe the attacks as if they were in some way part of a global '9/11' franchise is, frankly, bizarre.

less than three hours after suicide bombers attacked London's underground system in 2005. The attacks had come the day after London had been awarded the 2012 Olympic Games and the issue included such features as alternative London Olympic Slogans:

LONDON: Get it while it's hot.

LONDON: You can run, but you can't park and ride.

LONDON: Light the fire within, flee the fire without.

LONDON: Chariots of bombs.

LONDON: Where no matter what happens, and how many people are dead, there'll always be some twat with a camera phone taking pictures.

... and a list of possible suspects for the bombing including, at the top of the list, the French. I even penned a haiku for a feature we called 'Haiknews: today's news in just seventeen syllables':

> *London Olympics*
> *Transport regeneration*
> *Off to rocky start*

The Londoners who subscribed to *The Friday Thing* loved it and emailed in their hundreds to thank us for showing that the capital wouldn't be stopped by terrorists and would laugh in the face of danger. This was more true than they knew – I was staying at my girlfriend's flat at the end of one of the affected lines and had to walk eight miles back to my computer, through police cordons and pubs full of jubilant office workers, to edit and send out the issue.

Back in 2002, and with *The Friday Thing* starting to take off, I realised that writing jokes about the big news stories of the day was much more effective than a sarcastic web directory in making people laugh and, more importantly, getting myself noticed. Unfortunately it also turned out to be a much better way of getting pilloried in the press and almost thrown in jail ...

1.3

If you turned on the TV towards the end of 2002 you could have been forgiven for thinking that Britain had gone absolutely horseshit mental. Every week, it seemed, another pretty young girl from a nice family, who was happy and popular and always did well at school, was being kidnapped or murdered by what the *Sun* newspaper cheerfully termed 'evil paedo scum'. Naming and shaming was as popular a feature in the Murdoch press as Page Three girls and discounted holidays to Butlin's.

Of course you can't blame parents for wanting to keep their children safe; that's pretty much the job description of a parent. And, on the face of it, the tabloids were doing a public service in warning us about the paedophile menace lurking in our midst. The problem came when it turned out that a huge number of these concerned tabloid-reading parents were also absolute fucking morons. For every story of an actual sex offender being driven from their house by a baying mob there was one like that of Dr Yvette Cloete, a doctor at the Royal Gwent Hospital in Newport, South Wales, who returned home from work to find that a group of 'concerned parents' had daubed the word 'paedo' on her front door in bright red paint.

Dr Cloete was a consultant paed*iatrician*. Easy mistake.

If you're an absolute fucking moron.

And so it was that one hung-over morning, after reading yet another story about vigilantes who had threatened to stone Maxine Carr, the girlfriend of Soham killer Ian Huntley, to death during her high-profile trial for perverting the course of justice, I decided to set up a website parodying this collective national madness.

The result of two or three hours of hung-over labour was thinkofthechildren.co.uk, a spoof campaign site which claimed to offer a handy online guide for crazy vigilantes of all stripes to coordinate their crazy vigilante efforts. Although there are a few parts of the site I'm still a bit proud of, the majority of it was, I freely admit, satire of the lowest order. The frequently asked questions on the front page of the site read as follows:

Who are we?
We are concerned parents, many of whom have children of our own and who want the law changed to protect them. Every day in Britain happy, popular children who do well at school are being murdered by evil

paedophile scum. Well enough's enough! It's time the law got tough on child murderers.

What do we want?
We want the law changed to make it illegal to murder children and bury them in woodland. We want it to be made illegal for adults to work with children. We want an end to the ridiculous process of 'criminal trials' for suspected child killers.

When do we want it?
Now.

...

There then followed some essential advice on starting your own mob:

Placards
Once you've gathered a sizeable mob, you'll need to equip them with placards or banners. Placards – which are easily fashioned by fixing a large piece of card to a stick – should contain snappy slogans which are easy to chant. Good slogans include: 'die scum!', 'peedos out!', 'hang child killers!' and 'kiddie fiddler shitbag!'. Bad slogans include: 'You're the product of a complex series of social and psychological factors!' and 'I haven't really thought this through!'

and a list of upcoming mobs:

Event: The Soham Mob (Maxine Carr Trial)
Date: *TBC*
Type: *Taunting*

Details: *Please do come along to what promises to be an enjoyable afternoon's taunting. Children welcome. Our thanks to the Daily Express and Manchester United Plc for supporting this event.*

Event: The 'Not From The Home Counties' Protest
Date: *26 November 2002*

Type: Protest

Details: Protest march to demand justice for murdered children from troubled backgrounds who weren't 'happy' or 'popular' and didn't do particularly well at school. (Cancelled due to lack of support.)

Jonathan Swift it most certainly wasn't – but only a moron would look at it and not realise immediately that it was a spoof.

Things started slowly – the first hour or so after I sent the link to some of my friends the site got about a hundred visits, mainly from those friends or from people they'd sent the link on to. By dinner time, it had had a thousand visits. By the next day, ten thousand. Pretty impressive, but still chickenfeed compared to Jennicam and the Coffee Pot.

But then things started to get interesting. Several high-profile comedy and news sites linked to thinkofthechildren.co.uk, as did a couple of major sites specialising in finding new and interesting links – including the very influential B3ta.com.

Suddenly I had 100,000 visitors.

Gosh.

200,000.

Holy mackerel.

Half a million.

Holy shit.

Half a million people reading my stupid jokes!

It even got linked on to the *Daily Mail* discussion forums, where readers responded with a mixture of outrage and disapproval. One poster, in a bizarre twist of logic, even accused me of siding with child killers. The *Daily Mail*! My parents would be so proud.

And then ...

Nothing.

All of a sudden, thinkofthechildren.co.uk dropped off the Internet. It just vanished. One minute it was there. Next minute I clicked refresh and it was gone, in its place an error message: 'page not found'.

Irritated, I dialled the number of my web-hosting company, Host Europe. I assumed that the explosion of visitors in such a short space of time had exceeded the amount of traffic I was allowed on my basic cheapo hosting package, or that there had been some other kind of technical error.

I tried to be friendly with the person who answered the phone. It doesn't do to get upset about these things.

'Hello there, I hope you can help me. My site seems to have gone down.'

'Oh, I'm sorry, sir, can I take the address?'

'Yep, it's thinkofthechildren.co.uk. That's T-H-I-N ...'

But before I could finish – 'Can you hold, please? I need to put you through to my manager.'

This didn't sound good. This didn't sound good at all.

Suddenly another voice – a man with the same tone of voice as those little Nazis in ludicrous hats and luminous jackets who stand at railway ticket barriers waiting to fine you £20 because you've gone one station too far with your ticket.

'Hello, Mr Carr?' said the little Nazi, 'I'm afraid there's a serious problem with your hosting. At ten o'clock this morning we received a call from the Metropolitan Police's Obscene Publications and Computer Crime Unit asking us to shut down your web server. Apparently one of your sites was offering advice on setting up a vigilante mob ... *

He said the words 'setting up a vigilante mob' in the same way as an arresting officer might say, 'yes, Sarge, apparently he was just "*cuddling* the sheep"'. In exactly the same tone.

The Obscene Publications and Computer Crime Unit, he explained, had phoned Host Europe and asked for my site – my *spoof* site – to be shut down, without any kind of warrant, and Host Europe had complied without even bothering to tell me. This was bizarre. And I wasn't going to stand for it. I knew my rights!†

Unfortunately, the only response I could muster to communicate how little I was going to stand for it was a sort of gaspy yelping noise.

'M-m-uuuuhh–eeee?'

....

* Presumably as opposed to an officially sanctioned mob.
† I had no idea what my rights were.

I took a deep breath and tried again. 'But this is ridiculous. It's a joke—'

'It may be a joke to you, sir,' said the Nazi, 'but I assure you that we and the police take these complaints very seriously. There's nothing we can do; you'll need to speak to the officer in charge at the Met. His number is 020 . . .'

My next call, to the Obscene Publications Unit, confirmed my lack of faith in humanity.

'Yes, Mr Carr, we did ask Host Europe to shut down your site . . . No, sir, we didn't have to get a court order. We received a complaint about the site and, after investigating, I telephoned Host Europe and recommended that they take down the site.'

At this point I lost my temper.

'You recommended it? That's all it takes to censor something? A *recommendation*? Jesus, *Fahrenheit 451* would have been a much shorter book if the firemen just issued a bloody *recommendation* that books be burnt.'

For a moment I had forgotten that I was shouting at someone who probably had the power to send me to jail if I got a bit too lippy. He also didn't get the reference. But my point stood: 'On exactly what basis did you "recommend" deleting it?'

'I decided that it could be interpreted as inciting violence.'

Yes, officer, I wanted to say, you're absolutely right, it could be interpreted that way. If the interpreter was the type of baying, inbred, placard-waving, tabloid-reading *fucking moron* that the site was parodying in the first place.

'Did you even look at the site or did you just take the word of someone who saw the link on the *Daily Mail* forum and decided that Something Must Be Done?'

'Yes, sir, I did look at the site.'

'And you realised it's a parody?'

'In my view it wasn't clear. And the complainant believed it to be genuine.'

I was too angry to think straight. I couldn't believe how easily it had been for the police to get the site taken down, just because some idiot *Daily Mail* reader couldn't recognise a joke, compared to how difficult it would be to get a book pulped or a film banned in similar circumstances. I didn't care how unfunny thinkofthechildren was any more – I just wanted it put back up. Right. This. Minute.

'I'm sorry, sir, I can't actually make that decision. Host Europe were the ones who decided to take down the site. You'll have to ask them if they're prepared to reactivate it.'

In other words, in the absence of a court order Host Europe could have told the Met to sod off. But it chose not to. Instead, my friendly web host, to whom I'd paid hundreds of pounds to host my site, had complied with an informal request from the police – much like a puppy might comply with an informal request to 'roll over'.

Well, fuck that, I thought. I called my Nazi friend at Host Europe again, ready for a fight. Not only had they taken thinkofthechildren down, but they'd disconnected my entire server, including *The Friday Thing* and my own personal email account.

'So what do I have to do to get my server back up and running?' I asked Martin Bormann.

'You'll have to take down the thinkofthechildren site and give us an assurance that you won't put it back up.'

'And if I agree to that, you'll reconnect me?'

'Yes.'

'Okay, I agree – but you'll need to reconnect it first so I can delete the mob stuff.'

'Er ... All right then. But you're agreeing to take the mob stuff down?'

'Of course.'

Like hell I was.

'Thank you.'

'No, thank *you*.'

Click

Prick.

Now, I should say at this point that I was honestly, honestly, going to take down the part of the site that gave advice on setting up mobs. After all, it wasn't that funny. And the idea of being carted off to court for inciting violence when every chav in the country was standing outside the courts baying for blood didn't hugely appeal.

But the more I thought about it, the more I wanted to tell them where to shove it. Why the hell should the Internet be at the mercy of a humourless policeman and a dickhead hosting company having an informal chat?

Of course, what I also realised was that something being banned – whether it be a film, an album or a book – gave an absolutely guaranteed fast track to popularity. Surely by the same logic, *defying* a ban would be my passport to the satire hall of fame. This was going to be great!

The moment the server was reconnected, I put the site back online exactly as it was. Well, except for a small link at the bottom entitled 'An Open Letter to Host Europe and the Obscene Publications Unit'. Clicking on it took the visitor to a (*slightly* snotty) letter explaining that I had absolutely no intention of editing the site and outlining the various bits of the law that required them to get a court order for websites to be closed down. For good measure I put a note at the top of the page for anyone else who visited the site, inviting them to email the CEO of Host Europe, Jonathan Brealey, to tell him what they thought about Internet censorship. And then I sat back and waited for the shit storm.

I didn't have to wait long.

The first call came from technology news site *The Register*. Apparently some of the journalists were fans of thinkofthechildren and they wanted to write a piece about my 'fuck you' to the police. Then the *Guardian* called, and someone from the *Observer*. Then Spiked Online (formerly Living Marxism) asked me if I'd like to write something about my brave stand for freedom of speech. Even the *Christian Science Monitor* wrote a piece about me and my brave stand. If you've got the Christian Scientists on your side, you know you're doing something right.*

This word 'brave' that journalists kept using was starting to scare the hell out of me, though. I wasn't going for brave, I was going for cheeky. Cheeky people get judges wagging their fingers at them and are then sent on their way with a clip round the ear. Brave people go to jail and spend the rest of their days breaking rocks

....
* Unless you're a surgeon, obviously.

with sledgehammers. I wasn't brave. I was an attention-seeker in a strop. But it was too late to back down now – bloggers were saying I had 'balls of steel' (oh God), and the Christian Scientists had described me as a 'latter-day Jonathan Swift' (ridiculous, obviously, but of course I've dined out on the quote ever since).*

I put the worries to the back of my mind. I'd done my research and the law was pretty clear – the police could only shut down websites with a proper warrant, and with the press watching it would be a huge PR mistake for Host Europe to close me down again. I was sitting pretty.

And then my friend Sam Lewis rang, bubbling with excitement. Sam is a former journalist who had made a small killing not long before when he'd sold a magazine he'd started to a major publishing house. I'd met him when he was covering an Internet conference for an industry magazine and we'd since become good friends. He was almost ten years older than me, but we shared a similar sick sense of humour and I envied his ability to juggle being a good writer with actually understanding business. Whatever was going on in the industry – or in the media generally – he seemed to know about it first. Including this.

'Ha, mate! The *Evening Standard*! What a bunch of wankers, eh?'

I had no idea what he was talking about.

'Er ... mate ... I'm in Nottingham. I'm pretty sure they don't sell the London *Evening Standard* here. Why – what's going on?'

'Shit, you haven't seen it? You're on page seven of the paper and on the front page of the online version. You need to go online RIGHT NOW.'

'I am? For thinkofthechildren?'

'In a manner of speaking. Look, just go online NOW. I can't believe I'm the first person to phone you about it. Has no one else emailed?'

I hadn't checked my mail all day – I had been too busy sifting through the backlog of messages from when the server had been taken down. I scrolled up the list of messages in my inbox and, sure enough, there were half a dozen mails from friends with subjects

....

* Including mentioning it in this book.

like 'Evening Standards?' and 'Standard!' and 'Holy Shit!'. The *Standard* website finished loading and I scanned down the front page for a mention of thinkofthechildren. 'I can't see anything … there's just this big thing about Maxine Ca—

… oh …

… my …

… God …

… you have got to be fucking kidding me …'

But he wasn't. There, plain as day on the front page of the *Evening Standard* site (and apparently on page seven of hundreds of thousands of newspapers flooding the capital) was a four-column news story under the headline '"*Soham Mob*" *security fears as website urges violence at murder case court.*'

The story, by *Standard* reporter Danielle Gusmaroli, began:

Police today threw a security cordon around Peterborough Crown Court amid fears that an angry mob might try to attack Soham murder suspect Ian Huntley. The discovery of an inflammatory website encouraging protesters to use 'bricks, rocks and bottles'* prompted police to draft in 120 officers to guard the court for the second public appearance of the 28-year-old caretaker accused of the murders of Soham schoolgirls Holly Wells and Jessica Chapman.

And it went on:

The site lists the 'Soham Mob' among its supporters. They are thought to have been among the 500-strong mob that pelted Huntley's van with eggs and tomatoes as it left Peterborough Magistrates' Court last month after his first court appearance.

……………

* That's true, it did. In fact, what it said was *'During a mob gathering, anything which can be thrown should be thrown. Eggs, bricks, rocks and bottles make excellent missiles but use your imagination – it's your mob!'* It also covered fire-starting in some detail: *'Studies have shown that a paedophile is 90% less likely to return to his home if it has been razed to the ground so don't forget that paraffin! However, if you are planning to include an element of arson in your mob event, be sure to keep matches away from children.'*

I think I can categorically state that the Soham Mob were *not* among the five-hundred-strong mob who pelted Huntley's van, given that the Soham Mob were entirely fictional. In fact, they had a cast-iron alibi: they were inside my head the whole time.

And finally:

Attempts have been made to close down the website site [sic], *but its operators claimed that under the European Human Rights Act they have the right to freedom of speech.*

That last bit actually made me gasp. This woman – this *hack* – Gusmaroli had actually read my open letter about the fact that it was a spoof, and was covered by European freedom of expression rights, before she made up her story. And yet she'd still written a story as if the site was on the level. This was journalism, Jim, but not as we know it.

'M-m-uuuuhh–eeee!'

'Congratulations, mate. You're finally famous.'

'Yeah, as a vigilante, Sam. I'm famous as a *fictional* vigilante. I'm like the Lone Ranger for idiot chavs.'

'The Unsecured Loan Ranger.'

'You're not helping.'

'The Purple Loans Ranger.'

'Fuck off.'

'Oh come on, you know what Oscar Wilde said about being talked about.'

'Why am I spending two years in Reading jail when I've done nothing wrong?'

'That's fucking showbiz, man! No business like it. Good luck!'

1.4

Sam was right. After the brouhaha died down, thinkofthechildren turned out to have been a rather excellent piece of personal publicity. Thanks to all the press coverage – including a nice piece in the *Guardian* media section taking the piss out of the *Evening Standard* –

lots of journalists and commissioning editors knew who I was.

By the start of the following year I had left Nottingham (clutching my 2:2 in Law – a miracle of cramming) and moved to London where I was writing regularly for an eclectic mix of publications including the *Daily Star* and a sex magazine for women called *Scarlet* (where I reviewed adult DVDs on the basis of plot alone, making me the first person in the history of the universe to fast-forward through the sex scenes in porn films to get to the dialogue).

My biggest coup, though – and the one I was most proud of – was when I landed a regular freelance gig with the *Guardian* writing a regular new media column in my 'trademark satirical style'.*

If I'd learned anything from the thinkofthechildren incident – and I hadn't – it's that one man's 'trademark satirical style' is another man's first-class ticket to the dock, something I proved again and again at the *Guardian*, to the growing despair of my editor, Janine Gibson. Having narrowly dodged a complaint to the Press Complaints Commission for my first column in which I claimed that Madonna was pregnant again,† for my second column I'd hit upon the brilliant idea of taking on the ridiculousness of the English libel laws. How stupid and arrogant of lawyers and their overpaid clients – I wrote – to think that they could possibly keep anything secret in the era of the Internet. After all, what was the point of using court injunctions to cover their client's indiscretions when there was nothing to stop a foreign website publishing all the sordid details outside the UK court's jurisdiction? To prove my point, I decided to refer to a particularly juicy story that hadn't appeared in the UK press because of an injunction but had been widely reported overseas: that a particular clean-cut British celebrity was having an affair.

To prove my point, I first wrote a feature for *The Friday Thing* which didn't mention the name of the celebrity explicitly but did link to various foreign sites where it was revealed. I then boasted in the *Guardian* about how I'd done it, thus making a mockery of the injunction.

....

* Tough on facts, tough on the causes of facts.
† As above.

What I'd overlooked is that, in the English legal system, making a mockery of High Court injunctions has another name. Contempt of court.

The next day, as I was shopping in Budgens, my phone rang. It was Janine and she didn't sound very happy.

'Where are you?'

'I'm in Budgens buying a sandwich.'

'Well, you should probably get back in front of a computer. We have a bit of a problem.'

'Shit. We do?'

'Well, technically I don't. But you do, and the paper does, which means I do. Do you have a lawyer?'

'Um ... no ...'

'That's not good. You need to get one. We've just had a letter from ——— ———'s lawyers. They're threatening to sue both you and the paper for libel, and they're going to complain to the High Court that you are in contempt.'

'That doesn't sound good. Could I be fined a lot for that?'

'You could go to jail for that.'

'I should get a lawyer.'

'You should get a lawyer.'

In an astonishing stroke of bad luck, it turned out that the *Guardian* had decided to print my column right alongside an article about libel law written by none other than ——— ———'s lawyer! I can only imagine the lawyer sitting at his breakfast table, admiring his work only to scan across the page and see ... me ... underneath my gooning byline picture, sticking two fingers up at him and his stupid injunction. An injunction that the *Guardian*'s in-house lawyer later told me was 'one of the most restrictive and far-reaching' injunctions she'd ever seen. Brilliant.

I did the mature thing, of course, spending the next two days hiding in my girlfriend Claire's flat, avoiding phone calls from any number I didn't recognise and Googling for advice on how not to get raped in the prison showers. It wasn't until almost a month later – after spending the best part of £2,000 that I couldn't afford hiring a top-flight lawyer – that I heard the best news of my life: the other side had dropped the case.

Apparently they'd realised that they didn't have a case against the *Guardian* – just against me personally, and *The Friday Thing*. And as I didn't have any money, I wasn't worth the time or money to go after – despite all the 'irreparable harm' they claimed I had done to their client's reputation. I agreed to remove the article from *The Friday Thing* archives and the *Guardian* took the column down from their website. The matter was closed, but I was still £2,000 poorer and my future at the *Guardian* was hanging by a thread. To this day I can't see ――― ――― without wanting to punch the litigious little cunt in the face. Whoever he is.

After such a promising start, it's a miracle that I managed to hold on to my job for the next two years. Especially when every few weeks I'd manage to piss off someone important by attacking them through the column. Another enemy I made was Ian Hislop, the editor of *Private Eye*, who I decided to take the mickey out of mercilessly after he published a scathing article about a Labour MP named Tom Watson. Watson's crime had been to use his website to publish a hilariously ill-judged message to the 'youth' of his constituency. It began:

'Teens! We know that you're too busy fighting off your biological urges and being l33t hax0rs to Get Involved, but politics is cool, m'kay?'

Yikes! Hislop was right: it was pretty horrendous, and *Private Eye* republished it in full as an example of how massively out of touch today's MPs were with 'da yoot'. Unfortunately for Hislop, though, the message was a spoof, designed to prove exactly that point. It had been written by none other than Tom Watson's web adviser and my old friend, Tim Ireland.

Sensing comedy gold, I penned eight hundred words of open advice to Hislop about how Google was a great way to check out the origins of websites so as not to end up looking like a complete tit. The *Eye* was good at giving it out, but they very rarely found themselves on the receiving end of piss-taking so I felt very pleased with myself when I saw my column in print.

And then, a couple of weeks later, my phone rang. It was Sam Lewis again.

'Ha, mate! *Private Eye*, eh!'

'Oh, God. What now?'

'Honestly – do I have to do this for you every time? You're the star of this issue's "Ad Nauseum" column. They're pointing out that your piece suggesting that Hislop should use Google appeared on the *Guardian* website next to an ad for Google. They're saying it was deliberate product placement and calling you the "Google ad-man's stooge".'

'You're shitting me.'

'Ha hahaha. I swear to God.'

To be fair to Hislop, it was a beautiful piece of revenge and one that would have left the majority of *Private Eye*'s Luddite readership chuckling about how the *Guardian* had been caught out sucking up to an advertiser. The lesson couldn't be clearer: if you're going to attack another journalist, don't pick on one with a vast circulation and the ability to make you look like a complete twat in a magazine that all your mates read. I'd taken on the master, and lost. Game over.

I sent Hislop a letter congratulating him on his win, but explaining that for future reference accusing a new media hack of being in the pay of Google is like saying a motoring journalist is in bed with the internal combustion engine. He sent me a lovely handwritten postcard featuring a picture of Margaret Thatcher in return, thanking me for my advice and wishing me luck. The man is old school.

1.5

With regular money now coming in from the *Guardian* column, my regular contributions to other publications and the modest subscription revenue from *The Friday Thing*, I had been living something of the high life since arriving in London.

I had started hanging out with the great and the good of the dot com world: attending launch parties for new sites, going to parties to celebrate them staying in business for a whole year, eating their lunches, drinking their booze and learning their secrets while they tried to convince me to write about them in my column. Many of these online entrepreneurs had become my friends and I'd managed to find myself a new girlfriend – Maggie, a Welsh journalist who was a restaurant reviewer for a food and drink website. This was a brilliant blag: it meant we could eat at some of London's best restaurants and never pay a penny. Life was wonderful: *The Friday Thing* and the *Guardian* column meant that my plan to use the Internet to become hugely famous and successful was firmly on track, I'd made lots of new friends, and, on top of all that, I was getting laid and eating gourmet food for free. Even Sam Lewis was jealous, and he was rich.

Meanwhile, the people I was writing about were not having such an easy time of it. 2003 was a really strange time to be covering the 'new media' industry – mainly because no one was really sure for how long there would be an industry left to cover.

The dot com boom of 1999 seemed like a millennium ago: a period in history as crazy as the tulip craze or the South Sea Bubble look to us now.

The first signs of trouble for the industry had come in 2000. As the century turned, so had the market and – to use the parlance of analysts – the boom had turned out to be a bubble. And then the bubble had burst. The problem was that for years investors and the stock market had allowed the value of Internet companies to rise and rise, despite the fact that none of them was actually making any money. But then one day they decided enough was enough and with that: Pop! One company after another closed their doors, laying off hundreds of staff and causing the value of technology stocks to go through the floor.

During those post-bubble years, between 2000 and 2004, the entire industry was in turmoil. No one could agree whether we were seeing an industry in its death throes or whether the downturn was just (as many optimists claimed) 'a correction', a natural response by the market to weed out sky-high valuations and bad businesses. Generally, those who survived the crash remained firmly in the 'correction' camp, while those who had lost everything loudly declared that they were simply the innocent victims of an overhyped industry, fuelled by the high expectations of the press and the ridiculous overconfidence of investors. No one, they protested, could possibly succeed under those conditions.

It was that latter camp that most riled me, but also most appealed to my sense of Schadenfreude. These smug wankers who had grinned out from the front of business magazines and newspapers across the world, these young entrepreneurs, some not even out of school, who claimed fortunes (on paper at least) in the tens of millions.

God, I hated them.

God, I envied them.

But now they'd lost everything and instead of shrugging and saying 'ah well, it was good while it lasted, and fuck it, I'm still only twenty-two', they blamed the market, the press, the fact that they were ahead of their time. Anything to avoid admitting their complicity in the bullshit instant-fame machine that they thought would make them rich.

My favourite example of this phenomenon was Benjamin Cohen.

1.6

Benjamin – Ben – Cohen is one of that rare breed of people: someone I took a passionate dislike to from the very first time I heard his name, without even having met him.

Actually, I should clarify that – it wasn't his *name* that made me dislike him; that would make me sound like an enormous anti-Semite.* No, the reason I took an instant dislike to Ben Cohen is that he was everything I wanted to be: someone who during the dot com bubble had created a virtual media empire out of nothing and in doing so had managed to convince the press that he was not just a genius, but a rich genius. And all before he was twenty.

The story goes a little like this.

Once upon a time (1998) there was a sixteen-year-old boy called Ben. Ben decided that there was a gap in the market for a site offering everything the modern Jew-about-town could need: Jewish news, Jewish advice, a calendar of Jewish holiday dates, Jewish discussion rooms and so on. He called it soJewish, because that's

....

* In fact, some of my best friends control the media and killed Jesus.

the sort of name someone with no imagination whatsoever would call such a site.* Before long the site had become reasonably popular, with thousands of people visiting every week. SoFar, SoGood. But Cohen didn't just want to be an entrepreneur – he wanted to be a celebrity; and what better way for a slightly dorky kid to become a celebrity on the eve of the dot com boom than by becoming a teenage millionaire?

So that's exactly what he became.

And here's how he did it. He simply phoned up, wrote to and otherwise button-holed as many journalists as he could find and told them 'my company has been valued at millions of pounds'. Now of course, Fleet Street's finest are no mere hacks – so they went away and fact-checked Ben's claims, demanding proof of his self-confirmed valuation.

Just kidding. They are hacks.

'His company is worth millions!' they repeated. 'And if his company is worth that, and he owns the company, then that means he is worth millions as well! He's a millionaire! A teenage millionaire! Hold the front page!'

Even proper journalists normally known for their investigative work – journalists like Jon Ronson, whose work I love – were sucked into the hype. As he wrote in the *Evening Standard* at the time: 'For Britain's business journalists, Benjamin has come to represent the Internet world in all its wonder and bizarreness.'

Thanks, Jon. And to think they used to say 'if something sounds too good to be true, it probably is'.

But Cohen didn't stop there. After soJewish, he decided to expand his empire, creating a whole network of sites under the brand 'Cyberbritain.com'. And appropriately enough for a network with such a porny sounding name, the first two Cyberbritain sites were porn sites – Hunt4Porn.com and dotadults.com – both naked (sorry) attempts to attract the sticky white pound. The pitch? That the sites would provide the best way for one-handed surfers to find adult websites.† The reality? The site was just some tacky window dress-

---

* I would have called it 'Look! Jews talking'.
† Other ways include: close eyes, throw rock, hit porn site.

ing that Cohen had bolted on to an existing public-domain listing of hard- and soft-core smut.

But there was still a boom on and, again, the press lapped it up. Everyone knew that sex sells, and lazy journalists could only speculate what adding an 'adult' arm to a company already 'worth' 'five' 'million' 'pounds' would do to its valuation. But fortunately, they didn't have to – Ben was quite happy to tell them exactly what it did to his company's valuation. It increased it immeasurably, he explained. There was no doubt about it: he was now Britain's richest teenage dot com entrepreneur.

Even if he did say so himself.

Of course, all of this smacks of jealousy on my part. If I could have achieved even half of his success while still producing almost no original content or having any original ideas, I'd have done it in a heartbeat. Well, of course I would. Even if it meant having to use porn to do it, like Ben did. There is nothing inherently bad about online pornographers – as I've said before, they're basically responsible for inventing ecommerce and online video – and there is something only a little inherently bad about passing off other people's porn directory as your own. I had to admit it was pretty enterprising.

But ... and here comes the but ... BUT there is something very wrong about pedalling other people's porn, creating tons of artificial wealth on the back of it, and then pretending you hated doing it.

Which is what Cohen did the moment the market crashed and the hype dried up.

Four years after creating soJewish, Hunt4Porn and the rest, Cohen sent out a press release to journalists, marking the occasion of his twentieth birthday.

Reading through it, I was absolutely stunned. This was, after all, the guy who had spent the last half-decade or so relentlessly promoting himself and his media empire. The man who had gladly given journalists quotes about his wealth and how he was changing the world. A man who was quoted in a TV interview saying 'money has no morality'. And now, after the dot com industry collapses, he sends out this. A press release to mark his birthday. And what a press release ...

Once I'd finished reading the emailed press release, I immediately hit the forward button and sent it to Sam Lewis, annotated with my own comments. Here's exactly what I sent (the text in bold is from the press release; the italics are my comments) ...

To: Sam Lewis
From: Paul Carr
Subject: Total genius or unbelievable dick – you decide ...

The Last of the Teenage Dot.Com Millionaires is to Disappear ... He's turning twenty

A strong start. If the secret of a good press release is to grab journalists' attention with a strong title then he's played a blinder. When I read that title, my attention was immediately grabbed by the fact that I was suddenly vomiting involuntarily on my own shoes.

Benjamin Cohen has been at the forefront of one of the most innovative industries that the UK has ever seen, the dot com industry. Founder of soJewish.com, the community portal, he was thrust into the limelight at the tender age of 16.

Yeah, thrust into the limelight like Michael Douglas was thrust into Catherine Zeta-Jones. Or Harold Shipman was thrust into murdering old people.

Figures of £5m were quoted for his personal stake in the business. As it goes ...

as it goes? As it goes?! – another useful tip, Ben, don't get your press release drafted by a chirpy Essex builder.

... the company merged with the London Jewish News ... and then reversed into Totally plc on the AIM market. For a day Cohen was the youngest director of a publicly quoted company ever. His share in Totally was not worth anything like the £5m that was quoted two years earlier, it was valued at £310,000 ...

Hang on. Let me read that again. Is he saying he wasn't a millionaire at all? He's admitting it was never true? He lied in the title of his press release and then admitted it three paragraphs later? That's pretty ballsy.

... but had reduced to £40,000 when he came to sell his stake.

So in pounds sterling, he was actually a forty thousandaire. In what currency was he a millionaire? Yen?

Cohen was hyped from day one of his media debut. However, this was not by PR people – he had none – but by the press. Speculating at his stake in the business, Ben was made into a millionaire.

... and now the Oscar for most disingenuous paragraph in a bullshit press release. The envelope, please.

Cohen for his part never truly believed what was said about him and his bank balance and realised that at the end of the day he'd be very lucky to walk away from SoJewish.com with a few hundred thousand pounds.

Unlucky.

. . .

[Said Cohen] 'When I look back at the way that I was ... I cringe. I was at the top of an industry that was built on sand. I was carried away with the fact that I, a mere 17 year old had as much experience as anyone else at building an Internet company.'

'I can remember how rude I could be at times to journalists and people phoning up for advice. Back then, I could be as obnoxious as I liked and people would still come back for more, they had to, I was Benjamin Cohen, the Dot Com sensation.'

Also, Benjamin Cohen, the cock.

... Shortly after the [BBC2 *Trouble at the Top* documentary that followed Cohen and his 'businesses' as they struggled to make money] **was screened Benjamin says he grew up.**

'I realised the stupidity of what was going on, there was no concentration on key revenue streams, it was all about land grab

and not about money. I decided that the only way there would be a future was to start to cut back.'

. . .

Benjamin also decided to start a degree at King's College London in Religion, Philosophy and Ethics. This, he says, has also forced him to grow up.

'The added work load of a degree has made me focus a lot more when I am in work. I still manage to spend around 40 hours a week at work but it is a lot more focused on what can make money as opposed to what makes me look good in the papers.'

He added ... in a press release ... sent to THE PAPERS.

'I think that really I spent too much time flirting with the media and not enough time working in the early years.'

His three-page PRESS RELEASE continues.

The degree has also made Benjamin rethink his impressions of internet pornography, a subject that he has been criticised for in the past. CyberBritain.com owned Hunt4Porn.com, Europe's first and largest adult search engine. Destined to cause controversy, Cohen has always displayed mixed views towards this aspect of his empire.

'In one sense I still stand by the comments that I made last year about freedom of speech and the right of the individual to access pornography. Yet I have come to realise that there is really little money that I can make out of it.'

The above might actually be my favourite paragraph, not just in this press release, but in any press release ever sent. It's a heart-warming tale of Damascene conversion ...

God: 'You know, Saul, there's really very little money to be made in persecuting Christians.'

Saul: 'Good point, God. I think I'll change my ways. Call me Paul.'

Benjamin has grown up into a sensitive and sensible young man. He has dispensed of his obnoxious, brash manner of the past into quite the perfect gentleman. He has the ability to laugh at himself and realise his faults but most importantly, change them.

Seriously, Sam, I PROMISE I didn't make this up. 'Quite the perfect gentleman'!

'I prefer the new me a million [*] times more than the old one. I much prefer the calmer, sensitive and perceptive nearly twenty-something than the excitable temperamental teenager.'

*40,000.

Benjamin Cohen was the first and the last dotcom teenage millionaire ...

No, he wasn't. He's just admitted that. Do you think he even read this thing as he was writing it?

... sure there were many after he first appeared but they disappeared from the scene long ago. He's excited that the label will finally be dropped and he can become Benjamin Cohen, the businessman, student, media commentator and human being.'

Well, one out of four ain't bad. Although, if he's really off to university I can't wait for his next press releases ...

Benjamin Cohen: 'The media claimed I'd got off with my housemate while I was drunk, but that was just hype ...'

Benjamin Cohen: 'Why reports of my £4.5m student loan were greatly exaggerated.'

Benjamin Cohen: 'My mixed views on downloading tons of porn while I should be revising.'

Amazing.

P

1.7

It wasn't just Sam and I who were having fun at Ben Cohen's expense. The release was not exactly well received by the new media press, with many – including iconic geek news site *The Register* – simply printing the release verbatim and inviting readers to make their own comments.

You see, journalists will tolerate falling victim to hype; they'll tolerate overblown valuations and they'll even embrace precocious sixteen-year-old kids who claim to be worth millions of pounds, while the journalists themselves struggle to pay their rent. Yes, we're jealous and we're bitter, but we have a job to do and, in a boom, we're your bitches.

But when the market crashes and the same precocious kid sends a press release admitting that it was all bullshit: hoo boy, then your ass is ours.

As 2003 turned into 2004, more and more entrepreneurs who a couple of years earlier had treated the press like their own personal PR machines, found themselves calling up journalists and begging to take us for lunch. I knew that I was in exactly the place you should be during a flood. On the high ground.

It didn't matter how much money these people were losing; there were still plenty of stories to tell, and I was still going to be paid to write them, whatever happened. There was nothing that would make me envy the entrepreneurs I was writing about – nothing on earth that would make me want to trade places with them.

Nothing.

No way.

Not a chance.

And then I got the call.

Did I fancy a trip to Clapham?

2.0

'The interactive hit of the summer'

So this is what an undisclosed location looks like, I thought.

It was a balmy early spring evening in 2005 and I was standing outside an anonymous block of flats in south-west London. It was one of those buildings that originally provided affordable council housing for inner-city families but had since been bought by developers and turned into 'luxury apartments' to keep young professionals safe from the drug addicts and ASBO kids that, for some reason, inhabit the capital's streets. It was all key-pad access and CCTV, and yet with so much glass that it practically screamed 'throw a rock at me'. I managed to resist.

Instead, I found the number I was looking for and pressed a chrome buzzer.

Silence.

Did it even work? Was buzzing too working class for this place?

I pressed again.

A few moments later the door opened with a barely audible click and I stepped inside, pulling the door firmly closed behind me. I was on the inside now. Safe. Just a smooth lift ride was all that remained between me and the fifth floor: the gateway to Perplex City.

Everything inside Perplex City was overwhelming. The walls were painted a stark – almost blinding – white. Likewise the furniture – what little there was – and even the mugs in the kitchen were plain white. The open-plan flat was full of perhaps a dozen people, crammed together around the plain white desks, tapping and clicking away at their computers.

No one even glanced up from their work as I walked in.

Secrecy is everything at Perplex City. Secrecy and flat-screen monitors, literally dozens of which were crammed into that small, white room that acted as the top-secret headquarters for what would, one man hoped, become the most talked-about phenomenon of the coming summer.

The first anyone knew about Perplex City was when cryptic adverts started appearing in newspapers around the world, including the *Guardian* and the *New York Times*, appealing for help in finding a mysterious missing object known as 'the Cube'.

No contact information was given on the adverts – just a link to a site called perplexcity.com. Meanwhile, around the world hundreds of postcards simultaneously appeared in clubs, bars, shops and other public places, all containing subtle clues that led to the same website.

The chatter on the Internet was clear: something fucking weird was going down. And the reason I was in south-west London was because I was one of the few people who knew exactly what it was.

2.1

During the dot com crash of 2000, not every interesting Internet company had gone bust. Not every daring entrepreneur had lost everything – nor had all of them cashed in their millions just in time and retired to a south sea island while their peers went to the wall. A few (mainly those with the deepest pockets, who hadn't squandered their investment on flights on Concorde for senior executives, or office furniture made out of reclaimed airline parts) had seen the storm coming and adapted their businesses accordingly to ride out the crisis.

Two of these bright young survivors were Michael Smith and Tom Boardman.

Michael and Tom met at university and soon became firm friends, bonding over their twin passions of drinking and playing games. Well, three passions really: they also enjoyed playing drinking games. One day, while playing chess and drinking vodka, the idea came to them: why not combine their passions and replace these boring old chess pieces with shot glasses? Every time you took a piece, you took a shot.

Simple, but brilliant. They called their invention 'Shot Glass Chess'.

Before long, the brainiac twosome had rolled in their fourth love – making money – and had drawn up a business plan for a mail order company that would sell Shot Glass Chess, along with a whole host of other boys' toys. And how better to start a business, when you're fresh out of university and working out of your tiny rented flat, than by setting up shop on the Internet? After all, this was 1998 and there was a dot com boom going on.

To fund the business they pitched up at a dot com networking event called 'First Tuesday' clutching their business plan and – in a story that would become Internet legend – walked away a few hours later with a deal that would give them seven figures of venture capital investment to start their business. They decided to call the company 'Hotbox.co.uk' and their first logo was a little box with fire coming out of it. You couldn't fault their branding.

You also couldn't fault their flair for publicity. The company's first press cutting, which Michael and Tom still display proudly in their (now considerably larger and more opulent) shared flat, is a review of Shot Glass Chess from a Scandinavian porn magazine. It features two topless models getting drunk and playing chess. Swede dreams are made of those.

A couple of years later, when the dot com crash came, Hotbox was determined not to go to the wall. The company had low overheads, growing revenues and decent profit margins, and Michael and Tom were confident they could stay afloat if they expanded their business beyond the UK into the lucrative international market. Going international would mean making some big changes. For a start they would need to take the momentous step of moving from being the UK-centric Hotbox.co.uk to the world-beating Hotbox.com.

There was just one tiny problem: the name Hotbox.com was already owned by a rival site offering boys' toys.

Where by boys', I mean men's.

And by toys I mean hardcore pornography.

Hotbox.com was the home of 'Danni's Hot Box', owned by Danni Ashe, a forty-year-old former erotic dancer and probably the most famous and successful female Internet porn celebrity, unless you count Paris Hilton.

Using the Hotbox name internationally was a non-starter for Michael and Tom and so with a bit of thinking outside the – um – box, Firebox.com was born. With its new international client base, the company rode out the dot com crash like a mother. By 2004, Firebox was listed in the *Sunday Times* Fast Track 100 as the thirteenth fastest growing privately owned business in the UK. And it was in that same year that I first met Michael, all thanks to a phone call from my friend Emily Dubberley.

Emily's name will very possibly be familiar if you are a reader of any one of the zillions of women's magazines that Emily contributes to. She is what women's magazines charmingly call a 'sexpert', and a better example of the genre you'll struggle to find. That is, a woman whose job it is to have an enormous amount of extremely filthy, adventurous sex, and write about it, so that the rest of us might feel inadequate in both imagination and stamina. She is also the founder of Cliterati.co.uk, the UK's finest and most gloriously named repository of female-oriented 'erotic fiction' (porn stories) and was also the founding editor of *Scarlet*, the sex magazine for which I'd reviewed porn DVDs when I first arrived in London.

She is, you will have surmised, excellent company and a wonderful lush.

I always smile when I see 'Emily' flash up on my mobile's screen, knowing that when she calls there's a good chance it's to tell me a brilliantly indiscreet story about someone famous she's just kicked out of her flat, or perhaps her bed.

'Hello, darling,' she cooed, her vocal chords softened by a thousand blow jobs (she has run one-day courses at London's trendy Soho House, teaching Sloanes how to suck. I'm not making any of this up.) 'I'm in Soho with Michael Smith. I thought you might like to meet him.'

Now, if there's one thing Emily enjoys more than sex (and know this: there isn't), it's networking – making introductions between people who might be useful to each other in some way. She seems to know everyone, and not just in a biblical sense. Porn stars, entrepreneurs, strippers, actors, burlesque dancers, journalists, sex toy inventors, politicians ... you name them, she's got them on speed dial. I'd asked Emily to keep an eye out for anyone she thought might make an interesting subject for my *Guardian* column and she'd decided that Michael might fit the bill. Specifically, she thought I might be able to give him some coverage for his first new venture after Firebox.

And so it was that I ended up in the Lab Bar on Old Compton Street, supping a hugely overpriced rum and coke and watching Emily flirting her arse off with a young and phenomenally wealthy entrepreneur.

To be fair, it is hard not to be impressed by Michael – not just the head of the thirteenth fastest growing private company in the UK but also irritatingly good looking in that slightly dishevelled way that girls seem to like but which, whenever I try to emulate it, I just end up looking like I'm trying to sell them *The Big Issue*. He was also, thanks to Firebox, very wealthy indeed.

What an absolute cunt, I thought.

And to make matters worse, he was drinking orange juice. In the middle of the afternoon!

Naturally, I hoped whatever new venture Michael was setting up would turn out to be awful, an idea so bad that, when it launched, he would be scandalised in the press, lose all of his money and perhaps even his youthful looks. I am, you'll understand, the jealous type.

'So,' I asked, sipping my rum and coke, 'tell me about this new idea of yours.'

Putting down his orange juice – *cunt* – he reached into the pockets of his designer jeans and pulled out three or four brightly coloured pieces of cardboard, which looked to me a lot like giant trading cards. Each one had a different puzzle drawn on it: a maze, some kind of picture puzzle featuring a Manga-esque woman, a photograph of some biscuits, if I remember correctly.

'Puzzles?' I asked, aiming for dismissive and smacking head first into jealous.

Michael looked defensive, and sighed with the weariness of a man who gets that a lot. 'No, not puzzles ... Well, not really. I can't say too much, but basically we've created a new kind of puzzle game. It combines very special puzzles with a treasure hunt.'

'I get it,' I lied. 'How exactly will it work?'

'We're not saying yet.'

Of course you're not saying. Why would you tell me anything? It's not like I've come all the way across London and paid eight fucking pounds for a rum and coke just to hear about your idea. You just keep it to yourself and enjoy your orange juice.

Cunt.

The truth is, while I wanted so much – *so* much – to dislike Michael and his idea, I couldn't. On the contrary, I could see there were all sorts of possibilities in what he was talking about. Possibilities for combining puzzles with storytelling to engage with an audience in a really deep, emotional way. To use puzzles to actually allow a story to play out inside people's heads. I knew all of this because what Michael was describing was an Alternate Reality Game, or ARG.

2.2

When history considers the phenomenon of early twenty-first-century film hype, two letters will stand out like twin, towering, disappointing giants. A cinematic atrocity of World Trade Center proportions.

A 9/11 of mediocrity.

Those letters are 'AI'. Make no mistake, Steven Spielberg's 2001 robo-flick *Artificial Intelligence: AI* was by far the most grotesque example of overhyping and underdelivering effluent ever to be discharged from the Hollywood creative sewer. Horrible dialogue, a gushingly oversentimental plot and three – or was it four? – dire endings, each more of a mawkish non sequitur than the last.

I saw the film at university, sitting next to a girl I was head over heels in love with – more on her later – and I actually walked out of the auditorium to buy a hot dog. Anything to escape the tedium of the worst film ever made.

But to be fair to Spielberg, it is hard to imagine how any film could possibly live up to the very special kind of hype that preceded its release. While most films make do with an advertising poster campaign and some kind of fast-paced trailer with a dramatic voice-over, the marketing team responsible for *AI* commissioned Microsoft (the world's biggest computer company and inventor of the world's most condescending talking paperclip) to create a brand new kind of interactive advertisement.

Codenamed 'The Beast', it was not so much a piece of marketing as a totally immersive on-and-offline adventure game that grabbed players by the throat and threw them into a fantasy world of murder, intrigue and seemingly unsolvable puzzles.

It worked like this. Hidden in the posters and cinema adverts for the film were a series of dots that corresponded to a phone number. Cinema-goers smart enough to decipher the code and dial the number would hear a sinister message informing them that 'Evan Chan was murdered' and that 'Jeanine is the key'. Those who managed to figure out that clue – which involved a trip to Google – could then move on to the next phase of the game, and the next, and the next, until those who had proceeded far enough actually started to receive phone calls of their own. At home. In the middle of the night. All leading closer to the truth behind the murder of Evan Chan.

What those bemused players in 2001 didn't realise, as they trawled for clues on the web and waited for late-night phone calls from fictional characters, was that they were witnessing the birth of the alternate reality game, or ARG – defined by technology news site CNET as 'an obsession-inspiring genre that blends real-life treasure hunting, interactive storytelling, video games and online community'. The success of 'The Beast', both in terms of promoting a dreadful movie and in engaging players on a level never before seen in marketing, led to an avalanche of similar ARGs, to promote everything from 'urban' T-shirt brands to pulp spy novels.

But the level of round-the-clock commitment required by both players and marketers meant that most of the copycats vanished without trace, with only a handful – like Nokia's brilliantly titled 'Nokia Game' – registering as more than a passing blip on the cultural trend radar.

For a couple of years it looked as if ARGs were destined to join

Letsbuyit.com and Barcode Battlers in the e-dustbin of neat ideas that never really caught on. But then two things happened. First came the broadband explosion, creating a vast army of people who were now spending hours online every day looking for something to do. And then, not long afterwards, Dan Brown's book *The Da Vinci Code* shot to the top of the bestseller charts, introducing those very same people to the world of extreme puzzle solving. High-speed Internet access, a horde of puzzle freaks – it was only a matter of time before ARGs were back with a vengeance.

But what Michael was describing as we sat in the Lab Bar was an ARG with a difference. This was an ARG where the only thing it was promoting was itself – no secret movie or mobile phone brand to be pushed: the puzzles themselves were to be the product. It was, by any measure, a bloody good idea, and with the marketing and distribution might of Firebox behind it, it was hard to see how it wouldn't fly.

I ordered another rum and Coke and, dropping any pretence of aloof indifference, told Michael how cool his idea sounded. So cool, in fact, that I had a suggestion:

'Why don't you put a small section of a map on the back of each card? That way, when people have collected enough cards, they can piece them all together and follow the map to the prize.' It seemed like a pretty obvious step to me.

'That's a good idea,' he lied, pretending to write it down in his notebook.

With that, I left Emily to her flirting and promised to keep an eye on Michael and his puzzles, and maybe write something about them when he was ready to go public.

2.3

As it turned out, Michael and I ran into each other again a few months later, when he turned up at one of Emily's parties, thrown for friends and fans of Cliterati.co.uk.

Noted in society for their host's exquisite liquor cabinet, Emily's parties are generally considered to be both a great way to meet your fellow media types and the quickest and easiest way to get laid in north London. At the first one I'd been to, two porn stars showed up, along with early nineties Britpop icon Louise Wener, two magazine editors and a tiny woman dressed as a prostitute. Apparently the latter was actually a very famous burlesque dancer.

That same night I'd dragged along an old school mate of mine who had turned up with his very prim high school sweetheart. At the end of the night he ended up going home with his by now slightly less prim high school sweetheart *and* a very cute freelance journalist who was only supposed to be there to profile Emily for the *Metro*. The three of them slept together, in a variety of different configurations, for the next six months. Our other friends found the story unbelievable but it was all in a night's work for Emily.

The party where I ran into Michael was a slightly less sordid affair – but only slightly. Emily had promised to introduce me to some interesting Internet entrepreneurs who were going to be in attendance and who might make good column fodder, so technically I was attending the party for 'work', which is easier said than done when the only available seating options in Emily's living room included a sex swing and a space hopper with an enormous dildo attached.

Over bright green jelly shots containing God only knows what, I cornered Michael and begged him to tell me more about his idea. Forget shorthand and fake sheiks – plastic shot glasses full of alcoholic gelatine are the most important tools in the journalist's arsenal.

'Oh, come on, at least tell me something,' I pleaded. 'I promise I won't write about it until you're ready. You're one of the few people who was successful the first time round *and* is still launching a new company. You'd make a great story.'

Shot glasses *and* flattery.

My last memory of the evening is holding a plastic cup full to the brim with vodka while trying to remain focused on a conversation about vaginal casting with a stunning blonde girl, while Michael sat in a corner competing with Emily's *paramour du jour* to see who could recite pi to the greatest number of digits. Michael won by a healthy margin, reaching about twenty before we all passed out.

But before that, thanks in part to the jelly shots, I had managed to extract a few snippets of information out of him: things were continuing apace with his new venture, they had a name for the company and had even decided how the treasure hunt portion of the game was going to work. What they'd decided – and this is brilliant – is that each card was going to have a small piece of map on the back which, when put together with other cards, would create a much bigger map which would in turn lead to a clue which would in turn lead to the treasure.

The cheeky bastard.

Not only was he better looking than me, wealthier and able to remember pi to twenty decimal places (I got as far as 3.14 ...) but now he was going to make his fortune – again – and my brilliant map idea was going to help.

The bastard.

The utter bastard.

'You utter bastard,' I said 'You owe me.'

'Ha. Okay, what do you want?'

'I'll think of something.'

2.4

And so it was that I found myself, notepad in hand, standing in Michael's stark white rented flat on Lavender Hill in Clapham; the first journalist to have ventured inside Perplex City.

I'd pitched the idea to my editor as a red-hot exclusive double-page feature about a company that was going out of its way to shun publicity. In reality, during the year and a bit since we'd first met, Michael and I had become really good friends and I'd made him promise that, as soon as he was ready to go public with Perplex City, I'd be his first call.

The reason for the secrecy of the location, which I admit provided an element of excitement to the article, suggesting I had Bob Woodward-esque access to this secretive new business, had a slightly more mundane basis in reality.

As he sat down to be interviewed in the flat's single stark white bedroom, which had been converted into a makeshift conference room, Michael asked me for a favour: 'Er ... there's just one thing. The landlord doesn't know we're running a business from the flat – we've told him there's just two of us living here; so every time he comes round we have to hide all the computers and send all the staff away. You can't tell anyone where we're based or we'll get kicked out.'

'Don't worry, I'll just say it's somewhere in south London. Anyway, if I drew a map, you'd only steal it, you bastard.'

He laughed. As well he might.

Suddenly, from the other room came a shout. More of a yell, really.

'They've found it!'

To this day I've no idea if the moment was a set-up for my benefit – to this day Michael swears it wasn't – but at that exact point a staffer announced to the rest of the flat that one of the players had stumbled across the next phase of the game – an online newspaper called the *Perplex City Sentinel* (perplexcitysentinel.com).

Michael explained: a few days earlier his team had sent out clues which led smart players to the famous zebra crossing at Abbey Road. There, at a precise time, a character (played by Michael's actress sister, Anna) handed over envelopes containing clues to the next phase of the game. Twenty or so people had turned up in the flesh while a couple of hundred more watched from around the world, via webcam. Evidently they had managed to piece together the clues contained in the envelope because the fan forums were suddenly abuzz with talk about the *Perplex City Sentinel* and theories on what lay behind its mysterious subscription-only wall. And, of course, what it all meant for the search for the cube.

One player had even pointed out that 'sentinel' is another word for 'guardian' and was suggesting that the paper was involved. I laughed but did wonder for a moment whether I was in deeper than I thought. Surrounded by those white walls, with pictures of fictional people and maps of fictional places on the wall, it was almost impossible to know what was real and what was fiction. I was actually starting to get nervous, like Keanu Reeves in *The Matrix*. But in south London, in an illegal sub-let.

I got a few more good quotes from Michael about the game and then made my excuses and left, strangely relieved to be back in the gritty normality of south London's muggers and ASBO kids.

As I walked to the station to catch my train back to reality, my mind was racing. Michael's Perplex City game was exciting, for sure, and I genuinely thought it was going to be huge. But that wasn't why I was suddenly feeling a surge of adrenalin strong enough to make my head spin. Ever since I'd started writing for the *Guardian*, I'd been meeting people with interesting ideas that could very possibly make them rich if market conditions were right, and I hadn't cared. I'd seen it all before, the first time around. The promise, the hype, the bubble. It was all bullshit.

But standing in Perplex City HQ, seeing all those ultra-creative workers crafting a story that was already becoming an obsession among its players; hearing Michael's enthusiasm when he talked about bringing the Internet together with other media and knowing that he was having a ball doing it – I knew I was seeing something different.

These weren't Ben Cohens sitting in this stark, white flat; these were creative people and entrepreneurial people and technology people working side by side, building something that could genuinely become a phenomenon. And if Michael's past performance was anything to go by, they were going to make a killing in the process.

I was feeling something I hadn't felt for a while. And I was feeling it bad.

I was feeling jealous.

2.5

Of course, I'd like to believe that my article, in which I'd described Perplex City as 'the puzzle game gearing up to be the interactive phenomenon of the year', was entirely responsible for the success that the company had in the months that followed my visit. But I suspect it probably had more to do with the fact that Michael was offering prize money of £100,000 – or \$200,000 – to whoever successfully followed the clues and found the mysterious Receda

Cube. A cube which it was later revealed had been stolen from the very heart of Perplex City (a fictional place on a fictional planet) by person or persons unknown and hidden somewhere on earth.

What was clear, even in those early days, was that Michael was my kind of entrepreneur: someone who took every opportunity he could find to blow his own trumpet.

A few weeks after my article was published, Michael took me aside at a networking event and proudly showed me his new business card.

Another thing to know about dot com entrepreneurs is that they put in a huge amount of effort to get their business cards just *so*. In fact, if you're looking for the modern equivalent of Patrick Bateman – the lead character in Bret Easton Ellis' novel *American Psycho* – you'd do well to spend some time hanging around in dot com companies.

Michael's card was certainly very impressive. As is the dot com way, it was double-sided, in full colour, with company info on the front and a cool graphic on the back. On closer examination, the graphic turned out to be a scrap of newsprint containing a gushing review of Perplex City: 'the puzzle game that is gearing up to become the interactive phenomenon of the year ...'

He'd cut and pasted the words straight from my article.

First the maps, now this. The cheeky bastard.

3.0

'You can lead a leopard to dog milk ...'

At the beginning of 2005 I had honestly believed that I was happy, that I was proceeding nicely towards my goal of being famous and successful and rich. But in the weeks after my trip to south London I became more and more anxious; aware that, for all the fun I was having writing about people like Michael – and now seeing my words appear on their business cards – something was missing from my life.

Fame, say.

Or success.

Or wealth.

Or the likely prospect of achieving any of the above soon.

I'm wasn't entirely sure when I'd sleepwalked over the line, but while being a published author and newspaper columnist writing about the troubled dot com industry made me the envy of my friends at twenty-three, it was starting to mark me out as a bit of a loser at twenty-five. The money I was being paid by the *Guardian* was barely enough to cover my rent, and the royalty statements from the books I'd written since my initial eight showed that I owed Prentice Hall approximately £3,000 in unearned advances.

And, to make matters worse, the Schadenfreude I'd once felt writing about struggling dot commers and their attempts to steer their rickety old ships through the murky post-bomb seas of opportunity was fast wearing off. Perplex City might have been the first new company that made me feel jealous but I knew it wouldn't be the last.

There's no doubt about it, the industry was recovering – proper, stable businesses were being built and people who six months before had been struggling to break even were now starting to get more money from investors and even buyout offers from big media companies. The less Schaden they experienced, the less freude I felt. My jealousy was moving from mild, to strong, to intense to seething.

3.1

There was no single epiphany moment – no episode with me reading about a guy whose company had just been bought by Yahoo! for half a billion dollars that made me throw my laptop to the floor and shout 'enough!' before furiously starting to scribble the business plan that would make my fortune.

It would make a neat story if there was, but that's not how it happened.

How it *did* happen was that I had yet another conversation with Clare Christian about how bored and broke I was. It was a conversation we'd had many times before, and Clare always found a way to remind me that, actually, on balance, things were pretty great. This time, though, she was just back from another bout of maternity leave (seriously – for a woman with two children, she seemed to have been pregnant continuously for about five years) and was talking about how she wanted to spend more time at home with her children. The publishing house she was working for had been very accommodating – allowing her to split her time between home-working and the office – but the arrangement was far from perfect.

After both of us saying how we weren't entirely happy with our lot, for different reasons, we moved on to another subject we'd talked about a thousand times before: how we really should get round to pitching our *London by London* book idea to a publisher.

London by London was the sister publication to *The Friday Thing* and was a weekly ezine for people who lived in the capital. It had a simple format: every week people would email in their questions about the city, and we'd publish the best of them. Subscribers – there were about 15,000 – would be encouraged to provide answers to the questions and those answers would be published the following week, along with a new batch of questions. Simple.

Over the years, we'd built up a vast archive of questions and answers – ranging from the genuinely useful ('where can I hire a cinema for my birthday party?') to the utterly fucked up (one subscriber tried to recruit other readers to take part in the 'perfect' heist). As a publisher, Clare was certain that *London by London*'s huge archive would make a brilliant guidebook but we were struggling to get publishers to agree. Or at least they did agree, but only if we did it on their terms. A typical meeting would go like this:

Us: 'We have a successful email magazine with 15,000 subscribers, three years of archive material and between us we have years of experience in writing, editing and publishing. We'd like to make a book.'

Big publisher: 'We love it! We absolutely love it. We definitely want to do this.'

Us: 'That's great – and the best thing about it is that there's an existing audience for it. You don't need to change a thing.'

Big publisher: 'Exactly! And we wouldn't want to change anything. If it ain't broke, right?'

Us: 'Exactly!'

Big publisher: 'Okay, we'll just need to run it by some of the people in marketing and see what they think. Can we get back to you next week?'

Us: 'Sure, we look forward to hearing what they say.'

We'd walk away elated, certain that this time – *this* time – we'd found someone who loved the quirkiness of *London by London*, and its bizarre question and answer format as much as we did. And then the same follow-up call would come:

Big publisher: 'Good news! Marketing absolutely loved the book. *Loved* it. We're really keen to do this.'

Us: 'Excellent.'

Big publisher: 'There's just one thing. We're not sure about the format. We know it works really well on the Internet, but if it's going to work as a book, we need to position it next to the other travel guides.'

Us: 'But it's not really a travel guide. If anything, it's like a travel guide for people who already live here.'

Big publisher: 'Oh, no, we absolutely get that, but we just think it would sell more if it took some cues from other titles on the market.'

Us: 'For instance?'

Big publisher: 'How wedded are you to the Q&A format?'

* Click *

It was insane. How could these people not see how something with a decent-sized fan base on the Internet could really easily translate into a book? And how did they think that abandoning the big gimmick that made *London by London* unique – the fact that they were questions and answers provided by real Londoners – could possibly be a good idea? The answer, it soon became clear, is that the publishing industry at that time was scared shitless of the web. The Internet to them was this strange, mystical place where rules of popularity were different, where quirkiness was the order of the day. If something was going to make the transition from the web to books, it was first going to have to be made safe: wedged into an existing publishing format that didn't freak out the sales teams whose job it was to convince the likes of Waterstone's and Borders to stock it. The web was something that needed to be tamed, not understood.

We hit one brick wall after another.

I don't know whether it was having one meeting too many, or Clare's desire to spend more time with her family, or my jealousy over my friends starting to get successful again – probably a combination of all of those things – but in any case we made our minds up.

Like so many entrepreneurs have done, before and since.

Fuck it.

Let's do the show right here.

3.2

Juggling our day jobs, Clare and I began to write a business plan for a new kind of hybrid Internet and publishing company. One that would specialise in finding the hottest Internet talent and translating it into brilliant books, without losing the unique voice that had made it successful online in the first place.

In tribute to *The Friday Thing*, the first business Clare and I had collaborated on, we decided to name our news company 'The Friday Project'.

Our first challenge when writing the business plan was to figure out why big publishing houses were so scared of the web. It wasn't that there weren't rich pickings to be had on there. Thanks to the ease with which anyone could post their work online, the Internet had become a veritable pick and mix of brilliant new writers and illustrators (as well as some terrible ones). And yet – with only a few exceptions – every site that traditional publishers tried to turn into a book had ended up – to use a phrase so beloved of the web, sucking ass. We soon learned that our experience with *London by London* was just one example of what was happening to dozens – perhaps hundreds – of web authors and editors every year.

To be fair to the publishers, though, the Internet writers didn't do themselves many favours either. Most writers who published their work online had never had to be part of the mainstream 'system' – they had become used to being their own editors, and they hated the idea that they would have to adapt their 'unique' voice for a mainstream audience. Book publishing also suffers from ridiculous lead times of up to a year between submitting a manuscript (that is, the text of a book) and seeing the finished product on the book-shelves. To a web author used to the instant gratification of online publishing, waiting six hours, let alone six months, to see the fruits of their labours published was ludicrous.

On the strength of our business plan, and a pilot edition of the *London by London* book that we produced ourselves, we managed to convince Anthony Cheetham, the founder of Orion Publishing, to invest the money we needed to set up the business. He also agreed to become chairman of the company, giving us instant kudos. With Anthony involved, we were able to get a meeting with the CEO of Macmillan, Richard Charkin, who – unbelievably – agreed that Macmillan would handle the sales and distribution for our titles.

Suddenly The Friday Project was in business, and our launch announcement received a flood of publicity. Well, okay, a drizzle:

the two major book trade magazines, *The Bookseller* and *Publishing News*, ran nice features about this new 'web-to-print' publisher, and Internet journalists greeted us with a mixture of excitement and curiosity. The former wondered whether we were web folk trying to move into publishing, while the latter asked themselves whether we were publishers trying to move into the web. In reality, we were both, something that only really the *Guardian*'s coverage of our launch seemed to understand. But then it would: I wrote it.

Regardless of whether we were a publishing company using the web, or a web company using print, one thing was certainly clear – my days as a journalist were over. I had crossed over to the dark side. I was an entrepreneur.

3.3

My new career direction brought with it some major benefits. For the first time in my life I was being paid a proper salary. And a good one at that. Prior to The Friday Project, my monthly income *before* tax was less than £1,000 and, with rent of £650 a month, I was only able to live thanks to the sheer volume of parties with free food and drink that my job gave me access to.

My starting salary at The Friday Project was relatively modest by CEO standards but was more than enough to allow me to buy my own dinner. And buying dinner was certainly a concern as my year-long relationship with Maggie was long finished, and so were my free trips to the capital's finest restaurants.

There were other perks, too. During one meeting with our accountant it was revealed that, for some accountant reason that escapes me, Clare and I had been underpaid in the months immediately after starting the company. To make everything balance, we'd have to briefly increase our salaries by £10,000. Barely able to contain our glee, Clare and I went to the pub to celebrate – and afterwards, on my way home, I decided to send her a text message saying 'Holy fuck! Ten grand.' Just in case she'd forgotten.

Unfortunately, in my somewhat tipsy excitement, I texted the message to her landline number, where BT's text-to-voice technology magically translated it into a spoken message on her home answerphone. I can only imagine how traumatic it must have been for Clare's four-year-old son to check mummy and daddy's messages the next morning only to hear a demented Dalek voice chanting 'Ho-lee fock exclamation mark – ten graynd.' Clare was less than amused.

I laughed my arse off. Even if it was only very temporary, ten fucking grand was ten fucking grand.

Another advantage to the buzz that surrounded the launch of 'the world's first web-to-print publishing house' was that interesting people from other parts of the media started phoning us up. One such call came a few days after our big launch announcement.

I was about to jump on the tube from my new girlfriend's house into work. It was pouring with rain and I was about half an hour late – but it was an unknown number so I thought I'd better take the call.

'Hello,' said the unmistakably American voice on the other end of the phone, 'is this Paul Carr?'

'Speaking,' I said, walking through the station entrance and heading towards the escalators.

'This is Alison Benson calling from Pretty Matches Productions. I work with Sarah Jessica Parker here in New York. We've seen some of the press you guys have been getting and we're really keen to talk to you about a possible partnership.'

Soaking wet, late and blocking the way to the escalators, I didn't really register any of what Alison was saying.

'That sounds interesting,' I said, 'but I'm just about to get on a train. Can you call me back in an hour on this number.'

'Sure, no problem,' said Alison.

'Thanks,' I said, hanging up.

It was only when I got down to the platform that it hit me. Oh my God. Sarah Jessica fucking Parker's business partner wants to talk to me. And I just hung up on her. What kind of fucking idiot am I?

I wanted to run off the train to try to call her back, but it was too late. We were already moving. Oh God. What an idiot.

But then another thought hit me. Sarah Jessica Parker's business partner wanted to talk to me, but I'd told her I was too busy. Isn't that exactly what they teach you in celebrity school? Be cool. Act like you don't care. Make them think you're doing them a favour?

Yeah, right. I spent the entire journey pacing the carriage, willing the train to skip a few stations just so I could get to the surface quicker and call Alison back.

It wasn't just Pretty Matches that wanted to partner with us. Over the weeks and months that followed The Friday Project's launch, our phones barely stopped ringing with an amazing variety of offers and potential partnerships. It turned out we'd accidentally launched the company right smack bang in the middle of a feeding frenzy.

3.4

Earlier the same year, Orion* had published a book called *The Intimate Adventures of a London Call Girl*, written by a pseudonymous high-class hooker called 'Belle de Jour'. The book had been adapted from a blog of the same name and literary London was aflame with debate about whether Belle was really a call girl or just a brilliant hoaxer. Either way, her book was selling like hot cakes and so everyone was looking for the next Belle. And with The Friday Project claiming to have its finger on the pulse of the web, everyone thought we knew where she might be found.

Naturally, we claimed to know *exactly* who the next hot sex blogger was – but we were keeping the secret to ourselves, unless we received a very good offer. In reality, we didn't have a fucking clue. We were spending all our waking hours trying to set up a company – the idea of actually commissioning any books still seemed like a distant dream.

Terrified of missing the boat, I quickly wrote an email and sent it to everyone I knew. It read:

'Help! I need to meet some sex bloggers, pronto. Anyone?'

From all the replies I got back the same two names kept coming

....

* Who publish this book, too – hello, Orion.

up: 'The Girl With A One-Track Mind' and 'Mimi New York'. 'The Girl', as she called herself, guarded her anonymity fiercely, to the point that I later discovered that a friend of mine had actually been on a couple of dates with her and she'd refused to tell him even her first name lest he sell his story to the press or otherwise compromise her. All anyone knew was that she lived in north London, was in some way connected with the media industry and enjoyed having lots and lots of sex and writing about it. Emily swore blind it wasn't her.

Mimi New York wasn't strictly a sex blogger, even though she did work in the sex trade. Mimi – again, not her real name – was a Welsh twentysomething Cambridge graduate who had moved to New York on a tourist visa and then 'forgotten' to leave. Instead she'd arranged a false social security number and, after a brief stint as a waitress in a strip club and realising that there was more money to be made on stage than behind the bar, she became a stripper at Scores, Manhattan's most prestigious 'gentleman's club' (think Stringfellows, NYC). Her blog, detailing the life of an illegal immigrant pole dancer, had become something of a sensation.

I fired off emails to both The Girl and Mimi using the addresses on their blogs in the hope that The Girl might be up for a meeting in London to discuss book-related things and that Mimi might be planning a trip back to the UK at some point. They both replied within a couple of days, and the good news was that they were keen to meet. But there was a catch. Mimi absolutely positively couldn't leave New York because otherwise she'd be busted for overstaying her visa and The Girl was currently out of the country. In New York City.

3.5

Passport in one hand and credit card in the other, the next thing I knew I was boarding a plane for my first ever overseas business trip. My flight got in to New York on the morning of 11 September 2005. There were about two dozen people on board, all of them looking decidedly nervous.

I had arranged to meet Mimi in a coffee bar down the road from her club. Obviously as she was anonymous I had no idea what she looked like, so we'd swapped descriptions by email a few days earlier. I found this almost impossibly difficult: describing myself in purely objective terms without sounding either arrogant or pig-ugly. 'Erm ... I'm sort of average height, brownish hair ... erm ... I'll probably be wearing trainers.' She, on the other hand, didn't need to say anything. I was meeting her just before she started work: she'd be the one who looked like a stripper. I suppose the mental image I had in my head was of a dyed-blonde giant of a woman, with enormous fake tits, wearing a thong and perhaps some kind of plumage in her hair. Sitting in a bar, drinking a cocktail with an umbrella.

On walking in, there was no sign of anyone looking even remotely like a stripper. A bored looking barman wiped down his bar while a busboy scooted around trying to look busy. Perhaps Mimi was in the toilet adjusting her feathers or doing coke off the top of the cistern or something. I did a quick lap of the bar but still no sign of anyone stripperish – just the barman, the busboy and a tiny girl in sweatpants sitting in a yoga pose on a sofa in the corner, sipping a coffee.

'Hey!' shouted the yoga girl, seeing me looking around and apparently without appreciating that the café was empty and that shouting was completely unnecessary. I turned round, as did every-one else. 'Are you Paul?' Her accent sounded as if a Welsh girl and a New Yorker had been in an accident and had been chopped in half and welded back together again, half and half. A linguistic cut and shut.

'You must be Mimi,' I said, feeling ashamed of myself for making such tacky assumptions. Turns out strippers don't look anything like strippers when they're not at work.

'Ruth,' said Mimi.

We talked for an hour or so, with Mimi – Ruth – filling me in on her bizarre back story. How she'd lied about being able to cook in order to get a job as a chef on a boat sailing to New York; how she'd gone through immigration pretending she was on holiday; the trials and tribulations of getting fake documentation; the community of 'illegals' she'd become part of – a community which could only get work in kitchens and strip clubs and who at any moment could find themselves rounded up and deported. Then there was her Mafia clientele, the perverts who assumed stripper was simply a euphemism for prostitute (as the song goes: just cos she dances go-go, that don't make her a ho, no) and the time she had hidden a wrap of cocaine in her thong and ended the evening bouncing off the walls having ingested the entire contents through her vagina.

Finishing her coffee Muth – Rimi – apologised for having to cut the meeting short but she had to go to work. 'But hey!' she yelled from no more than two feet away, 'why don't you come and watch me dance later. I'll get you in to the VIP room. You can have champagne and I'll introduce you to some people.'

I can honestly say, in the years I was writing about dot com millionaires not one of them had ever closed the meeting by inviting me to come and watch them take their clothes off for money. Oh, brave new world!

3.6

'Do you think there might be a book in her?' asked Clare when I checked in that evening.

'Among other things,' I replied.

'What?'

'Never mind. Yes, I absolutely do. And we *have* to publish it. It's an amazing story.'

My meeting with The Girl wasn't till the next evening but I'd arranged to meet Alison from Pretty Matches that same afternoon to introduce myself and The Friday Project and to figure out some way that our companies could work together.

The strange thing is that I wasn't even really a fan of Sarah Jessica Parker – *Sex and the City* always gave me unpleasant flashbacks to nights in with ex-girlfriends, forced to watch episode after episode while enduring a constant running commentary: 'Oh, Samantha is *just* like me', 'I *love* her shoes', 'I would *so* definitely sleep with

"Big"' and so on and so on as, with every hour that passed, I died a little inside.

But I *was* a huge fan of HBO, the company that made *Sex and the City* and the company that was now backing Sarah Jessica Parker's production company, Pretty Matches. You only have to look at a list of the programmes they've been responsible for to see why I held them in such awe.

Six Feet Under
Deadwood
Band of Brothers
Sex and the City
Curb Your Enthusiasm
The Larry Sanders Show.

Hell, they were even first to broadcast both The 'Thrilla in Manila' between Muhammad Ali and Joe Frazier ... and *Fraggle Rock*.

'Dance your cares away *clap * *clap *.' What's not to love?

Delighted that, thanks to my meeting with Ruth – Mimi – I had found at least something to suggest that it might make a good TV show or movie, I jumped in a cab and asked to be taken to Sixth Avenue (I'd been warned not to describe it by its official name, Avenue of the Americas – apparently doing so is the mark of a tourist).

Pulling up outside the HBO building – an enormous white scoop-shaped skyscraper – I couldn't help but feel totally out of my depth. This was my first time in New York and everything about the city – including this building – screamed 'big time' and 'celebrity' at a volume made only louder by the fact that New York Fashion Week was happening in the park directly opposite and the whole street was awash with paparazzi and models. Jesus, what the hell was I doing there? Bumming around London, meeting Internet celebrities was one thing, but this was HBO and the person I was about to meet was Sarah Jessica Parker's gal pal and business partner. And she thought *I* was the one with the magic beans: the one who held the secrets of the Internet and knew the names and phone numbers of The Next Big Thing.

To be honest, at that moment I wasn't even certain of my own name.

Walking into the vast lobby, I discovered that they take security VERY seriously at HBO, presumably to prevent perennially single women who haven't coped well with the end of *Sex and the City* from penetrating the walls and staging a cry-in. A surly security guard demanded to see some photo ID before he'd allow me to sign in and wait to be escorted upstairs. I showed him my passport and waited while he typed the details into a computer, to be stored God knows where. Ten minutes later, Alison appeared.

Wow. Apparently not satisfied with turning me into a gibbering sack of nerves by inviting me to the most visually striking building on Sixth Avenue, opposite a marquee full of supermodels, to discuss the possibility of a TV partnership with a company owned by Sarah Jessica Parker, which was backed by a cable network I was in awe of, Alison had decided to up the stakes by being absolutely stunning. Originally from Arizona but now splitting her time between LA and New York, she had managed to be both West Coast beautiful – blonde, perfect teeth, yada yada – and also East Coast cynical. Oh, and she was funny. Very funny, in fact. I liked her immediately.

We spent an hour talking about The Friday Project, and Mimi and The Girl and all of the other titles we were hoping to publish in the next few months. She even let me look out of her floor-to-ceiling window where, almost a hundred feet below, I could just about make out the inside of the tent where the models were changing their clothes for the catwalk. After I'd finished perving, we turned back to business.

'You know the deal we should do?' she said.

Of course I didn't know what deal we should do. I knew absolutely nothing about television. Christ, I was still learning how the book industry worked.

'What do you think?' I said, trying to act like I knew exactly what deal we should make, but was waiting for her to say it first.

'We should do a first look deal.'

'Yes,' I said, doing that thing where you point at someone while also snapping your fingers. I immediately felt like a tit.

'A first look deal definitely works for us.'

Back at my hotel room, I fired up Wikipedia to find out what the hell I'd just agreed to. Apparently a first look deal is an arrangement whereby someone – say, a publisher – agrees to give a TV company a 'first look' at anything new they publish. It's a bit like an 'option', but much earlier and with no one getting paid. So what I'd agreed was that, for no money, Pretty Matches would have first refusal over everything new we published. But who cared about the details? The important thing was that we'd done a deal with Pretty Matches; Sarah Jessica Parker's production company! I was already writing the press release in my head.

But first I had to phone Clare to tell her the great news ...

'Great news,' I said, 'we've done a "first look" deal.'

'Great!' she replied. 'What the hell's a first look deal?'

Tsk! Honestly! 'It's an arrangement whereby someone ...'

With Clare up to speed and me giddy with excitement at having met both a stripper who danced for the Mafia and a hot, cynical TV producer who hung out with Sarah Jessica Parker all in the space of a day – *and* signed a first look agreement – I decided to hit the town. I'd arranged to meet a journalist friend in the East Village for a few drinks: and, God knows, I'd earned them.

3.7

I woke up the following afternoon with a grade A, Ivy League hangover. What the *hell* had I been drinking last night? I remembered pretty clearly arriving at the bar and meeting my journalist friend. I remember him ordering a Scotch on the rocks for us both and then me matching him – all six foot six former football player of him – drink for drink for three hours. I remember ... no, that's about it. I certainly didn't remember eating any dinner. I had definitely overcelebrated – and in about three hours I had to meet The Girl. I lay on my hotel room bed with the walls spinning around me, feeling absolutely awful. There was no way on earth I could meet anyone – even if I could have removed the smell and taste of booze from my body. I couldn't even find the strength to walk to the shower.

I turned on the light above my bed. And then I turned it back off again; the room was spinning even faster now and even the light from the crappy bulb of the hotel-issue lamp was making me want to vomit. I rolled myself out of bed and on to the floor with a thump and crawled – literally crawled – to my laptop which was parked on the windowsill. With the strength of Gunga Din, I opened up the screen – My Eyes! – and bashed out an email to The Girl.

'I'm really sorry,' I wrote, 'but I'm not going to make our meeting this evening. Something's suddenly come up. Can we reschedule?'

'No problem,' came the reply. 'Let's meet up when we're back in London.'

Thank God. No harm, no foul. I crawled back into bed and slept until dinner time.

3.8

Back in London it turned out that my no-show had in fact had some harm. Unbeknownst to me, The Girl had already been approached by a rival publisher and that meeting in New York would have been my last – and only – opportunity to sell her the idea of signing with The Friday Project instead. It wasn't until the book was published almost a year later, with reports that The Girl had been paid a 'six figure' advance, that Clare finally forgave me for letting the book go. There was no way we could have afforded even a five figure advance, let alone something north of £100k.

Missing out on The Girl, however, made wooing Ruth all the more important. We absolutely had to sign her book, whatever the cost. Assuming, of course, that the cost was less than about twenty grand. Sadly, Ruth had secured the services of one of London's hottest representatives: bald-headed super-agent Simon Trewin.

'Ruth being represented by Simon Trewin may not be the best news for you,' said one of our advisers – a man with decades' experience in the publishing industry – with admirable understatement. And so it wasn't. Despite a campaign of flattery, badgering, guilt-tripping, promising and cajoling of such intensity that by the end of it Ruth and I had become good friends, she opted to follow the money, accepting a very healthy six figure advance for the UK rights to her book, to be called *No Man's Land*.

'For what it's worth,' I emailed Ruth shortly afterwards, 'I think you probably did the right thing. We were never going to be able to afford you – and I think you deserve the money. You bloody greedy bitch. But when it all goes to shit with [your publisher] make sure we're your first call.'

She emailed back 'Thank you darling – and of course you'll be my first call, from my Caribbean island.'

I couldn't resist a quick PS. 'Oh, and the title is awful – I'd have called it: "Barely Legal: true confessions of a pole-dancing alien in New York". You're welcome. '

Her final reply: 'Actually, I agree about the title. I prefer "Lap Dogs".'

Brilliant.

I'd read a draft of the first chapter of the book by this point and it was everything I knew it would be: dark, honest, filthy, witty, incisive – and, if it weren't for the subject matter, you could easily mistake the author for a man. And that was certainly a positive thing in the face of shelves full of woman-as-victim misery memoirs that were designed to give men erections and women a feeling of 'there but for the grace of God'. But I also knew that, as much as I loved her writing, the publishing process was going to be a nightmare for Ruth. You don't pay a six figure advance and then not expect to mould the book into something ultra-commercial. Sure enough, the book was eventually published in the United States at the start of 2008, three new agents and two different publishers later.

3.9

There were times during my quest to become famous via the Internet that I envied people like Ruth and The Girl. There's no denying that being a woman who either has a lot of sex or – better still – who works in the sex industry gives you a massive head start in the whole Internet celebrity business. Even before signing their book deals, Belle, The Girl and Mimi had huge audiences for their blogs – comprising both men who got off on the sex talk and (in much greater numbers) women who were fascinated by honest accounts of worlds that 'nice girls' aren't supposed to be part of. Blogs had allowed girls like The Girl to be absolutely candid about their sexual desires and their bedroom adventures, and to do so behind a cloak of total anonymity.

But there is a tipping point; a point at which someone goes from being an 'Internet celebrity' to a full-blown celebrity – where their popularity is such that the mainstream media starts to get interested, and people start waving around lucrative book deals. And that's where things can begin to go wrong. Like it or not, once you start courting celebrity, you lose control of what people say about you. Like it or not, you become public property. That's the trade-off. The celebrity covenant, if you like.

The reality of that covenant was driven home to author and film industry worker Zoe Margolis one early August morning in 2006 when a man arrived at her front door, delivering flowers. The bouquet was huge and, like any single girl would be, Zoe was flattered that someone had sent them to her. It was only when she saw the note that she suddenly felt sick to her stomach. It read simply, 'Dear Zoe, congratulations on your book'. The card wasn't signed.

Zoe's sickness turned quickly to panic: this was the day her very first book was due to hit the bookshelves but no one, not even her family or her publisher, knew the real identity of 'Abby Lee', the pen name which appeared on the cover. All of the negotiations for the book had been done anonymously, through an agent. Perhaps two people involved in the book knew how to contact her, but they were both trusted friends and were sworn to secrecy. And yet now she'd received a bunch of flowers with an anonymous note. What the hell could it mean?

She didn't have to wait very long to find out. A couple of days later – at just after eleven on the morning of 5 August 2006 – an email arrived in her inbox. It was from Nicholas Hellen, the 'acting news editor' of the *Sunday Times*. The email read:

Dear Miss Margolis,

We intend to publish a prominent news story in this weekend's paper, revealing your identity.

We have matched up the dates of films you have worked on – Harry Potter and the Order of the Phoenix, Batman Begins and Lara Croft Tomb Raider – and it is clear that they correlate to your blog. We have obtained your birth certificate, and details about where you went to school and college.

We propose to publish the fact that you are 33 and live in [her address] – *London, and that your mother,* [her name], *is a* [her address] *-based* [her profession]. *The article includes extracts from your book and blog, relevant to your career in the film industry. We also have a picture of you, taken outside your flat.*

Unfortunately, the picture is not particularly flattering and might undermine the image that has been built up around your persona as Abby Lee. I think it would be helpful to both sides if you agreed to a photo shoot today so that we can publish a more attractive image.

We are proposing to assign you our senior portrait photographer, Francesco Guidicini, and would arrange everything to your convenience, including a car to pick you up. We would expect you to provide your own clothes and make up. As the story will be on a colour page, we would prefer the outfit to be one of colourful eveningwear.

We did put this proposal to you yesterday, but heard nothing back. Clearly this is now a matter of urgency, and I would appreciate you contacting me as soon as possible. To avoid any doubt we will, of course, publish the story as it is if we do not hear from you.

Yours sincerely,
Nicholas Hellen
Acting News Editor
Sunday Times

Zoe felt sick to her stomach. The delivery of flowers had been a ploy to get her to open her front door so that a paparazzi photographer hiding across the road could snap an unflattering picture of her. A similar stunt had been pulled on Cherie Blair the day after the new Prime Minister entered office in 1997. It was cruel then, and it was cruel now.

Abby Lee was one of two pseudonyms Zoe used to protect her true identity – the true identity that was about to be splashed across the pages of a Sunday newspaper.

The other was Girl with a One Track Mind.

For almost two years, Zoe had been sharing the deepest secrets of her sex life through her anonymous blog, always being sure to change identities and modify locations so as to ensure that even those she slept with couldn't identify her. Jesus, she'd even refused to give away her first name on dates. And now some scumbag 'acting' (definitely the operative word) news editor was going to out her for – for what? A cheap couple of pages of middle-class pseudo shock? If you close your eyes after reading his email, you can almost see Nicholas Hellen sitting at his desk, imagining he's Carl Bernstein phoning John Mitchell during the Watergate scandal . . .

'Sir, this is Carl Bernstein of the *Washington Post*, and I'm sorry to bother you but we're running a story in tomorrow's paper that we thought you should have a chance to comment on . . . and . . . um . . . we'd like a picture of you in a cocktail dress.'

It was vile and hideously misogynistic but in a way inevitable. By the time Zoe's book was published in late 2006, the line between Internet celebrity and just plain celebrity was blurred beyond almost all recognition. Musicians like the Arctic Monkeys and Sandi Thom were crediting their MySpace pages for making them stars (in reality, the Internet was just one part of a wider marketing effort; but with so many young consumers spending the bulk of their leisure time online it was a critical part). Bloggers were being invited to appear as talking heads on TV shows and each month dozens of artists, comedians, writers, journalists and filmmakers were making the leap from the web to the mainstream, helped, of course, by companies like The Friday Project.

The moment Zoe made that leap, from blogger to mainstream media player, she became fair game: just another puzzle to be solved by a journalist looking for an easy scoop. But unfortunately for Nicholas Hellen there was one critical difference between Zoe and the countless other people suddenly forced into unwanted tabloid*

....

* And in this instance the *Sunday Times* had proved itself to be precisely that.

celebrity. Zoe was a blogger. And the blogosphere had her back.

The first I knew about the *Sunday Times*' outing of Zoe was when I received a message from her asking for help. She had come up with a plan to get revenge on Nicholas Hellen, and she needed everyone who knew her and who had their own website to help. Hellen was going to become the victim of a Google bomb.

The Google bomb is a curiously modern but vicious form of weapon. Creating one is a simple process . . .

First you build a web page full of negative information about the person you wish to attack. In this case, Zoe put a page on her site containing the story of her floral doorstepping, and the text of Nicholas Hellen's subsequent email.

Then you email lots of high-profile bloggers and site owners and ask them to link to the page from their sites. The only rule is that all of the links leading from the blogs to the attack page must use *exactly* the same text. Usually the name of the target individual. In this case, then, bloggers were asked to write a short note about Hellen on their sites, with the words 'Nicholas Hellen' linking back to Zoe's page.

The result of Zoe's Google bomb was devastating; within a few days, Google's automatic search technology had noticed the sudden appearance of dozens of sites that linked the words 'Nicholas Hellen' to this one same page on Zoe's site. Google's technology assumed, quite reasonably, that Zoe's page must be the most important page for people searching for information on Hellen. Why else would it have so many links? From that day on, anyone typing Hellen's name into Google would see Zoe's site as the number one result, followed by dozens of other sites, all linking to the same place. At a stroke, Hellen's online reputation was toast. Much like Zoe's anonymity. An eye for an eye.

But even having exacted her revenge, the damage to Zoe's life was irreparable. She had to explain to her parents why their phone was ringing off the hook from other hacks looking to do a follow-up; she had to phone former lovers and apologise for what they now realised was a very public review of their performance; and she had to quit her job. Her old double life – media professional by day, secret sex blogger by night – was over.

She'd become more wealthy, yes, and offers of TV appearances and film deals were pouring in, but at the cost of her entire life up until that point. Whether she liked it or not, she was now a full-time writer, and a celebrity. Those would be the only jobs she would ever be able to get.

3.10

Zoe's outing made all of us at The Friday Project think long and hard about how we approached anonymous authors. To so many online authors, particularly bloggers, anonymity was a deal maker or deal breaker when they were considering moving into print. Up until then, we'd promised authors that we would guarantee their anonymity – and, true to our word, we'd been extremely careful to ensure that their identity was only ever revealed to a tiny number of people who were part of the publishing process.

Post-Zoe, we decided to tell authors something different – that no one can guarantee anonymity, no matter how hard they try. We would do everything in our power to try, of course, but if a journalist really, really wanted to know who they were, they'd find out. They'd be able to find a friend of the author, or they'd stake out our offices, or they'd pore through the book for clues (as they'd done with Zoe's, matching the work schedule she mentioned in her blog with her film credits) and then they'd follow those clues up. If you want anonymity, there's only one way to guarantee it, we'd say: don't write a book. Close down your blog, shut your laptop and write a diary. Then burn it. Other than that, there are no guarantees. And don't believe any publisher who tells you otherwise.

Our new policy received its first test sooner than we'd expected when The Friday Project made its first major signing: the A-list gossip blogger and media 'insider' known only as 'Mr Holy Moly!' (his exclamation mark).

Mr Holy Moly! ran a showbiz gossip site called holymoly.co.uk which prided itself on not just skewing celebrities, but marinating them in piss and vinegar and then barbecuing them until they bubbled. In addition to a weekly email full of foul-mouthed gossip, the site had two other popular sections: the glorious 'Cunts Corner' – a foul-mouthed directory of celebrities we love to hate and 'The Rules of Modern Life', a list of undeniable universal truths, including ...

'Under no circumstances should two men ever share an umbrella ...'

'Camouflage clothing is rendered useless in towns and cities ...'

'If you're going to fuck a leopard, make sure you duct-tape its back legs together. And that you're a leopard.'

and

'You should never try to milk a dog.'

It was this 'Rules' section that really excited us, and we were thrilled (and a little surprised) when Mr Holy Moly! agreed to allow us to publish a spin-off book called *The Holy Moly! Rules of Modern Life*, a collection of the best rules, brilliantly illustrated by artist Ben Aung. Mr Holy Moly!'s signing was proof positive that The Friday Project was doing something special; he could easily have secured a huge advance for the book from another publisher, but he was determined that the publisher he signed with had to 'get' the Holy Moly! site and not try to force the book to tone down for a mainstream audience. I'd been a fan of Holy Moly! from the day it started and we had no intention of toning anything down. No other publisher even got a look in.

The Holy Moly! Rules quickly became our first bestseller, even despite the fact that a scheduled appearance of the book on *Richard & Judy* was cancelled at the last minute when a producer found out that Richard Madeley had been featured in Cunts Corner.

To celebrate the publication of the *Holy Moly!* book and the official birth of The Friday Project, we decided to hire an entire floor of Soho House to throw a huge launch party. This was our big chance to set our tone to the rest of the publishing and dot com industries – and so we were determined to make the party as memorable as possible. One of the ideas we came up with was to create real-life versions of the illustrations from the *Holy Moly!* book: for example, having an ugly man dressed as a leopard handing out dog milk cocktails.

Despite what you might expect, it's a surprisingly simple matter, in London, to find an ugly man willing to dress as a leopard and hand out dog milk cocktails. In fact, there's an agency that does exactly that. It's called Ugly and it specialises in providing models with asymmetrical mouths, wonky noses and crossed eyes, many of whom are happy to dress up as big cats. For a price.

Ugly sent us over a batch of headshot photos to allow us to choose the model who would become our leopard. With Clare and me still running around setting up the company, we left the job of sifting through the photographs to our first proper employee, Heather Smith. Heather had previously been an editor at Prentice Hall, Clare's last employer, and we'd poached her essentially to look after the day-to-day aspects of publishing books while Clare and I went around raising more money to pay for everything. It's probably safe to say that, without Heather, The Friday Project wouldn't have lasted more than a couple of months before either Clare or myself dropped dead.

Apart from being completely indispensable, Heather was also one of the nicest, most professional people ever to have set foot on earth. Ridiculously hardworking and eager to please, she didn't have a bad word to say about anyone. In fact, she didn't have a bad word to say – full stop. She was so sweet that, just for fun, Clare and I spent the first three months of her employment trying to make her utter the word 'cunt', starting with bribery and moving on to trickery and blackmail. But no matter how hard we tried, her 'no swearing' in the office rule held firm to the point that she once scolded our online editor, Karl Webster, after he'd had an argument with some hapless tradesperson or other on the phone.

'Fucking motherfucker,' Karl had yelled as he'd slammed down the handset.

'Er ... Karl,' said Heather, smiling sweetly, 'I'd prefer it if you used the word "mother-effer".' Naturally this became a running joke in the office for the next few months.

Another brilliant example of Heather's niceness came as we watched her going methodically through the photographs from Ugly. She was feeling increasingly sorry for the poor unfortunate 'models' whose only chance at making it in show business was to trade off their wonky features.

'Awww ... this one's not actually that ugly ... Well, I suppose he's quite ugly. I mean I wouldn't ... but ... awwww ... he's sweet ... sort of ...'

Eventually Heather found someone she decided would look ideal dressed as a leopard and, after a quick trip to a costume-hire shop to pick up the costume (including a fake moustache, for some reason), we were all set.

3.11

The big night arrived and, right on time, our ugly man reported for duty. But whereas in his headshot he'd looked bright-eyed and enthusiastic, in the flesh he appeared to be on the brink of death. Pale, trembling and barely audible, there was no way he'd be able to hold a single glass, let alone a tray of dog milk cocktails (actually White Russians).

Seeing our concern, he explained that he was a practising Muslim, and that, as it was now Ramadan, he couldn't eat a crumb of food or drink a drop of liquid until a very specific time: 7.23 p.m. The party didn't start until 7.30 so he'd have plenty of time to wolf a sandwich and a cup of sweet tea and all would be fine.

And so it was – except that for the first twenty minutes of the party guests were greeted by a pale, trembling leopard who looked as if he might collapse at any moment. And then, once the sugar rush kicked in, we almost had to scrape him off the ceiling he was so high. At least we could be confident that we were the only book launch party that year to feature a giant ugly leopard wearing a fake moustache and showing all the symptoms of bipolar disorder.

I had also had a brilliant idea for the music. Instead of a disco or something similarly naff, we'd hire an Internet celebrity called Adam Kay to sing live. Adam Kay – or Dr Adam Kay, to give him his full title – is almost certainly the world's only singing, swearing gynaecologist. He had achieved Internet 'fame' with a spoof song called 'London Underground' which mocked striking London Underground workers in a variety of colourful and offensive ways, to the tune of the Jam's 'Going Underground'. The song had been a huge hit, downloaded over six million times, and we'd quickly snapped up the rights to distribute Adam's album and also to publish a spoof medical book written by him the following year. This made him, I decided, the natural choice of entertainment to mark out the differences between a Friday Project party and, well, one organised by any other publishing house. How many of our rivals would have a singing, swearing gynaecologist at their launch party? I'd guess not many.

The party got off to a swinging start. I'd bought my very first suit for the occasion – £500, a snip with my new salary! – and Clare had put on her best party dress. Heather, of course, looked absolutely perfect and utterly unflappable despite running around behind the scenes to make sure everything was ready. It was essential that the evening went exactly to plan given that we'd invited the great and the good of the publishing and online industries. The waiting staff, including our leopard, were instructed to ensure that the champagne and dog milk flowed freely. And so it did. As I looked around the room, I couldn't help feeling a huge sense of pride that we'd made it.

There, on a table in the corner, was a pile of *Holy Moly!* books fresh from the printer, and next to them, piled high on the floor, were the goody bags we'd put together for the night, including a voucher for copies of our other upcoming books, some hilarious *Holy Moly! Rules* beer mats, a branded mug, various other freebie knick-knacks and the bag itself – a really nice canvas thing printed with our new logo. To anyone walking into that room ...

... seeing the CEO of Macmillan deep in conversation with both the former CEO of Orion and the former head of Simon & Schuster; and across the room Mr Holy Moly! (incognito, of course) mingling with the founders of two of the UK's other coolest cult websites – Popjustice and B3ta – all surrounded by almost a hundred people from various parts of the media. And the press! Both of the major publishing trade mags had sent reporters, as had the *Guardian*, *The Times* and the *Independent*. A photographer flitting around taking dozens of those ridiculous pictures you always see at launch parties of people standing in a perfect arc, chatting effusively and unnaturally for the camera ...

... to anyone walking into that room, The Friday Project was, without doubt, a proper, professional company. We were grown-ups.

Dr Adam cleared his throat and took to the microphone. We'd hired him a huge electronic piano for the night, with two enormous speakers to really fill the room with sound. As he played his opening chord – 'bllluuunnngg' – a hush fell across the room. The great and the good of the publishing industry waited to be entertained.

It was at that exact moment – 'bllluuunnngg' – that I remembered one small detail about Adam the singing, swearing, gynaecologist. The thing that had drawn me to his songs in the first place, but that, with the benefit of hindsight, made him absolutely unsuitable for an audience of people who work in publishing; which is to say an audience that was at least 70 per cent women. Adam was also probably the world's only *misogynist*, singing, swearing gynae-cologist. Some of the songs on his album were unbelievably sexist – perhaps as a reaction to his day job, or perhaps just a sign that Adam hated women. But surely tonight, looking around the room, he'd stick to safer stuff.

I closed my eyes and said a silent prayer.

Things began safely enough, with a rousing chorus of 'London Underground' to get everyone in the mood. Sure, every time Adam sung a line about the drivers being 'lazy fucking useless cunts', Heather's face contorted into a frown and I could tell it was taking all her strength not to shout 'Er, Adam, I'd prefer, lazy effing useless cees' but the audience as a whole loved it.

'Gosh, this is edgy,' thought the publishing types. 'Not this fucking song again,' thought the web people who had heard it a thousand times when it was doing the rounds of the nation's inboxes. Then, encouraged by the positive reaction in the room, Adam moved on to his second web hit: a song sung to the tune of Tom Lehrer's 'Vatican Rag' ...

Its title? 'The Menstrual Rag'.

Oh God.

Once a month your girl's upset
She goes to Boots to buy Lillets.

I looked around the room at the sea of shocked publishing faces –

70 per cent of them women. Oh please God tell me they're just listening to the tune. The acoustics aren't very good in here. Please God, please God.

Who was I kidding? We'd hired two mother-effing speakers. He was louder than God – and even more of a misogynist.

It happens every twenty-eight days,
When she's in her luteal phase.

Around the room, now, no one was talking any more. Wide eyes. Open mouths.

All she does is moan and nag,
You go five days without a shag.

I closed my eyes and necked two dog milk cocktails in quick succession.

There's no cunnilingus
You can only use your fingers
When she's using a menstrual rag.

And on and on it went. The Internet people were loving it, of course. There was Mr Holy Moly! hiding in the shadows but unmistakably tapping his feet. There was Peter Robinson, founder of Popjustice.com; he seemed to be enjoying it rather a lot, too.

And there were the publishers. Silent. Mouths agape. And there are my parents, who had come along to support my new venture, delighted that I had a proper grown-up job at last . . .

Oh God. Oh God.

Heavy flow or gentle spotting,
Running down her legs or clotting
All that lining that she sheds leaves
Nasty patches on your bedsheets.
Just don't waste your efforts pleading
You won't be shagging when she's bleeding
The Methenamic acid means you might as well be flaccid
When she's using a menstrual rag.

At least he was medically accurate. God knows it's not easy to find a rhyme for Methenamic acid. The man has real talent.

Four songs later and Adam took his bow. I cheered wildly, as did at least 30 per cent of the room. Everyone else looked horrified. I wondered whether I should introduce the leopard to Emily, who was standing by the bar ordering a Screaming Orgasm, just to create an even more awkward moment.

Suddenly I felt a hand on my shoulder. It was Sara Lloyd, Business Development Director for Palgrave Macmillan. Sara was an extremely important person and, unmistakably, a woman. 'Well, I can honestly say,' she began, choosing her words carefully, 'that I've never – ever – been to a book launch like this.'

I necked another dog milk cocktail, grabbed Emily and a few of my web friends and headed over the road to the pub for a post-mortem.

In the final analysis, it was clear to me where we'd gone wrong with the party. It wasn't that we'd misjudged our audience. No, that wasn't it at all. The problem was that everyone in publishing has got so used to book launches being staid affairs, perhaps even without a gynaecologist singing about menstruation, that they were just unprepared. If we were going to make the publishing industry realise we were a cool and edgy Internet company, we'd have to keep throwing parties until it sank in.

And so it was that we decided to throw our second party a few months later, just in time for Christmas. But this time we'd be a bit more low key; ease people back in gently. Just some mingling, a festive glass or two of cheap house wine and not an ugly leopard in sight. What could possibly go wrong?

3.12

In hindsight our mistake with the Christmas party – if we wanted it to be low key and low cost – was to host it in a champagne bar smack bang in the centre of London: the International on Trafalgar Square. I'd been to another party at the bar a few weeks earlier and I'd assured Clare that, while it was definitely upscale, it was also on one of the busiest tourist corners in London and so was perfectly able to cater to the cheap end of the market as well. If we stuck to house wine, and strictly limited the amount of money we put behind the bar, we could make the whole thing very affordable indeed.

The event kicked off at 7.00 p.m., which would have been exactly the right time had we not decided to have our team Christmas lunch immediately beforehand, at the St Martin's Lane Hotel. Given that we started on our first pre-lunch cocktail at noon, and drank at least four bottles of wine between the four of us over food, by the time we rolled up to the International, half an hour or so before the advertised kick-off time, we were already pretty drunk, even by our standards. Which is to say we were verging on hammered. And with a little while to go before the first guests were due to arrive, Clare and I decided to order one quick bottle of house champagne for ourselves and the team, to round off the afternoon's celebrations.

'We'll have finished it before everyone gets here,' Clare reasoned. 'And after that we'll just buy cheap wine for everyone as they arrive.'

'Good thinking,' I agreed, swaggering over to the bar, my credit card in hand. Just one bottle. Something modest. Best not repeat the bar tab from the first party, I thought.

No sooner had we popped the cork on the bottle than our first guest arrived, one of our newly signed authors, James Lark. Rude not to give him champagne while we were all drinking it, we reasoned. One more bottle won't hurt as long as we switch to wine after that. And with that, I grabbed James and demanded 'Right! Follow me! You're having champagne.'

'Are you guys drunk already?' he asked, not realising that, as we'd started at noon, there was no 'already' about it.

'Not in the slightest,' I slurred, throwing his scarf over the bar.

In the interests of accuracy, I should say that Clare and I have different recollections of how the evening ended. For example, she insists I scared away the head of sales of one of the major publishing houses by falling over a footstool and landing on him. I maintain he was leaving anyway and that he took my toppling in good spirits. Clare insists that she didn't offer James thousands of pounds for the rights to his first novel; I insist that I had to stop her from giving him a contract right there and then, drawn on the back of a cocktail napkin. But we do agree on one thing: neither of us has any real recollection whatsoever of how the evening ended.

Other things we do agree on . . .

A couple of hours into the party, the house champagne ran out.

We started drinking the next least expensive. Until that ran out. The last three bottles of the night were bottles of Cristal. We drank a champagne bar dry. We're still proud of that.

At the end of the night, Clare handed over her credit card, only to be taken to the manager's office to speak to the bank. The final tab was so large that the bank needed special authorisation to process it.

Clare left the bar without her credit card. Having successfully remembered her mother's maiden name and authorised the transaction, she simply turned on her heel and walked out of the building. She has no idea how she got back to the hotel she'd booked for the night to avoid having to travel home. I had to pick up the card the next day, after a meeting with our very unamused accountant.

I got into a heated argument with the Russian bouncer over whether it was acceptable to kneel down in the middle of a crowded champagne bar when there were no seats. I then got into a second argument about whether it was possible to be thrown out of your own party. The Russian bouncer won both of these arguments, by a mile.

Adam Kay, the swearing, singing doctor turned up at one point, and immediately had a bottle of champagne thrust into his hand by someone. He later arrived back at his girlfriend's house in the early hours of the morning, miraculously clutching a full glass of champagne.

It was a hell of a night.

3.13

Starting The Friday Project had given me access to almost as many parties as I'd gone to as a journalist, even if Clare and I were the ones paying for them, but it had also given me something even more valuable: ownership of shares in a company. Or 'equity', as entrepreneurs insist on calling it.

This equity was the thing that had really transported me from one side of the fence to the other. In the evenings I was still hanging out with the same dot com entrepreneur mates that I spent time with when I was a journalist – still drinking the same overpriced beer – but now, rather than being an observer and friend, I was part of the equity club, too. We were all on the same team.

With every book The Friday Project published, so the value of my 'equity' increased. Hell, I didn't even have to write the damn things: someone else did all the hard work and we packaged their words and sold them. I had none of the disadvantages of being a columnist – the crap pay, the living from week to week, the having to have your own ideas and write your own words – and all of the advantages – namely being schmoozed by people with more money than God and slowly increasing my personal wealth. And as a nice added bonus, the PR girls in publishing are *astonishingly* hot, compared to the slightly less hot dot com ones I met through my *Guardian* column. In PR, as in life, the pretty girls preferred literary types over web geeks. There's no doubt that, by combining publishing with the web, I had found my ideal career.

There was just one slight problem.

Me.

3.14

For all the downsides, the life of a freelance journalist is by no means an arduous one. Breakfast is at noon, your hours are set not by some all-seeing boss, but by the daytime TV schedules (as a freelance, I tried to have lunch at around *Diagnosis Murder* o'clock, with elevenses around quarter past *Columbo*) – and the equivalent of dressdown Friday is not putting your dressing gown on over your boxers. Evenings tend to be spent attending press parties or hanging out with other journalists, bitching about mutual friends.

For all of publishing's reputation as an industry that survives on boozy lunches and inflated expense accounts, it turned out that running a small publishing company was actually astonishingly sensible – and bloody hard work. This is something I hadn't really anticipated.

While covering the dot com world, I'd visited companies like Yahoo!, with its free jelly beans for visitors, and Google, with its free meals for all (cooked by the chef who used to serve the Grateful

Dead) and its giant space hoppers in the lobby. This was how I imagined start-up life to be.

At the end of one dot com party I'd found myself at, the founders had decided to drag the last remaining guests off to a strip club in Farringdon to round off the night. I'd never really understood the point of strip clubs and why they were better than normal clubs, which were cheaper, less sleazy and there was at least a slim chance that you might end up going home with the person dancing in front of you. But an after-party is an after-party.

On arriving at the club, the bouncer decided that one of our group couldn't come in as he was wearing jeans and trainers.

'You can't come in wearing that,' he sneered.

What he didn't realise was that the scruffy oik had just signed a deal that would make him a millionaire many times over. Unfazed, the young founder simply pulled out his black Amex card and a huge wedge of £50 notes and sneered right back at the bouncer, 'This is what I'm wearing. What exactly is the problem?'

As is by magic, the dress code suddenly became far more relaxed and the group was welcomed with open arms. The life of a young entrepreneur.

They say that the Queen thinks the world smells of fresh paint, because that's all she ever smells; to a journalist covering certain aspects of the dot com world, the whole thing smells of parties, jelly beans, booze and fun. It's 80 per cent fun, 20 per cent hard work. And sky-high valuations. And my job had been to hang around with these people, then to roll up at my desk at noon and work through the night. Like many hacks, I always managed to achieve far more between the hours of 6.00 p.m. and 6.00 a.m. than I could during normal working hours.

And that's what I went into The Friday Project thinking I could replicate. Thinking that Clare and I would be able to create some-thing akin to a crazy Internet company that just so happened to publish books. A sky-high valuation, but with all the security and (gasp) revenue of nice, safe old publishing. And I still wanted to get to my desk at noon and work through the night after everyone had gone home.

Yeah!

No.

What it turns out what we'd created – with our publishing investors and our roots in 'old media' – was a traditional book publishing company that happened to understand the Internet a lot better than any other traditional book publishing company. And as a traditional company, there were rules that needed to be abided by.

For a start, forget what you've heard: the boozy publisher's lunch is a myth, as are the red-nosed publishing execs who arrive at their desks at eleven, lunch at noon with an author and spend the rest of the day schmoozing and boozing. In reality, people who work in publishing today are by a huge majority young, female graduates from good universities who have an absolute laser-like focus on advancing their career. They are very dedicated, very smart and absolutely fucking terrifying. These people think nothing of arranging a meeting at 9.00 a.m.! 9.00 a.m.! To me that's not a meeting; that's a court date.

Also, as far as I could tell, every single one is called Emma or Clare.

I'm not kidding about the Clares: in our small company of five people, we had two Clares. We had as many Clares as we had men. I'm prepared to believe that's a ratio that stands up industry-wide.

But still, despite my initial shock at being expected to do a grown-up job for my new grown-up salary, I was determined to keep the dream alive to some extent, by ticking a few of the sensible boxes while Trojan Horsing (yes, as a verb*) some dot com fun in the back door. I'd come in for the early meetings, and I'd put on a suit for the investors and I'd do my damnedest to learn what business things like EBITDA[†] meant and why, in publishing, when someone talks about turnover, they mean the amount of money that bookshops take from customers for your books – not how much of that money the publisher actually receives.[‡] But then, by night, I'd still hang out with my dot com friends, finding new possible authors

---

* In the Internet era, all nouns have become verbs. If you don't believe me, Google it.

[†] Earnings before interest, taxes, depreciation and amortisation.

[‡] I still have no fucking clue; it's insane and totally meaningless.

and plotting ways to make our books more interesting and exciting and, oftentimes, more offensive than anything else on the market.

The road to hell is paved with such good intentions. Try as I might, 9.00 a.m. meetings just didn't work for me at all. My body was absolutely incapable of adjusting to a normal working day and as a result I'd often be found still at my desk at three in the morning, eating cold takeaway and catching up at work, knowing full well that, factoring in an hour's journey home to my flat in Crouch End, there was no way on God's green earth I'd be back when everyone else arrived the next day, bright-eyed and bushy-tailed. My working habits were summed up perfectly when the *Bookseller* wrote a profile of me which began and ended as follows:

Paul Carr is by turns the professional entrepreneur and the overgrown student hurling himself into whichever wacky scheme catches his attention. He got outrageously drunk at the Nibbies; is 'pathologically late' for meetings; and confesses to being an 'arrogant little shit' but he must be doing something right . . . Carr's enthusiasm is transparent: 'I love it. If I were able to get bored in this environment, I'd be mentally ill.' His enthusiasm is to be believed: according to Macmillan c.e.o. Richard Charkin, he regularly emails at 3am. 'He is an extraordinary young man; incredibly bright and incredibly hard-working,' he says.

The Nibbies are the very prestigious trade awards of the book industry. Held annually in the God's waiting room that is Bournemouth, I defy anyone to survive them without getting outrageously drunk. And, frankly, you haven't lived until you've woken up in the wrong hotel room, wearing a tuxedo, and with pockets full of sand.

When the profile appeared, my friends were entirely split as to whether it was positive or negative. Generally, my publishing friends thought it was a stitch-up – 'outrageously drunk!' 'arrogant little shit!' – I can't believe they said that.

'They didn't,' I protested, 'it was me who said that, they were quoting me.'

'You described yourself as an arrogant drunk? To a reporter?'

'Um . . .'

My web friends, on the other hand, thought it was brilliant. To them, Oscar Wilde's maxim had always stood them in great stead. To them, in an industry so driven by hype, every additional column inch was an additional few thousand dollars on their company valuation. I was very firmly in their camp and I immediately pinned up a copy of the article behind my desk, next to the *Evening Standard* article about thinkofthechildren.

3.15

By the time January rolled around, I'd basically given up trying to impress the publishing people and had decided on another tack. Business was going well – we'd published three books in the last two months of 2005 and were on track to publish an impressive twenty-five titles in 2006. Our priority now was to raise more money, and we'd decided to do this by becoming a public company, which basically involved spending a lot of time with lawyers and accountants and then convincing people to buy shares in us.

It seemed pretty logical that Clare would take charge of schmoozing the publishing people while I concentrated on mixing with the web types and generally creating a bit of hype. I was certain that, if everyone was talking about us and we'd attracted the coolest web brands to publish with us, then a sky-high valuation would surely follow.

It certainly seemed to be paying off. If the publishing industry wasn't sure whether The Friday Project was a new kind of hybrid dot com/publishing company, the media certainly was starting to make its mind up that we were. We were getting a ton of press, with a new article appearing in some newspaper or other every week claiming we were the future of publishing.

But, if the media was lapping up our image as 'the publisher of choice for the web generation' (our words, reprinted in the *Observer*), then surely our next announcement – which came just before the start of our Public Offering process – would blow their minds, and change The Friday Project forever.

It started with a story in the *Bookseller*. Scott Pack, whose job as head buyer at Waterstone's had led to him being thought of as 'the most powerful man in publishing',* had announced his resignation. What was curious about the story was that Pack had apparently no plans as to what he was going to do next. He'd just decided that he'd had enough of his present job and wanted to see what else was available. At the same time as I was reading the article, across London Clare was doing exactly the same. When I phoned her she beat me to the punch before I could even get a word in: 'Have you seen that Scott Pack is leaving Waterstone's?'

'Yes! That's why I was calling. Do you think we should invite him to lunch?'

'That's what I was wondering,' Clare replied. 'But there's no way he'll join The Friday Project. Everybody will be trying to get him.'

And she was right. The Most Powerful Man In Publishing would, at this very moment, be drowning in a sea of emails and fruit baskets from every major book chain and publishing house in the country inviting him for lunch as they tried to schmooze him into working for them. It's hard to think of a bigger coup for a publishing house than having Scott on board as the ultimate gamekeeper-turned-poacher.

'It's worth a shot, though – no? I mean, nothing ventured. And, hell, we're cooler than everyone else anyway. We can let him create his own job and he'll have more fun with us than fucking WH Smith or Orion or someone.'†

I sent him a short email. Would The Most Powerful Man In Publishing be interested in having a chat about possibly coming to join The Friday Project, in exchange for a sack of shares and a huge amount of autonomy in shaping the commercial side of the business?

When his reply came the very next day I was amazed. Amazed he'd even bothered to reply at all. We'd met Scott a couple of times to try and persuade him that Waterstone's should buy vast quantities

....

* The first time I met Scott, I wrote up the experience on The Friday Project blog, describing him as 'the man a publisher like me would gladly fellate if it would make him more likely to buy our books'.

† Again, fucking Orion are the publishers of this book. Hello again, Orion.

of our books and he'd always been a model of courtesy and professionalism. In fact, we were always amazed to discover that he'd actually bothered to read the books we'd sent him, before deciding whether to order them. You'd think this would be a basic requirement for a head buyer, but with an estimated 206,000 titles being published in the UK each year – more than in any other country – he'd be forgiven for skipping a few. And as professional as he was, we thought this might be one time he wouldn't bother answering.

And yet he had replied: 'Always up for lunch and a chat.'

Over the best mixed grill in west London (the Kew Grill, Scott's favourite restaurant, near Waterstone's HQ: we'd done our research) we explained to Scott how him joining The Friday Project would be a partnership made in heaven – we would get someone in the business who actually knew about money, and how to spend it sensibly, and he would get to channel his years of experience in creating bestsellers into a different path: talent-spotting new authors. The Most Powerful Man In Publishing politely listened to our pitch and asked all the right questions, but we all knew – Clare, me, Scott – that there was no way on earth we could compete with the big boys. Still, just by having the meeting we'd shown ourselves able to fight on the same battlefield as the major houses. We were nothing if not plucky.

A few weeks later, at about ten at night, my phone rang. It was Clare, chasing, I thought, some publicity material I'd promised to have finished that afternoon but was only just getting started on. I almost didn't answer in case she told me off.

'I know, I know, I'm almost done,' I said, not allowing her to get a word out.

'Have you checked your email?' she asked. She sounded breathless and somehow high-pitched, like someone who had just won the lottery, or lost a 100 metres sprint.

'Um, no ... what's up?'

'Just check your mail.'

'Um ... okay ...'

Click .

Click .

Pause.

Click .

Pause.

'Oh. My. Fucking. God.'

The following day we told everyone in the office the news. After serving out his notice period, The Most Powerful Man In Publishing would to be joining The Friday Project as commercial director. Of all the big fucking deals there have ever been in my life, this was the biggest fucking deal of them all.

The only catch was, we couldn't tell the press for a month or so until all the details had been finalised. I was like a three-year-old with the world's coolest secret. It was excruciating.

When the news finally broke, a few short weeks before our Public Offering closed, we couldn't have hoped for a better response from the press. The *Observer* said it best ...

Last week, Carr and Christian made a move that [William] *Caxton, a world-class hustler, could hardly have bettered. After weeks of rumour, The Friday Project sent the literary blogosphere buzzing announcing the appointment of a 'commercial director'. Who could this be? Was he a net-head? An internet geek? A coke-snorting nerd in trainers? No, he was ... Scott Pack, former Waterstone's executive and enfant terrible of British bookselling.*

During his tenure as chief buyer at Waterstone's Mr Pack became a love-hate figure in the book trade, admired for his energy, loathed for his brash outspokenness and apparent indifference to traditional book culture ... Where the new energy will take the Project is anybody's guess, but, overnight, the company has transformed itself from an interesting start-up to a serious player and one that understands the rules of the game.

A serious player.

3.16

While we waited for Scott to work out his notice period and arrive in the office, our party schedule continued apace. The first *Holy*

Moly! book had been such a success that we decided to publish a sequel a few months later, which, of course, called for another extravagant launch– this time on the roof terrace of the Century Club on Shaftesbury Avenue.

For the months following the publication of the first book, Mr Holy Moly! had been waging an online war with the *Metro*'s showbiz columnist, Neil Sean, who Moly! relentlessly mocked for simply recycling celebrity press releases and branding them as 'exclusives'. This was a perfectly fair accusation, as anyone who has ever read Sean's column, 'The Green Room', will testify.

But despite basically deserving everything he got, Sean had reacted angrily, threatening to call in the lawyers if Mr Moly! didn't quit with the name-calling. There was just one catch – poor old Sean didn't know who Mr Moly! was. He was anonymous, after all. And so he hatched a plan – he would gatecrash Holy Moly!'s book launch and confront him on his own turf.

The party was in full swing when he arrived, with about three hundred people crammed into a space designed for half that number. I spotted him first, and ran – literally ran – across the room to tell Clare.

'Tell me, please God tell me, that's who I think it is at the door.'

'Where?'

'The door, the door! Look'

'I can't see any – Oh, brilliant!'

When they make the movie of that evening, the entire room will, as one, go silent, a piano player will stop playing and there will be an audible gasp as the rest of the room notices crap gossip royalty walking among them, searching in vain for his nemesis. In reality no one really gave much of a shit. But I did; I gave an *absolute* shit. If this didn't get us in the diary columns the next day, and raise our value by a few quid, I didn't know what would.

At the launch of Toby Young's book *The Sound of No Hands Clapping*, about his attempts to break into Hollywood, two guests had ended up having a fist fight, guaranteeing column after column of coverage in the New York press. There was a very real possibility, if Sean managed to track down Holy Moly!, that tonight we'd witness the very first Friday Project murder.

I bounded over and shook him warmly by the hand. 'Hello, Sean,' I said, introducing myself.

'Neil.'

'Sorry?'

'My name's Neil, it's Neil Sean. You called me Sean.'

'Oh, yes, sorry Sean. Sorry. Neil. Sorry, Neil.'

I attempted to keep Sean talking while our PR girl, Charlie, went off to warn Holy Moly! what was happening. As we talked, it became clear, to my absolute delight, that Neil Sean is almost exactly as much of a tool in person as he is in print. Our conversation – and I will never forget it as long as I live – went like this:

Neil Sean: 'The thing you have to realise is that I really don't give a shit about what people say about me.'

Me: 'Which is why you're here. To tell Holy Moly! that he hasn't bothered you.'

Sean: 'Exactly. Thing is, at the end of the day, I know I'm successful and I get paid a lot of money – and at the end of the day, that's all that matters when you look back at your life. How much money you've made.'

Me: 'Quite right. What matters is what you take with you when you die. At the end of the day.'

Sean: 'Exactly.'

I wanted to like him – really I did – I wanted him to be different from Holy Moly's caricature. But no, as I watched this man flitting around the room, trying to find someone who could identify his online tormentor, I couldn't help but think he deserved everything he got. And as soon as Sean left that's exactly the point I made to the anonymous figure who had been standing behind us the whole time, listening to our conversation. And Mr Holy Moly! completely agreed.

3.17

Scott's arrival at The Friday Project led to a huge burst of publicity – to the point that, by the time we'd closed our Public Offering, we were so oversubscribed with people wanting to buy shares that we had to send back more than £50,000 to people who we couldn't accommodate. There simply weren't enough shares to give to everyone who wanted to buy them.

In the end, the offering raised over half a million pounds and turned The Friday Project into Friday Project Media Plc.

Scott couldn't have been more valuable to the company: he knew more about why books sold – and why they didn't – than anyone else in the country; he knew what covers worked, what types of books people bought at what time of year, and how best to spend marketing money to get the optimum results.

His head for figures, his innate understanding of the publishing industry and his clear benefit to the valuation of the company weren't the only ways in which he and I diverged. We also differed in that Scott understood that expensive launches and PR campaigns rarely shifted a single extra copy of a book, especially compared to the same money spent to promote a book in store. Launch parties were basically an ego stroke for authors and a chance for publishers to get drunk in the name of work; in publishing it was sales – revenue – not hype that meant success.

He was absolutely right. We'd launched the highest-profile new publishing company in Britain, we'd published some amazing books, we'd built a killer team and we'd had a fucking great time. But now the party was over, and in the most literal sense. It was time for us – me – to grow up and get on with the hard work of running a public company.

I should have been happy but of course I wasn't. I wasn't in it for the money – I wanted the fame, goddammit, and the truth is, with every day that passed, that goal seemed more and more at odds with what was best for the company.

But what was the alternative? Quit? Walk away from my first proper salary because I wanted my face in the papers and to be feted at parties? What was I, twelve years old? And if I didn't want to be running a proper company then what exactly did I want to run? A pure web company? Who says that would be any more fun anyway?

The truth is, I was being pathetic. I'd seen a great idea turn into a proper company – with proper revenues and a proper staff – and there I was itching to leave; to have a new idea; to do something else. What the hell was wrong with me? I resolved for once in my life to be grateful for my lot and to sit down and get on with it.

And then two weeks later, 9 October 2006, this happened ...

YouTube.com, the video-sharing site started by Chad Hurley and Steve Chen the previous year, was sold to Google for $1.65 billion.

One. Point. Six. Five. Billion.

A company founded four months before The Friday Project.

A company that mixed old media (video content) with new (the web).

And the kicker?

Chad Hurley was – and still is – two years older than me. Chen is a year older. And there they were, on the front cover of every paper, from the *New York Times* to the *Financial Times* to *Newsweek* to *Time* magazine.

All my jealousies – my burning ambition to become a web celebrity – came flooding back.

One. Point. Six. Five. Fuck. Right. Off. Billion. Fucking. Dollars.

Just to put that in context, according to *Forbes* magazine, Blockbuster Video – an actual company with actual shops in every continent of the globe except Antarctica, actual paying customers and millions of actual videos and DVDs in stock – was worth 'just' $710 million, or $0.71 billion. Based on the price Google had paid for them, YouTube was worth the same as two Blockbuster Videos. After just eighteen months.

That's just bizarre.

4.0

'Jealousy is the mother of invention'

In his book *Adventures in the Screen Trade*, William Goldman (most famous for writing the screenplays of *Butch Cassidy and the Sundance Kid* and *All the President's Men*, if you're a boy – or *The Princess Bride*, if you're a girl) sums up his industry in three words:

Nobody knows anything.

He was talking about Hollywood but the same maxim could easily be applied to Silicon Valley and the rest of the Internet industry. And if there's any single aspect of the Internet industry in which knowing nothing has been elevated to an art form it's the calculation of what companies are worth.

In business if you want to work out the value of a company you have a few options. If the company is a public one – that is, one listed on a stock market – then all you had to do (I'm simplifying very slightly) is take its share price and multiply that by the total number of shares that the company is split into. As the price of each share goes up, so does the overall value (the 'market capitalisation') of the company. Using that calculation, the highest valued companies in the world are, at the time of writing (in billions of dollars):

1. ExxonMobil (oil & gas) $410.65
2. General Electric (everything) $358.98
3. Microsoft (talking paperclips) $275.85
4. Citigroup (banking) $247.42
5. AT&T (telephony) $229.78.

A second method, if a company isn't listed on a stock market, is to look at its revenues. That is, the amount of money that comes into the company from customers.*

Say a company is bringing in £1 million a year in revenue, a potential investor would multiply that figure by a magic 'x' number to work out a valuation. This is sometimes referred to as an 'x times revenue' valuation. The value of x depends on a number of factors: the nature of the company, what valuation similar sites have received ... that kind of thing.

There's just one small problem with an 'x times revenue' valuation – they are prone to being total bullshit. So prone, in fact, that they've become enormously popular among start-up companies that don't have any revenue at all but want a nice juicy valuation to attract investors without having to give too much of their company away.

I know this because I've been in the room when entrepreneurs have been working out their valuations. The conversation tends to go like this.

Entrepreneur: 'What are we saying revenue is for year one?' (Bear in mind this is a total guess – at this stage the company hasn't even launched.)

Business partner: 'A million.'

Entrepreneur: 'Okay, let's do three times revenue – three million?'

Business partner: 'Can we say 3.5?'

Entrepreneur: 'Okay. 3.5 times revenue. We'll value the company at three and a half million.'

Business partner: 'Another drink?'

Entrepreneur: 'Can we make it a triple?'

But while in traditional businesses that kind of bullshit can be controlled by ensuring that a company's 'x' value is roughly the same as similar companies in the market, the Internet doesn't allow those kinds of comparisons.

Internet companies are the Emo kids or Goths of the business world: they might all look and smell basically the same but, actually, they're all So Freaking Unique that they defy categorisation. Accord-

....

* Unless you work in publishing, in which case just make up your own batshit definition and write it here: ———

ing to its own figures, YouTube brought in a total of $15 million in revenue for the whole of 2006. In big business terms, that's chickenfeed: the same amount of money that Exxon brings in every *twenty minutes*. And yet YouTube, we're supposed to believe, is worth $1.6 billion – which is 107 times its revenue, give or take. Meanwhile, Amazon, which is traded on the stock market and had revenues of $10.7 billion for 2006, currently has a market capitalisation of $37.74 billion. So if Amazon was valued based on its revenues, it would be worth less than four times revenue. Two Internet companies – one worth 107 times its revenues, the other less than four times.

Welcome to the wacky world of Internet valuations, where the only accurate value of a privately held company is what some idiot will pay for it.

Another example: about a year before the YouTube deal was announced, auction site eBay decided it wanted to buy a two-year-old company called Skype. Founded by Janus Friis and Niklas Zennström (a Dane and a Swede), Skype's service was as simple as it was ingenious. In brief, it allowed Skype users to make free phone calls to other Skype users via the Internet. All you had to do was download the special (and also free) software and the Skype service would take care of the rest. As an added bonus, Skype users could also make and receive calls to and from the traditional global phone network for a small extra cost. This cost was far, far below the normal cost of an international (or even a national) call as that part of the call was connected across the Internet, with only the last few local miles needing the normal phone network.

Clearly Skype had the potential to annihilate traditional telecoms companies, and eBay decided it wanted in on the action. At the time the deal was done, the service had a modest turnover – some $30–$50 million a year – so some experts expressed surprise when eBay offered to pay $2.6 billion in cash and stock up front, plus a further $1.5 billion if Skype met certain financial targets. A total of $4.1 billion.

Madness.

Or perhaps not. What if Skype did rise to a position of dominance in the telecoms market? Remember AT&T's valuation of $229.78

billion? Suddenly $4.1 billion for Skype starts to look like chicken-feed. Who can say whether $4.1 billion was a bargain or a fortune?

And to take one more example, who knew if the $580 million Rupert Murdoch paid for social networking site MySpace (along with its parent company) the same year was a bargain or whether he got shafted?

No one knew anything. Even Barry Diller – former chief executive of Paramount and Fox, owner of QVC and Ticketmaster and one of the leading media players in the world – was forced to admit in an interview: '[Murdoch] has either bought these things very cheap – or they're worthless.'*

As it happened, when it came to Skype even eBay had no idea whether they'd got a good deal or not: in October 2007, two years after the sale was agreed, the company reduced Skype's valuation by $1.43 billion.

The industry shrugged its shoulders.

Nobody knows anything.

Do Skype's Zennström and Friis care that their company turned out to be totally overvalued? Of course they don't – they're already working hard on their next business: a service called Joost, which promises to be the future of television and which has already attracted $45 million in funding. Some experts are already suggesting that, thanks to deals with media giants like Viacom to distribute content through Joost, the company could one day be worth twice as much as YouTube.

Or it could be worth nothing at all.

Nobody knows anything.

4.1

With news of YouTube's $1.65 billion dollar valuation still sinking in, I phoned Sam Lewis to see if he fancied a drink. He was in the middle of writing a business plan for a new business – a site that

....

* He said it at the 2005 O'Reilly Web 2.0 conference, a Mecca for entrepreneurs involved in the second dot com boom/bubble.

hoped to change the way people socialise, using mobile phones – and I was keen to hear how he was getting on. I also knew I could rely on him to bring me back down to earth when something was bothering me. We arranged to meet at the Chandos, the pub across the road from the International bar.

'So how about YouTube?' he asked, before we'd even sat down. 'Sick with envy? Puking your guts out with jealousy?'

'Fuck off,' I said. 'You know the two of them are only a fraction older than me. In comparison with them I'm a total failure.'

'Mate, I'm thirty-five,' he replied. 'How do you think I feel?'

'Yes, but you've had one successful business. And your new thing could turn out to be the next YouTube – easy. Or at least easier than The Friday Project could. Do you think anyone will pay a billion for a publishing company.'

'Perhaps not. But that's not what this is about and you know it,' he said.

'No, it's not—'

'It's about the fact that you want to be famous – and you don't think anyone will ever become famous starting a publishing company. You're jealous that Chen and Hurley are on the front of the papers and that everyone's talking about them. And that no one gives a toss about you.

'I'm not jealous.'

But I was, of course I was. Bitterly so. How could I not be?

'So why don't you launch a web service? What is it you always say – writers have ten ideas before breakfast? So have a fucking brilliant idea. Stop fucking moaning about it.'

'It's not as easy as that.'

Have a fucking brilliant idea – what kind of advice was that to give someone? *Have a fucking brilliant idea. Win the fucking lottery. Trip over a fucking cure for cancer and land inside a fucking supermodel.*

But, actually, he had a point. A brilliant idea was all the YouTube founders had had eighteen months ago; a brilliant idea was all it took Alex Tew to become rich and famous. And, wait a minute – I *did* have a brilliant idea.

Sort of.

4.2

For the last couple of months our online editor Karl and I had been working on a plan to develop the online arm of The Friday Project. The suggestion had come from Anthony Cheetham who thought having a web service of our own would boost the company's valuation during the public offering.

I'd kicked around a few possible ideas for a site but the best one I'd come up with – the one that everyone in the company had agreed to let me spend the grand total of twenty grand developing – was a site we'd codenamed Fridaycities. Fridaycities would be an exciting and hugely ambitious reinvention of the *London by London* newsletter: a site that would allow people who lived in any city in the world to come together to swap information about every aspect of the place they lived, in real time.

Say you lived in London, and wanted to know where the best oyster bar was, or the best place to buy a viola – you would post your question on the site and within a couple of minutes you'd have a couple of dozen answers from other users. No more waiting a whole week for the newsletter to arrive. Users could also set up personal profile pages, detailing their likes, dislikes and areas of expertise; and this information could be used to suggest questions and answers they might be interested in.

What I envisaged was a kind of MySpace for the grown-up city dweller. But unlike MySpace, we'd employ professional editors to ensure some basic standards of grammar and spelling: I'd always suspected that the sign-up process for MySpace somehow disabled all the vowels on your keyboard; that's the only explanation I could think of for the levels of illiteracy one sees on the average MySpace page.

Rather than bringing me back down to earth, my chat with Sam had only made my mind race faster. With work already under way on the Fridaycities site, it was quite possible that, without realising it, we'd already started building the next YouTube.

Sam had a hot date that he needed to get to so we agreed to catch up the following week when I'd had more of a chance to think. I, too, had to run: I was late for a networking event that I was supposed to be attending.

As I walked across Trafalgar Square and down the Strand towards Adam Street, I passed a man dressed in purple handing out free copies of the *London Paper*. Without thinking, I grabbed a copy and carried on walking. The top showbiz story on the front page concerned a star whose drunken behaviour had been uploaded on to YouTube for the amusement of the world.

Bloody YouTube. It was everywhere.

4.3

The Adam Street private members' club lies behind an anonymous looking black front door, just off the Strand. The only indication that you've come to the right place is a small brass plaque with an engraving of a bowler hat, the club's logo. London has dozens of these private clubs, from showbiz haunts like the Groucho Club on Dean Street and Soho House around the corner on Greek Street, to distinguished old-school gentlemen's clubs like the RAC* on Pall Mall and the Garrick on Garrick Street. But Adam Street has an interesting gimmick: it caters specifically for entrepreneurs.

The club was founded in 2001 by James Minter (Jamie to his friends) when he took over some basement vaults underneath a row of terraced houses owned by his father. It boasts a bar and an excellent restaurant, which are open to both members and guests, but the real draw of Adam Street is that it offers countless opportunities for networking. Walk into the club at any time of the day or night and you'll see them – either hunched over a laptop in the library or attending a working dinner in one of the club's two private dining rooms or dancing the night away after a networking event in the basement function room. Adam Street is the place that London's new wave of entrepreneurs calls home. It also helps that the club bans lawyers, accountants and other professionals from

....

* Unlike the Garrick, the RAC does actually allow women inside, providing they don't get too uppity.

touting their services in the club in the same way that the Groucho and Soho House ban paparazzi.

Since moving to London, I'd spent a huge amount of time in Adam Street, partly because it's where all of my friends tended to spend their free time and partly because of the club's late opening hours and excellent cocktail menu.

Tonight, though, I was here strictly for work; for an event called 'The Next Big Thing' where a group of successful entrepreneurs and investors would take to a small stage in the basement function room to share their predictions for the future of the Internet. The range of speakers was incredibly impressive, including venture capitalists Sean Seaton-Rogers and Nic Brisbourne, veteran entrepreneur Angus Bankes and web wunderkind Alex Tew.

Arriving late, I'd just missed Angus Bankes's presentation but made it just in time to see Michael Smith take the platform. In his opinion, The Next Big Thing would be companies that kept things simple rather than building complicated web services which most people couldn't understand and wouldn't use. An interesting view from a man who invents puzzles for a living, I thought.

At the end of the evening a microphone was passed around, I introduced myself as a former journalist-turned-book publisher, made a weak joke about getting drunk on Alex Tew's tab and we all headed off to dance the night away at the Gardening Club.

It had turned out to be a great end to a great night, with Alex being chatted up by a group of four very pretty girls who had read about The Million Dollar Homepage and were suitably impressed to be in the company of a real-life millionaire. At a pound a drink, he could buy them a hell of a lot of vodkas and tonic. Not wanting to be outdone, I got chatting to a stunning blonde American girl at the bar and decided to pretend to be Tom Anderson, the founder of MySpace. Despite my complete lack of American accent, she was almost convinced that I was telling the truth, especially when Michael – who had been standing behind me listening – tapped me on the shoulder and yelled over the music 'Hey, Tom – let's do shots!' For that stunning bit of wingmanship, I finally forgave him for the map.

But I didn't do shots with Michael and the others – in fact I stayed remarkably sober. I had too much on my mind to start mixing it up with drink. The YouTube deal; the ovation that had greeted Alex Tew; Sam's encouragement to *have a fucking brilliant idea*. Jesus, why couldn't I just put my ego away and be happy with what I had? What the hell was wrong with me?

4.4

What happened next is something of a blur, but on 7 December 2006 – my twenty-seventh birthday – I announced to the world that I had negotiated a buyout of the online arm* of The Friday Project for an undisclosed sum.

The sum was undisclosed because it was basically tiny. I'd have to give up some of my Friday Project shares and pay a year's worth of four figure monthly instalments. Friday Project Media would retain a 10 per cent stake, and I'd step down from the board of FPM Plc. 'An undisclosed sum' always sounds far cooler than the truth, and, sure enough, the trade press lapped it up.

But, of course, I couldn't start an entire business all on my own, so Karl and I went out for a drink to talk about the future. Of course he would come, too, he said – taking a stake in the new company, even though it meant giving up his Friday Project salary and any semblance of security he'd managed to build up. It was an amazing display of loyalty and one that made me feel much better about what could easily have been the most reckless decision I've ever made. We also convinced Savannah Christensen, a friend of mine from law school who was now editing a start-up independent newspaper called *The Penny*, to join us as the site's new head of community – the person who makes sure that the users are looked after and that vowels are used at all times.

The fact that we had no office space, no business plan and, most critically of all, no money in the bank, didn't faze us. After a few

<hr />

* Which, by this point, consisted of a very basic skeleton version of Fridaycities with a few thousand test users, plus a mailing list of several thousand people who subscribed to *London by London*.

meetings in my living room to sketch out a business plan and divide up between the three of us the dozens of jobs that needed to be done in a start-up, we were utterly convinced: Fridaycities was going to be the next YouTube.

We couldn't fail.

At least that's what we told ourselves.

In reality, we were terrified.

4.5

But terror would have to wait. With the buyout just a week or so old, we knew we had a huge job ahead of us if we were going to finish building the test site and start populating it with test users.

Our first, and most important task, was to raise some start-up capital and, given that I'd just kissed goodbye to my salary, and was still paying rent on a flat I couldn't afford, it was time to start begging.

Over Christmas I put together a set of financial forecasts that basically showed we could set up the new company and finish building the test site for just over £50,000. On the strength of the business plan and no small amount of familial loyalty, my parents and my uncle Hugh agreed to become our first investors, each putting up half of the money. This injection of cash gave us enough working capital to survive for the first three months of 2007, by which time we'd either have to have found an additional investor or we'd end up on the streets.

Despite our modest capital and the uphill task ahead of us, our confidence was rock solid. Fuck it – weren't business plans and projections so last century? YouTube had gone from launch to $1.65 billion in a year and eight months, almost by accident.

I already had the contacts in the industry; I had the big idea; we had the beginnings of a management team. Okay, so I'd never actually run a pure Internet business before, never actually raised money for one, but I'd seen enough people of my age who had. And I had one big advantage that no other first time dot com entrepreneurs had: for four years I'd basically been a spy – first at the *Guardian*, where entrepreneurs would gladly let me peek inside their businesses; reveal their secrets in the hope that they might translate to a few favourable words in print. And then at The Friday Project where I'd had even more access: acting as a sounding board for their future ideas and plans and listening while they tried to convince me that these plans could provide material for book spin-offs. If anyone knew the secret of what made a successful – or unsuccessful – new media business in London, surely it was me.

But, of course, nobody does know the secret of what makes a successful new media business. Nobody knows anything.

Duh.

5.0

'Children, animals and the love of your life, oh my . . .'

A confession.

Describing Savannah as a friend from law school is a bit of an understatement.

Quite a big understatement, actually.

It is certainly true to say that I met Savannah on the first day of my first week at law school. That much is certainly, verifiably, true. I still have the notes from that first day when a quirk of surname meant we were forced into the same group for a horrendously patronising treasure hunt the faculty had arranged for us to 'get to know each other'.

Having barely had the chance to say hello to the people we would share lecture halls and seminar rooms with for the next three years, we were bundled into small groups and turfed out on to the streets to look for clues around the city. Here we all were, away from home for the first time and beginning our lives as proper grown-ups – and they were sending us on a bloody treasure hunt. This was law school?

In what turned out to be a foretaste of our entire attitude to our studies, Savannah and I decided to leave the rest of the group to traipse around the city hunting for clues while we spent the afternoon in the pub.

But the treasure hunt wasn't the reason I wanted to spend the afternoon with Savannah, and the quirk of surname wasn't the reason we ended up becoming friends. In fact, I'm pretty sure we could have been studying different courses at opposite ends of the city – perhaps even the country – and I'd still have found her.

It helped that she was American, blonde and stunningly beautiful. Those were three of my boxes ticked right there, before she'd even opened her mouth. And when she did, she was easily the most naturally funny girl I've ever met. Arguably, in fact, the only naturally funny girl I'd ever met, given that I'd grown up in Kent where girls are taught not to speak with their mouths full, meaning that from the age of thirteen they're essentially mute. Savannah also had a great line in acerbic put-downs, most of which were aimed at me as we sat that afternoon in the pub, getting to know each other. Before we'd ordered our first drink, I was charmed by her. By the end of pint number one, I really fancied her. By pint number two I was crazy about her.

Pretty soon I was looking for any excuse to spend time with her, to the delight of my girlfriend of two years, who, by a quirk of UCAS points, was also starting the same course at the same university as me. Fortunately, spending time with Savannah was easy as we were in every one of the same classes and her university digs were not two hundred yards from mine.

Whenever I was with her, I wanted nothing more than to impress her – just to see her smile or make her laugh. If I'm a bit of a geek today then in those days I was basically an extra from *Revenge of the Nerds*. I still had my high school haircut, and my high school girlfriend and a dress sense that could best be recreated by replacing a blind man's entire wardrobe with ill-fitting jumpers. I was far from being a catch, especially to this Californian goddess with her surfer boyfriend. But I did have a secret weapon: I knew I could make people laugh – and so that became the basis of my plan to win her heart. Getting a haircut and losing the jumpers would have helped, too, but that would have to wait until the second year. No sense going overboard.

There was just one hitch in my plan – two if you count the fact that I had a girlfriend and she had a boyfriend: there was no way in hell I could tell her about the night job I had in those days, writing dorky books about the Internet. I mean, how could I ever get her to fall for me if she knew I made money by running a website? And then writing books about it? What a geek! Her boyfriend was a surfer, for God's sake. A surfer who worked in a bar. How the hell was I supposed to compete with that?

Unbelievably, I managed to keep my deep, dark Internet secret from Savannah for almost a year, through a combination of changing the subject and out and out lying, but I knew that in the end, one day, she'd find out the horrible truth.

It was the day of her twenty-first birthday and I was going to have to skip her birthday party to go to London to meet Clare for a progress report on the books. I went round to her house in the afternoon to explain that I had to be in London (an all too common excuse for missing appointments with her) for the evening, and that I was really sorry I wouldn't make the party, but that I'd try to see her later.

I'd made similar excuses a dozen times before and she'd always accepted them with a mixture of resignation and confusion, clearly not wanting to pry into my personal business, if I wasn't going to tell her what I was up to.

But that day, for some reason, her reaction was different. All of a sudden, her face turned very solemn and concerned; that look girls normally give you when you make a joke about child abduction.

I was suddenly very aware that she was staring at me. And that neither of us was talking.

Finally she broke the silence.

'Um, Paul, can I ask you something? You don't have to answer if you don't want to.'

'Sure . . .'

Oh God, here it comes.

'Is everything okay?'

'Of course. Why wouldn't it be?'

'Well, these trips to London, and the strange phone calls you keep leaving the room to take, and the fact that you never turn up to lectures . . .*

. . . I mean, you know you can tell me anything, right?'

I sighed, took a deep breath, and prepared for the worst. This was the moment I'd been dreading. I could hear her roaring with laughter already. Looking down at my shoes, I told her everything – about the website, the book deal . . . everything. It was like admitting to your mum that you like dressing up in her clothes while she's at work. Possibly more embarrassing.

For ten seconds, maybe longer, she stayed silent, still fixing me

....

* That was true; in two years I'd been to a grand total of three lectures, including the treasure hunt one.

with her annoyingly beautiful eyes. Eyes which had already started to fill with tears of laughter and pity.

Except, no.

Something was very wrong with this picture.

They weren't tears of derision – they were just tears. Normal tears. Normal girl tears.

'Oh, thank God,' she sobbed. 'I've been trying to work out for weeks what it was you were hiding. All my friends have been guessing.'

'And what did you come up with?' I asked.

'We thought you had a gay lover in London who was dying of AIDS.'

'What?!'

'Well, it was the only thing I could think of.'

All this time and she'd thought I had a gay lover in London. That's why she thought I wouldn't let her meet my 'girlfriend' and why I kept running off to London instead of partying with her. That was the *only thing she could think of*? And at that exact moment she became the love . . .

'Hang on . . . you run a website . . . and you've written books?! Oh my God, that's soooo cool, why didn't you tell me? You have to show me!'

. . . of my life. All I had to do now was convince her to dump her boyfriend and live happily ever after with me.

Sadly, that particular goal proved only partially successful. After university, while I moved to London to start my career writing about my fellow geeks for cash, Savannah moved to Exeter with her now even longer-term surfer boyfriend to carry on studying law and presumably spend the weekends watching him surf and then nights on the beach and . . . GAAAAAAAH.

We stayed in touch, on and off, with just the occasional phone call where I'd tell her about my life as a singleton in the big city (I'd split up with my high school girlfriend, and hadn't yet met Maggie, so I was busy making up for lost time in a huge way, basically sleeping my way around the city. This had become slightly easier since I dumped the jumpers and got my hair cut.) In return, she'd tell me how happy she was with her boyfriend and how they were going to buy a pub together in the country, and run it as a couple. I was deliriously happy for them both, of course, and probably only spent a couple of hours a week typing 'surfing accident statistics' into Google.

And then one day – almost two years later – I received the best text message of my life.

'Hey you. I'm moving to London in June. On my own. Want to come house hunting with me?'

Praise Jesus. Praise Buddha. Of course, the fact that she was moving to London on her own didn't mean she had split up with her boyfriend. And even if it did – obviously it bloody did – it didn't necessarily mean we'd get together. I mean, she was just stating it as a fact. A piece of news.

Yeah. Right. The angels were singing, the sun was shining. Savannah was coming to London and within weeks we'd be married. No other outcome was conceivable.

'Sure. Let me know when you're coming to town and I'll see if I'm around.'

I am so fucking cool.

As luck – wonderful, wonderful luck – would have it, one of my flatmates was moving out of the shared house I was living in. By July 2004, Savannah and I were sleeping under the same roof. By August, we were sleeping under the same duvet.

Praise Mohammad.

For almost a year I was the happiest man in the world. I was writing for the *Guardian*, arsing about writing books, editing *The Friday Thing* and dating the love of my life. Sure, she had basically moved straight from one live-in relationship into another, but that was fine.

We'd work through it.

5.1

We didn't work through it.

5.2

Not even slightly.

5.3

But fuck it. Those twelve blissful months we were together made me happy enough to make up for a lifetime of miserable comparisons to come. And anyway, we'd got together weeks after she'd come out of a live-in relationship. She only needed some time; I'd get her back in the end. We were meant to be. A matter of time, is all.

Unless of course – a couple of years later – we suddenly found ourselves working together in the same office, in the stressful environment of an Internet start-up. That would be suicide. Madness. Idiocy. It doesn't matter if she's brilliant, and talented, and that I'd get to see her every day. Working together would ruin everything.

'You're hiring Savannah?' Sam wasn't so much asking as despairing.

'Yep, she's brilliant with people. She's just finished launching an independent newspaper for London and wants a new challenge. She's smart and she's a million times more organised than Karl and me put together. She's perfect.'

'Yes, I know all that. You've been saying how brilliant she is for three years. But you know if you work with her, you'll never get back together, right? I mean ever.'

'Of course,' I lied.

I'd figure it out somehow.

5.4

Karl was a considerably less dangerous proposition. He and I had also met while I was at university, but under somewhat different circumstances.

In my second year, with my academic workload starting to get a bit heavy, I decided it was time to hire a few more writers to contribute to *The Friday Thing*. I wrote a short advert for the next issue inviting people who could 'write good jokes for not very much money' to email in samples of their work. About two dozen people responded, and Clare, Charlie and I sat down to sift through the hopefuls. By and large the quality was less than inspiring. Dire, you might say.

Most of the people who replied seemed to have misread the ad and were asking us for a lot of money in exchange for some not very good writing. One hopeful even pitched the idea of a fake agony aunt column – always the last refuge of a failed comedy writer. We divided the submissions into four piles – 'unfunny', 'laughably unfunny', 'so bad they're funny' and just 'funny'. That last pile was the smallest by a mile but left us with a list of maybe four possible hires, including two particularly good efforts, one from an Italian-based English writer called Graham Pond and another from a chap in Sunderland called Karl Webster. Graham Pond was the best by a nose, having sent a genuinely hilarious piece about Easter that he'd written for an English-language magazine in Bologna. In a close-run vote, we picked Graham for the weekly gig, but we also sent Karl a nice email inviting him to send in more stuff, promising to pay him for anything we used.

A few weeks later we hired a pub on Fleet Street and hosted a party to celebrate the first birthday of *The Friday Thing*, and we were very excited when Graham said he was going to fly over from Italy to attend. He'd been submitting really great stuff every week and I was keen to put a face to the jokes. He finally arrived about two hours late: tall, in his early thirties and with a slightly grizzled look that was somewhere between Hunter S. Thompson and Tintin.

'You must be Paul,' he said, striding over to me and throwing his rucksack at my feet. 'And these ...' his voice dripping with a writer's contempt, 'must be the readers ...'

'And you must be Graham,' I replied, kicking his bag under the table. I liked him immediately.

'Actually it's Karl.'

'Karl?'

'Karl Webster. It's a funny story actually ...'

And so it was. It turned out that Karl was so keen to secure the gig with *The Friday Thing* that he'd sent in six different entries, under six different names. All four writers in our short list had been him, including Graham Pond. It's hard not to be impressed by that kind of chutzpah. And I was impressed, to the point that when Clare and I set up The Friday Project he was the natural choice to take over the editorship of *The Friday Thing* and *London by London*, and to head up the company's online arm.

To avoid any weirdness or jealousy, and to underline the fact that we were all in this together, I insisted that Savannah and Karl would each have equal shares to me, and that we'd all have the same salary. Despite the fact that the start-up money had come from my parents and my uncle, we were all risking the same thing: our futures. So it was only fair that we all had an equal say. There are few things more certain to end long-term friendships than arguments over money.

5.5

On the freezing morning of 1 January 2007 we dragged our new landlord out of his hung-over bed to let us into our brand new offices in the converted Battersea Studios in south London. I had arranged to meet Savannah at Victoria Station at noon, but naturally we both arrived late and very hung-over. We always had very different styles of being hung-over: Savannah always managing to look absolutely radiant and full of life, while I always looked like I'd been raped by a hedge.

And so began a new year and the first day of Fridaycities.

I'd found the office space on the Internet and it seemed perfect for a start-up with very little money. For a start it was dirt cheap – tenants paid for room in the open-plan space for just £100 per desk per week, which included all bills: telephone, electricity, Internet, meeting room rental – the works. A bargain, we thought. Also, the space was very cool looking, having been created by an extraordinarily camp (but totally straight, he insisted) interior designer called Peter, who had designed every aspect himself.

Peter's flair for design and order would prove to be, putting it mildly, a mixed blessing. The space was certainly stunning to look at, with expensive designer furniture, fingerprint access and an enormous wooden Buddha greeting guests at the door. But Peter was also just a touch too house proud for comfort. In fact, when it came to rules, he made the guards at Alcatraz look laissez-faire. For a start there was to be no clutter on desks – no personal knick-knacks or photos of any kind; no papers left lying around and (on pain of death) absolutely no pot plants. He had, he explained, arranged for fresh flowers to be brought in weekly and that any additional greenery would ruin the 'look'. But his ultimate bugbear was teaspoons. Peter hated teaspoons. The office had a smoothie machine, a coffee-maker capable of producing five types of hot beverage and a shelf containing at least twenty little silver tins, each with a different type of tea. But nary a spoon with which to stir them.

Instead, Peter had invested in thousands of those stupid single-use wooden splints you get in Starbucks. By going down the disposable route, he explained, there would be less need for washing up and so fewer overheads. He was barking mad, clearly, and on several occasions I thought Savannah was going to physically assault him with one of the wooden stirrers. But the space was cheap and the lure of fingerprint access was simply too great for a geek like me.

As we waited for Peter to arrive with our new keys on that first morning, I examined the gigantic map in the lobby, showing the other offices in the building and who inhabited them. What I discovered was definitely a good omen.

By a strange coincidence, our immediate neighbour in the building was a company called Mind Candy Design, otherwise known as the company Michael Smith had set up to run Perplex City. We would be working ten feet away from Michael – so close in fact that I could look out through the giant windows and see his giant TV and Playstations from my desk. I could smell his success without even opening the door.

Another good sign – literally – was the one that I noticed as we walked up the stairs to our new office. Standing outside the Mind Candy office was a huge vinyl banner promoting Perplex City.

There in two-foot-high lettering were the words 'Perplex City: the puzzle game that is gearing up to become the interactive phenomenon of the year. – *Guardian'*.

Two years on and he was still dining out on that article.

The cheeky bastard.

6.0

'What's a nice girl like you doing at a sausage fest like this?'

The next time I ran into Alex Tew after our evening at the Gardening Club, he actually ran in to me.

More accurately, he ran across a crowded nightclub and jumped on my back.

I had been invited to a party for 'Imperial Entrepreneurs', a group of young business people, particularly technology entrepreneurs, who attend Imperial College in London. It's hard to imagine a group more geeky than young technology entrepreneurs from Imperial College and so it's not entirely surprising that the crowd was 99.9 per cent male and – um – conservatively dressed. I swear you've never seen so many checked shirts in your life. This wouldn't have been a problem had the organisers not decided to host the event in the basement of Paper, the sickeningly hip nightclub underneath the Café Royale, just off Regent Street.

The cool venue was the only reason I'd accepted the invitation so readily: the club has a reputation for attracting astonishingly attractive and wealthy women – quite unobtainable, of course (and a gold-digging nightmare if you were successful) – but very nice to look at and great fun to flirt with at the bar.

The event was due to kick off at nine and by the time I arrived, just before eleven, a queue of checked shirts had formed, snaking halfway down the street. It didn't seem to be moving. I noticed the organiser standing towards the front of the queue – even he was queuing. That wasn't a good sign.

I wandered up to find out what was going on.

'What's going on?' I asked.

'They're not letting anyone in.'

'But I thought you'd booked the whole floor for the party?'

'We have, but the bouncers say they want to keep the balance of men and women about the same through the whole club.'

'But that's stupid. This is an event for Internet entrepreneurs – there'll be about ten women here in total if you're lucky.'

Even that was optimistic. Internet networking events are so legendary for their awful women-to-men ratio that in San Francisco they've been nicknamed 'sausage fests'.

'Yeah, but what can you do?'

'Why don't you find a girl?' I suggested.

'Why?'

Clearly this wasn't going to be easy.

'Look, hang on,' I said, pulling out my phone. There was only one thing to do: I called my friend Kate who lives a five-minute walk from Regent Street. Kate works in television and in the two or three years I'd known her she'd become used to getting phone calls from me at all hours of the day and night inviting her to come and crash parties with me. Having agreed early on in our friendship that there was no way she'd be stupid enough to sleep with me, and after I'd exhausted all my efforts to convince her otherwise, she had become the ultimate friend date. She had also become my unofficial PR rep, hyping me to her attractive female friends and assuring them that – for the right woman – I'd be a great catch.

'Carr! What can I do for you this evening?'

'Hello, darling,' I said. 'I don't want anything. I was just calling to see how you are. It's come to something when a fellow can't call his friend of an evening to see how she is.'

Silence.

'Okay, okay. I need a favour. Can you put on something sexy and come to Paper on Regent Street?'

'What? No. I'm watching *CSI: NY* and they're about to start cutting open the body. And, anyway, what are you doing at Paper? It's awful. All fake tits and permatans.'

Duh, I thought, that's why I'm here.

'I know, I know. But this is an emergency. I need you to be my sexy date to this geek party thing. They're not letting men in on their own.'

'And so you want me to be your plus one? To some sausage fest geek party?'

'Yes. Please.'

'Sorry, got to go, they're using the special electric brain saw.'
Click

Clearly Kate wasn't going to be any help. Just wait till she phoned me in the middle of the night asking me to be her plus one to a party full of sex-starved women. I'd show her.

Just then I noticed three extremely glamorous-looking girls – all fake tits and permatans – tottering towards the front of the queue in the confident way beautiful girls who know they're going to get waved through velvet ropes do.

Fuck it. Nothing ventured ...

'Excuse me,' I said, trying to act as nonchalantly as possible, as if approaching footballers' wives was something I did every day.

They looked at me through their four layers of mascara, and then looked at the other two hundred geeky men standing in the queue next to me. I swore one of them was about to Mace me.

'Yeah?'

'I know this is really cheeky ...' I leaned in, conspiratorially. The smell of perfume was unbearable; Mace would have been blessed relief ... 'but I've been forced to go to this party with all these nerdy guys. It's for work. I'm a journalist, you see ...'

I tried to keep my voice down. If my plan was going to succeed, there was no way the girls could think I was there voluntarily. That I was one of *these* people.

'... and they're only letting one man in with every girl.'

'So?'

'So, would you mind awfully if I tagged along with you ladies, just till we get through the door?'

They looked at me with a mixture of pity and fear.

'I'll buy you all a drink, if you do. Please, it would really help me out.'

(Little-boy-lost face. Never fails.)

'Okay. But we're drinking champagne,' they cackled as one. It was terrifying, but it had worked.

Once inside, and having spent nearly £25 buying three drinks – £25! – I looked around the room. Sitting on a huge banquette were a dozen or so of the prettiest girls you've ever seen, wearing the

121

shortest skirts. Scary beautiful – the type of women who can only be models or high-class hookers. It was like they were auditioning extras for *Anne Summers: The Movie*. And they were all tall. So very, very tall.

And also this. Terrified.

They had clearly turned up at their usual haunt, expecting it to be full of the usual crowd of Premiership footballers and boy band members. But, instead, their territory had been overrun by a hundred or so young technology entrepreneurs, most of them still students, ferociously networking with each other and barely giving the women a second glance. Which was probably absolutely fine by them.

It was at this point that I was assaulted by a drunk millionaire who ran across the room and jumped on my back.

'Paul Carr!' Alex Tew shouted, nearly knocking me off my feet. 'Thank God you're here. You got past the bouncers then? Man, I fucking love it when I see you at parties – I know we're not going to stop until the next morning.'

I was flattered, even though he was essentially calling me an alcoholic who didn't know when to call it a night. I was delighted to see him, too – someone human, and fun, at an otherwise potentially horrific party.

'So, how's it all going?' I asked.

'Great! I'm about to announce my next project. It's going to be even bigger than The Million Dollar Homepage.'

'Let me guess,' I joked, 'The "Two Million Dollar Homepage"?'

'Funny you should say that ... Come on, let's get a drink ...'

6.1

Turns out that Alex's big new idea was, essentially, The Two Million Dollar Homepage – but with a twist. Called Pixelotto, the new site would again allow advertisers to buy one of a million squares on a giant web page. But this time, instead of each square costing a dollar, they would cost *two* dollars – one dollar of which went to Alex and the other into a prize fund. Every time a visitor to the site clicked on a square, he would be entered into a prize draw to win the entire fund. It was, once again, beautifully simple – users were encouraged to click more often by the promise of a huge prize, giving advertisers a better return for their squares and Alex even more advertising bucks as a result.

Given how many people clicked on the ads on the original Million Dollar Homepage – the site is littered with testimonials from satisfied customers – it's hard to see how Pixelotto could possibly fail. And, indeed, Alex boasted, lastminute.com, the online travel company specialising in late deals, had already agreed to buy the block of squares right in the middle of the site. He was making money before the damn thing had even launched. Money for nothing – just a concept. Now *that's* being an entrepreneur.

Dr Linus Pauling, the great American theoretical chemist, once said, 'The way to get good ideas is to get lots of ideas, and throw the bad ones away.' If Alex Tew is anything to go by, Pauling was bang on the money.

A short time later, at yet another networking event, I decided to ask Alex what his secret was to knowing whether a business idea was good or bad. The Million Dollar Homepage had spawned hundred of imitators, making it that Holy Grail of inventions: one that not only launches a new business but an entire new format. I wanted to know his secret so that I could apply it to Fridaycities.

'There's no secret to having good ideas.'

'Thanks, Alex. That's a lot of help.'

'Seriously – there isn't. What I do is get a notepad and write a list of every idea I can think of that might make money. That's the first criterion – can it make money? If not, it's a waste of time. Then, when I've got my list, the difficult part starts – choosing which idea to follow. Which one has the best chance of succeeding for the greatest possible reward? When I did The Million Dollar Homepage I had a list of, like, ten ideas that might work. The Homepage was the best of them. And it worked.'

I couldn't argue with that.

'You know,' I said, 'that party we went to with all those people in checked shirts gave me a great idea for you: next time there's a geek party, you should offer to sponsor all of the shirts – you could sell each check for £10 to an advertiser and split the money with the nerds. Call it "the thousand check shirt party".'

'Yeah,' he deadpanned, 'that's a good example of an idea that wouldn't make it off the page.'

Fuck it, it was worth a shot.

6.2

It's actually not at all surprising that I'd run into Alex at Paper or that Michael Smith happened to be in the same building as us or even that, a few weeks later, another acquaintance of ours, Michael O'Shea – founder of kids' toy site Wickeduncle.com,* took a desk opposite ours at Battersea Studios.

The thing you need to know about the London Internet scene (and it is a scene) is that it's absolutely tiny. And it's made to feel even tinier by the number of connections there are between the major players. There can be very few sectors of the media where at any given party or networking event you'll find almost all of the key players in the same room. At an Internet event, one bad tray of hors d'oeuvres could wipe out the entire industry.

And, boy, are there a lot of events. In London alone, in any given week, there are at least half a dozen – ranging from sensible breakfast gatherings to Bacchanalian late-night parties where 'getting to know your peers' is meant as much in the biblical as the commercial sense.

Whichever type of event you choose to attend, if you want to succeed as an Internet entrepreneur then being part of the 'scene' is a must. The more networking you do, the more likely you are to meet the guy who invested in the guy who got bought by the guy who will become the guy who gives you $10 million to start your business. I knew that if I was to have a hope in hell of succeeding

....

* Wickeduncle, incidentally, is a great example of the dangers inherent in choosing a company name. To Michael, Wickeduncle – a site designed to help relatives buy toys for young children, thus making them 'wicked' in a cool way – was a brilliant piece of youth branding. To me, it always sounded like a gift site for paedophiles.

with Fridaycities I was going to have to spend a lot of time networking, and so I decided to attend as many of these events as possible. It was a tough job, but I was prepared to make the sacrifice.

The first event I went to after moving into the new office was one of the most grown-up examples of the genre. If the London Internet scene is a tight network then Saul Klein is right smack bang in the middle of it. A venture capitalist by trade, he has invested in a whole host of successful dot com companies, including Michael's Mind Candy, and is also on the board of directors of Skype. If you're trying to raise money for a company in London, he's a very useful person to know. And there are few better ways to get to know him than by turning up at his weekly morning networking event: Open Coffee.

Open Coffee is a strange beast, basically an impromptu coffee morning for entrepreneurs and investors. Every week, between the hours of ten and noon, a certain central London coffee shop suddenly starts filling up with men and women in smart suits with laptop bags slung over their shoulders. It happens slowly at first, almost imperceptibly, but by 10.30 it's unmistakable. For a start, everyone in the shop is standing up, walking around, working the room. Any normal customers who stray in suddenly find themselves having a business card thrust in their faces, or their tables being overrun by laptops. At the very centre of this madness are the venture capitalists, Saul and his colleagues from London's various investment houses all standing, like cheerleaders at the prom, fending off approaches from would-be suitors. In truth, very little business is talked at Open Coffee; instead, it's all about making introductions. The best most entrepreneurs can hope for is a quick shake of a royal hand, a thirty-second explanation as to why your business is going to change the world and, if you're lucky, an exchange of business cards and the promise of a follow-up which may or may not come. And then it's back to the outer orbits, to spend the rest of the morning talking to other entrepreneurs and trying to pretend you're far more successful than they are.

And so it was that, despite not being by nature a morning person, I stumbled, bleary-eyed into a Starbucks somewhere near Oxford Street. I'd dragged Savannah along with me too on the basis that a) she was much better at mornings than I was so she'd ensure I got there on time, b) she's much prettier than me, so increased our chances of getting attention from the assembled male investors by about a million per cent, and c) if we couldn't find anyone to talk to, we could always talk to each other.

After ordering a couple of tall, wet, skinny lattes, or something equally preposterous, we began to 'work' the room, which was already ridiculously crowded. In a far corner, I spotted Saul who was talking to another extremely important person, Danny Rimer.

'Don't look, but the dream team is standing over there,' I whispered to Savannah.

'Where?' she shouted back, over the deafening networking gaggle.

'In that corner. Those two.' I nodded with my head. 'Don't look!'

'The geeks?' Savannah shouted, louder this time. To Savannah, anyone involved in the web industry was a geek. This, despite the fact that, of course, she herself was now involved in the web industry.

'Shhhhhh. They're not geeks – that's Saul Klein and the guy he's talking to is Danny Rimer. Danny works for Index Ventures and invested in – well – everybody. Skype, Joost, MySp ... Jesus, he was like thirty-fifth in *Forbes*' list of the most powerful people in technology deal-making.* He is a Fucking Big Deal.'

'Well, he looks like a geek.'

'He does look a bit like a geek,' I conceded.

'I probably shouldn't mention that to him?' she asked.

'Probably not, no.'

But, frankly, at this stage the chances of getting near enough to either of them to say anything were looking extraordinarily slim. Between us were about a hundred hungry entrepreneurs. We needed some kind of secret weapon. And fortunately, at that moment, one walked up behind me.

'Paul!' I felt a huge hand on my shoulder. It could only be one person. Robert Loch.

'Robert!' I shrieked with a mixture of surprise and relief. Robert –

---

* He was actually thirty-fourth in *Forbes*' list, I found out later.

more about him later – had mentioned a few weeks earlier that he knew Danny and had offered to arrange an introduction should I ever need one. Boy, did I need one.

'No problem . . .' he said, and off we marched through the crowd, scattering entrepreneurs left and right as we went. Robert is well over six foot, which is an incredible advantage if you want to get from one side of a crowded room to the other.

'Saul, I want you to meet Paul and Savannah,' he said, not even waiting for the two men to finish their conversation. 'They're looking for funding for their new company, Fridaycities. They're a really good team, and their business is very interesting. But all you really need to know is that – like all the best teams – Paul is the funny one and Savannah is the pretty one.'

Yeah, thanks, Rob – exactly the right level of professionalism. We had been aiming for platonic power couple, but we'd suddenly become one of those hot wife/funny husband couples you get in American sitcoms. Still, it was an in and we managed to blurt out a few sentences explaining Fridaycities and why it was going to change the world. Rimer, to his credit, pretended to give a fuck – even going so far as to suggest that we should hook up a meeting when we had a proper presentation to show him. We had our business card swap and we were away. Not a total disaster, but hardly a resounding success. But, then again, I'm not a morning person.

6.3

After my lukewarm success at Open Coffee, I'd decided to redirect my networking efforts to the evening events and parties: not only am I very much a night person but evening events also had the twin benefits of informality and alcohol, which is always a good thing to have around when you're trying to win new friends and influence people.

Saul Klein very rarely attended late-night events – and rumour had it that he didn't approve of the organisers of these often hedonistic parties, believing that they fuelled media clichés of young, drunk entrepreneurs partying their way into a second bubble. The party organisers, for their part, believed exactly the opposite – that a critical element of any industry, particularly a media-related one, was its social scene. In all other areas of the media, much of the real business was done on the party circuit, with people making new hires based on people they'd met socially, not during a sober early morning introduction at Starbucks.

The truth was probably somewhere between the two – yes, the evening parties were often attended by journalists, who liked to go back and report that the Internet sector was 'partying like it's 1999' (natch) but there was also no denying that late-night events tended to attract a far higher calibre of attendee – successful entrepreneurs and investors who weren't there to network, but just to have a good time. It was when they were off duty that they were at their most approachable.

And so when, a couple of weeks later, Robert Loch called me with his news, his timing couldn't have been better.

6.4

'Mate, guess where I am.'

When Robert phones you asking that question, it's generally unwise to try to guess. Imagine Prince Philip calling you up and asking 'guess who I've just offended'. Life's too short to list all the various possibilities.

'I have no idea. It's not even noon, so presumably you're in bed.'

'No ... Guess again ...'

I first met Robert when he was co-founder and 'product architect' at a business networking website called Soflow. Imagine a kind of Facebook for business people, but with significantly fewer users, and you've basically got Soflow. The company's main investor was Martin Clifford, an entrepreneur who sold his first business – a dating site called uDate – for $150 million in 2003. While most dot com entrepreneurs preferred to base their operations in Silicon Valley, or San Francisco, or London, Clifford opted to run Soflow from his villa in Barbados. In what was certainly the sweetest corporate retreat of all time, Robert and the rest of the Soflow team spent their time shuttling back and forth to the Caribbean for strategy meetings held in Clifford's outdoor swimming pool. Despite the site's relatively small user base and heavy competition from rival services like LinkedIn.com, Soflow was determined to use its diminutive size to its advantage – focusing on entrepreneurs rather than trying to reach all business people. On the Internet, niche sites work.

Unless they don't.

Soflow didn't, despite raising $5 million in funding.

Robert left the company in 2006 and Soflow.com limped on for a few more months before being rebranded and relaunched as Wis.dm (yuck), a site that allowed users to answer simple yes and no questions such as 'Do you wonder why men would be attracted to mermaids when it would be impossible to have sex with them?'* and 'Have you ever taken a folding chair on to an elevator?'* Of course, with its new highbrow focus and audience of brain surgeons and rocket scientists, Wis.dm took off like a rocket.

Meanwhile, realising that there's more fun to be had helping other people raise money than doing it yourself, Robert set up a new company – 'Internet People' – that would bring together entrepreneurs and investors through 'informal networking events'. And by 'informal networking events' what I mean is that Robert very quickly got a reputation for organising the best parties in the dot com world.

Let me be clear here: we're talking *killer* parties – both in the sense that a lot of entrepreneurs would kill to be there, and also because there's always a slight risk that someone would end up dead before the end. Robert's were parties that you'd fly in *from* Barbados to attend.

The formula for Internet People was simple: find a killer venue, fill it with top people in the industry, choose an interesting theme and then mix in some young, female models to taste. No sausage fests, these events. Robert had befriended a group of South American models who, in exchange for some drinks, would happily dress up in tiny outfits and mingle with his party goers.

....

* These are actual examples, taken at random from the site's front page.

So, when it comes to knowing how to throw a good party, Robert is no slouch. But even by his standards, the news he was calling to give me that morning was unbelievable.

'Okay, I give up. Where are you?'

'I'm just on my way to pick up the keys to Mr Rong's.'

'That's great!' I replied. 'No. Wait. Hang on. Who is Mr Wrong? Do I want to know?'

'It's spelt R-o-n-g-s, without the W. It's our new club.'

'We have a new club?'

'Yes, it's in Soho, near Chinatown. So we're calling it Mr Rong's.'

'Hang on. *We?*'

'Yeah. You're one of the founding members. It's going to be a club for Internet people to hang out in. Network. Get drunk. That kind of thing. Like Adam Street, but it's ours. It's me, you ...' he rattled off a list of perhaps a dozen more entrepreneurs, 'and of course the Brazilian girls and their friends have been given free membership.'

My alarm clock went off. Noon. I sat up in bed.

'Er, Rob. Couple of things ... when did you decide to buy a club? And how the fuck are you going to afford it? No – more to the point, how the fuck am *I* going to afford to join? Oh, and ... did you say it's in Chinatown?'

'Yep.'

'Okay, well, ignore all my other questions – you do realise you're going to be cut into tiny pieces by triads? You don't just open a drinking den in the middle of Chinatown.'

'We'll it's not exactly Chinatown, it's Soho; the Chinatown end of Soho. And it's not a drinking den. It's a networking venue. With drinking. And don't worry about the cost; I've got it covered. You just have to bring booze when there's an event on. It's got three floors, with a dance floor and a bar. Oh, and two hot tubs.'

Much as I was trying to be the voice of reason, this was fucking amazing news. Robert and I had first talked about the idea of a members' club for entrepreneurs – and other social outcasts – the previous Halloween. We were pretty drunk and, if I remember correctly, at least one of us was dressed as a zombie and drinking a very strong White Russian. Or possibly the other way around.

The plan would be to rent a huge loft space somewhere in the centre of town and split the rent between a dozen of us. Technically it would be a residential flat – to avoid tricky licensing issues – but it would host Internet People events and would also be available to 'borrow' for other events, for a fee. In our fantasy world there would also be bedrooms to avoid having to get the last tube home – and (we joked) a hot tub, creating a much more honest environment for the real purpose of these kinds of events: making the organisers rich or getting them laid. Preferably both. We were going to call it 'The End Game', at my suggestion, because of our theory that money, drinking and sex were, basically, the end game for the entrepreneur.

Of course, to the rest of us The End Game was just a drunken joke. A projection of our Playboy delusions of combining business with decadent pleasure. But one of the great things about Robert, like so many Internet people, is that he refuses to accept that there's any kind of gap between reality and fantasy. Not even a sliver. And so, in the intervening months, a mystery benefactor (an entrepreneur who had made enough money to be able to afford such things) had been found to help share the not inconsiderable costs of renting the 'club'. And now Rob was on his way to the estate agent's to pick up the keys to the flat, situated next to a Chinese restaurant and now apparently tiptoeing the line between comedy and racism with its new name 'Mr Rong's'.

Finally, London had a permanent venue for Internet entrepreneurs, and I had access to a hot tub and all the rum I could drink. How could that not improve my productivity? I reasoned. After all, it was a damn sight cheaper than Adam Street – and I'd be going there for Work.

Yeah, right.

No good could come of this.

Absolutely none whatsoever.

6.5

The first big event to be held at Mr Rong's was a networking event organised by Robert, entrepreneur Oli Barrett and Michael Smith, who had got himself into the event organisation game with a regular Schmooze-fest called 'Second Chance Tuesday'. The name was a backhanded tribute to 'First Tuesday', a successful networking event held during the first dot com boom, which eventually became a poster child for everything that was ridiculous about the investment bubble. First Tuesday was also the event where Michael Smith and Tom Boardman raised the money for Firebox, so when Michael and his friend Judith Clegg, a successful business consultant, decided to start a similar event for the second dot com boom, Second Chance Tuesday was the perfect name.

Being the first 'Rong's' event, the party promised to be a hell of a night. The sort of night that, had Caligula been hosting a networking event downstairs, he'd have probably come up to ask us to keep it down a bit because we were frightening the horses.

Needless to say, I was looking forward to it immensely. And, needless to say, I planned to do very little actual networking there. That could wait. I 'accidentally' forgot to tell Savannah that I was going – she might now be my business partner, but she was also an ex-girlfriend and nothing was going to cramp my style that night.

The best thing about Rong's – especially given the risk of triads – is how invisible it is from the street, situated at the very top of a nondescript block, between a Chinese restaurant and a nondescript pub on a nondescript street in a nondescript part of Soho. Arriving outside, the only clue that I was at the right place was the dim, persistent thump of bass from a distant stereo and the strange red glow coming from the upstairs windows. To anyone walking past and looking up, it looked a bit like the scene in a horror film when the evil scientist plugs his monster into the lightning conductor machine for the first time.

It's aliiiiivvve.

Confirmation that I'd got the right place came as I rang the doorbell and a champagne flute whistled past my ear, shattering into a thousand pieces next to my feet. 'Sorry,' came a voice from somewhere very high up.

Yep, this must be the place.

A terrifying lift ride to the top of the building – the car had barely enough room for a single person and rattled alarmingly – and with the dull thumping getting louder with each floor, I was in.

The first thing that struck me about Mr Rong's was how bright everything was – bright yellow walls, neon tubes everywhere, spelling out various feel-good slogans like 'You have nothing to fear but fear itself' – and also how vast the place was. Split on to three levels, the main downstairs space comprised a dance floor with an enormous wall-sized cinema screen. Then there was the bar, with its giant illuminated lettering spelling out the word 'Now', for reasons that were not entirely clear. And in the corner, next to the bathroom, was the first hot tub. But tonight, while still undoubtedly a tub, it wasn't at all hot. Because it was filled to the brim with ice and magnums of champagne.

I wandered over to the table on the far wall, where rows of name badges sat waiting to be claimed. Looking through the names, one thing was clear: all the big names on the London dot com scene were going to be in attendance, including – and here was the best bit for me – several of the A-list of venture capital investors. Getting to them over coffee was hard, but now they were in my domain; surely if there was any environment in which they'd have their guard down and agree to have a meeting with us about Fridaycities, it would be in Mr Rong's after drinking a bathful of champagne.

Unfortunately, any hope I had of schmoozing a venture capitalist was dashed the moment I climbed the stairs to the second level – the outdoor deck where the main party was going on. I swear to God, you have never, ever, seen a space so crowded in your life. We're talking Black-Hole-of-Calcutta-with-Added-Neon crowded. If anyone had so much as coughed too fiercely someone could easily have fallen to their death. That explained the champagne flute. Word had clearly got round; possibly about the networking opportunities, probably about the champagne, certainly about the hot tub.

As if to cement the club's status as the Mecca for the reborn London dot com scene, Channel 4 had sent along a film crew to cover the event and there were reporters from *Business Week* and the *FT* in attendance, too. The *FT* journalist would later rave about the party, describing Robert as 'the Hugh Hefner of London'.

Skulking back downstairs I spotted Michael, who for some reason looked a lot like a Roman emperor, perched as he was on a big plastic throne-like chair surrounded by unfeasibly attractive women hanging on his every word. 'Michael!' I shouted, to no response.

'Michael!'

Nothing. I was just about to throw something at him when I noticed he was posing for a photographer. 'What's the photo for?' I asked someone standing in the background.

'It's for *Business Week* magazine – they're doing a feature on the "swinging" London business scene and they've decided that that guy is going to be the focus.'

Michael, the jammy bastard, had been instructed by the photographer to pose with a gaggle of incredibly hot women, to demonstrate ... actually, who cares what? Jammy bastard. Suddenly one of the hot women turned around: 'Paul!'

Fucking hell. It was my Maggie, my ex-girlfriend. And there she was, a fawning extra in Michael's photo shoot. Was there nothing the man wouldn't steal from me?

I decided to try to track down the *Channel 4 News* reporter who was apparently interviewing people on one of the other floors. Anything Michael could do, I could do better. If he was going to be in *Business Week*, I was going to get myself on to *Channel 4 News*.

Grabbing a glass of champagne, I headed for the bright spot-lit corner and the gaggle of entrepreneurs all hoping for their moment on camera. Barging past Simon Woodroffe, Yo! Sushi founder-turned-*Dragons' Den*-star-turned-hotel entrepreneur, I forced my way towards the front of the crowd.

And that's when I saw him. The brand new technology correspondent of *Channel 4 News*. The king of the made-up valuation. The former porn entrepreneur.

Benjamin

bloody

Cohen.

Somewhere in the background, over the cacophony of party noise, I swear I could hear Michael and my ex-girlfriend sharing a joke.

6.6

The party was still in full swing, and the hot tub on the top floor was just starting to heat up, but being surrounded by quite so much success in one room was making me giddy. I felt like a total fraud; wasn't I still just a publisher posing as a dot com entrepreneur? With only my parents' money in the bank and my friends as my only partners? How could I even show my face at these networking events when I still had so much work to do?

I headed back to the lift and descended into the streets of Soho. As I took the night bus back to my flat I knew it was time for me to up my game in a big way.

What I needed was a proper way in; someone on the inside of the industry who believed in Fridaycities and who would add an air of legitimacy to our whole operation. Someone – not just a blood relative or a friend I'd known for years – who would put his or her money where my mouth was, proving to the world that this was for real. Otherwise wasn't I just a latter-day Benjamin Cohen – five years after the event – someone whose only success came from telling people he was successful?

I needed an angel.

7.0

'There must be an angel ...'

Begin talking about your business to any fellow entrepreneur and he is guaranteed to ask you one of the following questions:

'How are you guys funded?' or

'How much money did you raise?' or

'Are you still looking for funding?'

These are our obsessions, like men comparing cars or penis size. And, just like with cars and cocks, there are two options when faced with one of these questions – either tell the truth or lie through your teeth.

Raising money is the thing that keeps dot com entrepreneurs awake at night. In an industry where it's possible to sell your company for hundreds of millions of pounds despite not having ever made a penny of revenue, it's critical to have a decent pot of money to spend while your business gets established sufficiently to secure proper venture capital funding. How you answer the funding question will absolutely shape how other entrepreneurs see you and your business – and can also be the kiss of death when speaking to potential investors. In a perverse catch-22, no investor wants to be the first, or only, person to invest in a company that hasn't got any money.

After all, if your company is so hot, why on earth has no one else realised yet?*

The very first task for any new media mogul, then, is to raise some initial start-up money, either by raiding their savings or tapping up

---

* The only possible exception to this rule is if you're running a site that has been raking in profits from day one, despite having absolutely no external investment. Something like The Million Dollar Homepage. It's a piece of cake to raise money if you don't need, or want, it. The parallels between casual sex and money could fill a book.

friends and family. This process is known – creatively enough – as a friends and family round, and tends only to work if you need a small amount of money – £50k, say – to buy computers and rent an office. In the case of Fridaycities, I'd spoken to my parents and my uncle and begged them for money. When they agreed, we had completed our friends and family round.

That was stage one. The easy part.

After the friends and family round comes your 'angel' round, which is where the fun really starts. An angel round is just like a friends and family round, but where your uncle or your parents are replaced by a private investor (often a successful entrepreneur with money burning a hole in their pocket) who gives you a wodge of cash (maybe a couple of hundred grand, rarely more) in return for shares in your company. As one of the earliest investors, they tend to take quite a large stake – sometimes as much as 25 per cent – for their money. If you've ever watched *Dragons' Den*, you've seen an angel round.

Quite why these early investors feel the need to call themselves 'angels' is not entirely clear, but, frankly, if someone is giving you a couple of hundred grand, you'll call them whatever they want you to. 'Who's your angel?' 'You are, you big, generous hunk of money, you.'

The major benefit of the angel round, apart from bringing in much-needed cash for luxuries like salaries and printer paper, is that it makes your company legitimate.

Now when a fellow entrepreneur or, more importantly, a venture capitalist, asks you the big funding question, you can answer honestly: we've secured angel funding from ——— ———. If your Mr X happens to be a name they recognise – or, better yet, a drinking buddy of theirs – you've got instant credibility. It's a pack game, and the theory goes that if you've managed to convince someone of the worth of your idea, then you must be on to something. Unless you're talking to a potential investor – who will check your story before he commits to putting in any of his own money – you can lie about the amount. No one will believe you anyway. The point is that you've shown that *someone* believes in you.

Suddenly, with an angel investor or two in the bag and enough money to get your business launched, doors start to creak open. Doors that lead to the third stage – the Holy Grail of funding – the venture capital round. Venture capitalists – the Saul Kleins and the Danny Rimers – are the big men of investment. They represent funds of many millions of pounds, and they're the people you go to when you want to raise two million pounds in exchange for giving away a huge chunk of your company.

Unlike angels, they don't just offer the benefit of their experience; they insist on giving it. When you have venture capital money, you are – and don't you ever forget this – no longer your own boss. Oh, sure, they'll let you keep your job title – CEO, founder, whatever – but they'll take a seat (maybe two) on your board, and when the company 'exits' (that is, gets bought by Google, or floated on the stock exchange), they get their money back first. Any questions?

No?

There's a good entrepreneur.

But I'm getting ahead of myself.

I still needed to find an angel.

7.1

Following my encounter with Angus Bankes at Adam Street a few months earlier, he and I had become good friends. Part of the reason he liked me, I suspected, was that he saw me as a curiosity: a journalist who drank, partied and managed to upset people, just like his former business partner, Nick Denton. In fact, several times he'd jokingly referred to me as 'the British Nick Denton' (Denton is British, but he now lives the life of a media mogul in New York). When I first told Angus about Fridaycities, he offered to try to hook me up a meeting with Denton in New York, in the vague hope that he might be of some commercial use, perhaps even as an investor. 'I'm sure Nick will see you,' he said, confidently.

Unfortunately, Nick had other ideas. Having now established himself as a permanent fixture on the New York media scene (he's rumoured to count Michael Stipe among his personal friends, and Fred Durst of Limp Bizkit once sent him flowers), frankly he doesn't need to waste time schmucking about with the likes of me. After a number of emails from me suggesting a meeting, he eventually palmed me off with a meeting with his business development manager. A clearer fuck off you will never get. But bless Angus for trying.

As I sat in our new office, stirring my coffee with a biro and drawing up my list of possible angel investors, one name kept coming back. If Angus was happy to introduce me to friends of his, people he trusted, surely that must mean he liked the idea. Why else would he risk the embarrassment?

It was worth a shot.

I picked up the phone. Angus was the first name in my phonebook. A good sign, I thought.

'Angus, it's Paul Carr.'

'Oh, hello. Funny you should ring – I was just talking to someone in the office about Fridaycities.'

Another good sign.

'Brilliant! All good, I hope. Actually, it was Fridaycities I wanted to talk to you about. Things are really starting to move here – we've got our new office in Battersea.'

'Isn't that where Michael Smith is?'

'Yeah. He's across the hall. I can smell his success from here.'

'Ha! How's the fundraising going?'

'Good. Good. We've just closed our friends and family round. Actually, that's why I was calling. I was wondering whether you might be interested in being – and this is just a thought – but whether you might be interested in coming on as our non-executive chairman?'

Coming straight out and asking Angus for investment would be madness, not to mention rude. And, also, that wasn't what we wanted from him. Not when he could offer so much more as a non-executive director.

Ah yes, the non-executive director. A quick explanation of what I mean by that ...

At the head of any limited (or public) company is the board of directors, responsible for driving the direction of the company. In a small business the board might consist of just the founder (usually called the managing director in the UK, or chief executive officer (CEO) in the US) and the company secretary, who is in charge of all the financial and legal crap. In a large business the board is often the size of a small army – bursting with people in expensive suits boasting job titles like Vice President of Corporate Responsibility and Senior Director of Job Title Invention. They are the people who represent the shareholders, and are responsible for the smooth running of the company. The bucks stop with them.

To make matters more confusing, board members can be either executive or non-executive. The former are usually actual employees of the business – they have a day-to-day job, actually running things. The latter are more akin to advisers. They come to the board meetings, sure, and they give input to the running of the show, but they probably don't actually do anything for the company on a nine to five basis.

And yet, despite not being actual company employees, non-executive directors can be very useful indeed. Imagine you're the owner of a company that makes frozen meals. You want to establish yourself as a class act, both to customers and to the business world. So you phone up your favourite celebrity chef. 'Jamie,' you say (Gordon ... Gary ...), 'how do you fancy joining our board as a non-executive director?'

'What do I have to do?' asks Jamie.

'Nothing,' say you. 'Just come to the board meeting every month and tell us what you think. Oh, and maybe let us use your name in our annual report. And possibly think about endorsing what we make. We'll pay you ten grand a month, and you can have five per cent of the company.'

'Once a month?'

'Yep.'

'Pukka.'

Everyone's a winner.

So, back to the phone call ...

I reckoned Angus would make the perfect non-executive director for us. He had already made an effort – by contacting Nick Denton – to help us raise money, and having shares would only encourage him to do even more. God knows, he might even invest himself.

But the biggest plus was his experience in raising money for Internet businesses that went on to sell for – say – $30 million. He'd been around long enough to know almost everyone in the Internet investment community, and for everyone to know him. With him at the table, we'd have instant credibility. And if I could convince him to go one step further – to become non-executive chairman (effectively, the head of the board) – then the business would look even better. In fact, it would be a Big Fucking Deal along the same lines as hiring Scott at The Friday Project. Most start-ups would kill to have Angus on their board, so I was under no illusions as to how tough a job I was going to have to convince him.

'Well, I'm flattered.'

'Sorry?'

'I really like the business. Send me the business plan and an email with what you're offering. But, yes, I'm definitely interested.'

And that was that. An email, a lunch and a couple of weeks later we had a non-executive chairman.

'And I suppose I should start thinking if I know anyone who might put some money in.'

And with that, we had the beginnings of an angel round. Fridaycities was real. There was no turning back now.

Holy shit.

7.2

With Angus on board, and our legitimacy established (for a few weeks at least), it was time to get on with the serious business of raising cash.

The first weird thing about raising money for a start-up company is that it feels like you're actually running two companies: the one that you're raising money for, and a totally separate one that exists purely to raise money for the first. And, as a founder, it's the second one that's most important, the one that takes up most of your time. Because without that one, the other one has no money and no future.

In terms of the actual Fridaycities site, my role at first would be closer to that of architect than actual builder. Having had the big idea (a site that allows city dwellers to share information), mapped out how we'd achieve it (a monster of a Microsoft Word document, written over about three weeks that explained everything I thought the site should do) and, finally, found someone to build it (a particularly talented freelance programmer called Dan Webb), my main job was to manage the fundraising and to build partnerships with other companies that might be useful to us. The actual day-to-day running of the site was down to Savannah and Karl – Savannah managing the users, deciding what questions appeared on the site and deleting those she thought were just slightly too obscene, and Karl writing a daily editorial to encourage users to keep coming back to the site, day after day.

The second strange truth about raising money for a start-up new media company is how much of it is dependent on personal contacts. If you want to get a bank loan to start a fruit shop, there isn't a bank in the world that will refuse to see you. You phone up your local branch, you tell them you want to start a business and need a loan, you draw up a business plan, you put on a suit and tie and you make an appointment. Possibly not in that order. The hard part comes after you get through the door and have to convince the twenty-five-year-old 'small business manager' to agree to lend you five times his salary.

By contrast, in the world of angels and venture capitalists, the hard part is finding the door in the first place and getting through it. And that's where our non-executive chairman would come in. Angus had agreed to make introductions to some investors he knew, including both potential angels and also some venture capitalists who specialised in early stage investment. But first he wanted to see our presentation: the PowerPoint slideshow I'd prepared, explaining the company to potential investors.

In the unlikely event that you're unfamiliar with PowerPoint, it is basically Satan's own office tool. For a former writer, there is almost nothing more horrific than having to boil down everything you want to say into a ten-page PowerPoint presentation. The way it sucks everything down to bullet points. The supremacy of style over substance. The fact that PowerPoint presentations All Look The Fucking Same. It's utterly, utterly vile. But, as I discovered, it's also absolutely essential. If you want to raise money, you are going to have to pretend to love PowerPoint. Investors expect, nay, demand, it.

Which is why it made perfect sense for Angus to want to see our presentation before he lined us up any meetings with possible investors.

There was just one slight problem.

We didn't have a presentation.

I didn't even know where to start. What even goes in these things?

There was only one thing for it. I called Sam.

Twenty-four hours later, we were back in the Chandos and I was about to pick Sam's brains again. I returned from the bar with two pints of Pure Brew, the pub's premium house beer. It was the least I could do for the man who was, over the next hour or so, going to teach me everything I ever wanted to know about PowerPoint presentations. What Sam didn't know about PowerPoint you could fit on to, well, a PowerPoint slide.

'Okay,' I said, flipping open the brand new Moleskine notebook I'd bought specially for the occasion, 'tell me everything.'

'First up, the secret of a good PowerPoint is K-I-S-S. Keep it simple, stupid. These people see dozens of these fucking things a week. The last thing they want to see is another one. So don't just write down everything you want to say on the slides and then read them out. That's the mark of an amateur.'

I was scribbling wildly, trying to write down everything he was saying. Sam grabbed the pen out of my hand.

'Jesus. Look . . .' He wrote right across two pages of the notepad . . .

'Keep. It. Simple. Stupid.'

Touché.

'Okay, do you have any good press quotes about Fridaycities you can use? They're always handy.'

'Um . . . yes, sort of,' I replied. 'We had a nice piece in the *Guardian* the other week. Just saying that the site was launching and that it looked interesting.'

'Perfect. Did they say anything you can quote?'

'They described us as "MySpace for adults".'

Actually, what the *Guardian* had really said was that we were *claiming* to be 'MySpace for adults'. The quote had come straight from our press release.

'Perfect!' said Sam. 'Quote laundering is your friend! Stick that quote on your first slide. Nice and big.'

The lesson continued ...

'Your second slide needs to be an introduction of who you are and what you've done before.'

This was going to be a bit trickier as I was the only one of the three of us (it was too early to include Angus) who had ever run an Internet business before. Sure, Savannah had a law degree and had managed and edited a small alternative newspaper, and Karl was a great writer with lots of experience, but in terms of things that a VC would care about, we had a problem. Hell, even I was struggling with just The Friday Project under my belt. But on the other hand, we were writers, so we could quite easily tart ourselves up a bit.

Instead of the plain old Friday Project, I could use the company's proper corporate title, Friday Project Media Plc. That always sounds more impressive. Like in that old British Telecom ad, where Maureen Lipman plays the proud grandmother who decides that, even though her grandson failed everything except sociology, he was still a success. 'You have an ology? You're a scientist!' I had a similar theory: you ran a PLC? You're a fat cat!

Karl, meanwhile, thanks to a splash of artistic licence, became a critically acclaimed writer, courtesy of the four books he'd written (two that I'd commissioned him to write while at The Friday Project, one about the Internet that we'd co-written together, and a last one – *Birth Marks and Love Bites*, that, while strictly speaking a novel, hadn't actually been published. But we could take a punt and say on the slide that 'His novel, *Birth Marks and Love Bites*, will be published in 2008'. That seemed like a good enough bet. Who can say what will happen in 2008?

Savannah was the easiest polish of all – drag out the *Penny* newspaper stuff (Savannah was also editor of *The Penny*'s spin-off website, Pennylondon.co.uk), big up the law degree and post-graduate degree and she was golden. Before we knew it, and thanks to the brevity of PowerPoints, we would all have ologies.

Sam was impressed. 'Perfect . . . you're getting the hang of this.'

The next stage of the presentation, Sam explained, would be to outline what the site was and who was going use it.

'How do I know who will use it? It's for everyone,' I said, like an idiot.

Sam was exasperated: 'Jesus, you really are an idiot, aren't you? The answer to that question is *always* twenty to thirty-five-year-old young professionals. It doesn't matter whether your site sells incontinence pads by post, or offers downloadable colouring books. The audience – sear this into your brain – is twenty to thirty-five-year-old young professionals. In marketing speak these are members of the "ABC1" socio-economic group. Your investors are going to be ABC1s. You are all ABC1s. Advertisers fucking love ABC1s.'

In fact, even advertisers who hate ABC1s and actually want to reach, say, DEFs (the old, the students, the unemployed and the dead) will still pack their adverts with ABC1s. Don't believe me? Look at the adverts for those 'all-purpose loans' that bail out chavs who have spent their benefits on one too many PlayStation 3s. The ads that sit between *Diagnosis Murder* and *The Jeremy Kyle Show* in the schedules. Ever wondered why, instead of being skint peasants, the people in the adverts always seem to be middle class with nice houses and lovely soft furnishings? In other words, people who don't actually need a fucking loan?

'ABC1s?'

'ABC fucking 1s. Everyone either is one, or aspires to be one, even if it means borrowing money they can't afford to repay.'

Across the two notebook pages I wrote 'ABC1s' in huge letters.

'Are you taking the piss?'

'A little bit. Sorry.'

'Right – the last things to think about are your revenue and investment requirements. This is where any last pretence of accuracy or honesty should be abandoned. The company doesn't exist yet, it has no users, customers, readers, whatever – it is a totally imaginary beast. You might as well try to guess the height of your pet unicorn. In short, you can say what the hell you like about how much the company will make, and how much you will spend making it. As long as you can justify it through maths. And as long as you – and I can't emphasise this enough – as long as you believe it. What's your business model?'

I explained that Fridaycities aimed to make its money through what we called 'premium services'. The vast majority of users could access and use the site for free – they could sign up, ask their question and get answers – all without spending a dime. But if they happened to find someone else on the site who they wanted to contact privately, then they had to get out their credit card. In the presentation, I was planning to show a hypothetical example of someone who was starting a book group in London who wanted to use private messages to invite other users to join. That person would surely be prepared to pay £12 ($25) a year for the ability to send private messages to other book lovers on the site.

'Bollocks,' said Sam. 'Book groups? You know what anyone listening to you talk about private messages will actually hear?'

'No ... ?'

'Sex, sex, sex, sex, sex.'

Sam was right. It's a sad fact in the new media world that most people will only pay for two types of content ... sex and gambling. That's it.

Think about it ...

Millions of people pay for porn online – sex.

Millions of people pay for subscriptions to dating sites – sex.

Hundreds of thousands of people pay for subscriptions to financial information sites and share tips – gambling.

... but the rest is slightly more subtle ...

Tens of thousands of people paid to subscribe to Friends Reunited, the site dedicated to bringing together old school friends. Why? Because they wonder what their best pal is doing now? No. Because they want to see if the kid who stole their lunch money is in jail yet? Uh-uh. People subscribed to Friends Reunited for one reason and one reason only ... because they want to know if the pretty girl they kissed when they were twelve is now a pretty woman. And if she's single. And, if so, then they want to contact them. Why? Sex.

In fact, you could argue that even the gambling sites are really about sex. Why else does anyone want to get rich quick?

Bluntly, if you want to raise money for a site that relies on people paying for premium services, you better hope that when you go through your presentation, investors hear this when you talk about revenue in your presentation ...

'Sex, sex, sex, sex.'

By giving users the ability to contact people who live in their city and send them private messages, you'd better believe that's what they'd be hearing. And just in case that was too subtle, we had added an extra twist – one that I thought was maybe in the top three ideas I've ever come up with ... The Quick Tick.

The Quick Tick was as simple as it was utterly brilliant. When you visited another member's page on Fridaycities, you'd see a list of five tick boxes. Next to each one was a sentence ...

This person makes me laugh [   ]

This person scares me [   ]

I like the cut of this person's jib [   ]

I've met this person in real life [   ]

If you ticked one of those boxes on someone's profile, the recipient of your tick would get an email saying that someone had ticked them. We would then add up all the ticks and show a leader board of the funniest, scariest (etc etc) users on the site. It was a quick and simple way for users to give each other a nudge, without going to the effort of writing a whole message.

And if you're not hearing 'sex, sex, sex, sex' yet, it's because I haven't told you the final box.

I quite fancy this person [   ]

Boom. If you ticked that box on someone's profile they would immediately get an email saying that someone – could be anyone, it's anonymous – quite fancied them. But here's the kicker: if they became a premium member (just £12/$25 a year) they could find out *who* ticked them.

Imagine you were registered on the site and got that email. Someone had looked at your profile and they quite fancied you (we spent days trying to get the exact wording right, to encourage casual ticking). Tell me, honestly, you would be able to resist paying £12 to find out who?

'Sex, sex, sex, sex.'

147

Sam continued ...

'So, if you know where your money is coming from, we can start to make up some maths. Let's start with users. You're going to attract – let's say – eight hundred thousand users in the first eighteen months.

'Eight hundred thousand?' I asked. 'Isn't that quite ... a lot?'

'Nonsense. That's very achievable. MySpace has over a hundred million users – eight hundred thousand is chickenfeed. Now, of those eight hundred thousand how many will pay for premium membership?'

He ran through some possibilities as I sat, silently making notes, amazed by how utterly believable Sam sounded as he zipped through the numbers, having a conversation entirely with himself ...

Ten per cent? Too high.

Five per cent? Too round.

Four per cent? Perfect. Modest and scientific.

So, that's 32,000 users in eighteen months, paying £12 each.

That's £384,000.

Except – and here's the next rule – no one uses pounds. The web is international. And, despite the American economy's best efforts to become worthless, the dollar is still the global currency. On the day we did the maths, the dollar was basically worth two to the pound.

'$768,000 revenue. Pretty damn respectable.

Impressive even.

Scientific.

Total bullshit.

But scientific.

You getting all this?'

'Yep,' I said, my hand aching as I tried to keep up.

'Good. Right – last questions – how much money are you trying to raise?'

'Well, to cover our costs for the first year we need ...'

'Pfff ...' he cut me off with a wave of his hand. 'Another classic beginner's mistake. Don't even start to work out how much money you actually need. Not since the beginning of time has anyone ever been able to successfully predict how much money they will spend setting up a new media company. How much do you *want*?'

He had a point, again. Alex Tew set up The Million Dollar Home-page for, basically, nothing. Angus raised millions for Moreover and still, to this day, the company hasn't spent it all. It was nearly impossible to work out the actual amount of money you'd spend setting up your business.

'No, the only real question is how much can you get in return for the amount of the company you're prepared to give away to the investor. Your angel round is probably going to be the most expen-sive money you'll ever raise. You've got no business, no customers, no proof of anything and investors stand a damn good chance of losing their shirt. As a result they'll want a big stake in the company, for as little money as they can get away with putting in. But at the same time, they'll want to give you enough money to give you a fighting chance of success. So, the trick is to decide how much money you need to get you through to your next – bigger – round of funding.'

The mighty venture capitalist round.

We decided £300,000 was a good amount, based on how much I knew we were spending and the fact that we were confident of finding a larger investor within six to eight months. But, of course, we would put in the presentation that we needed £500k.

'Everyone negotiates,' explained Sam. 'The question is how much equity £300k will buy for your new – as yet entirely hypothetical – investor. And here's when the biggest piece of bullshit of all crashes through the door. The valuation.'

'How do you think we should value the company?' I asked.

'£1.2 million.'

'£1.2 million? Based on what?'

'Based on the fact that I've just said it. £1.2 million, post-money.'

There are two valuations, he explained, pre-money and post-money. In short, the pre-money valuation is the value of the company *before* an investor puts his money in. Our pre-money valuation would be £900,000. The post-money valuation is the value of the company, once the investor's money is in. So, if we were worth £900,000 pre-money then after the £300,000 was added to the pot, the post-money value of the company would be £1.2 million.

There was method in this plucking-a-number-out-of-the-air madness. Putting £300,000 into a company that was worth £900,000 to start with would give the investor a third of the company pre-money, or a quarter of it post-money. Both well below the 51 per cent level which would give the investor control of the company, but, importantly, also low enough to ensure that we could raise even more money at a later date, and a higher valuation, without giving too much away in total.

With six pages of notes, I had more than enough to get cracking on the presentation, but as it was already past ten and we'd had almost half a dozen pints each, it would have to wait until tomorrow.

'Come on, let's go to Adam Street,' suggested Sam. 'Apparently Daniel Bedingfield's going to be there for some party or other.'

'Daniel Bedingfield? God, I hate that prick.'

'Exactly, come on . . .'

7.3

Adam Street, 2.00 a.m. And while Bedingfield was a no-show, a couple of Sam's business partners had turned up and we'd managed to get over our disappointment by getting wasted on Mojitos.

'So,' I slurred to Sam, mixing together mint leaves and ice with my straw, 'I forgot to ask you earlier; how's the fundraising going for your new business?'

'Yeah – great,' he replied, even more drunk than me, thanks to the Pure Brews from earlier. 'Actually we've got a meeting tomorrow morning with ——— [one of the hottest players in the London VC world, and renowned for being very, very serious].'

'Tomorrow morning? You don't mean *this* morning?'

'Yeah, in about . . .' he checked his watch '. . . six hours.'

'Jesus, mate,' I said. 'You're still going to be pissed in six hours.'

'Yeah – and we haven't even finished our presentation yet. I've got to go home and do it. I think I'll probably just stay up all night and go straight to the meeting."

And this was the man I was relying on to make our presentation professional?

I drained the last of the rum from my Mojito and nodded at the waitress to bring me another.

7.4

The next afternoon, hung-over to crap, and hunched over my laptop trying to stop the room spinning long enough to make my Power-Point slides, I couldn't resist phoning Sam to see how his meeting had gone.

'Great! We got the investment. Ten million.'

'You are fucking kidding me!'

'Of course I'm fucking kidding you. P— [his technical adviser who had been out with us as well] was still drunk in the bloody meeting. We told him before we went in that he wasn't allowed to say anything, but he kept interrupting us even when I kicked him under the table. I nearly fell asleep and S— [their other partner] couldn't remember any of the presentation. It was a fucking train wreck.'

'Oh. I'm sorry, man.'

'Nah, doesn't matter. They were never going to invest. But by only arranging meetings with people who are never going to invest we can drink till four, do the presentation and not have to stress about whether we'll get the money or not. We know we won't anyway.'*

His logic was impeccable, in a way. And he'd made enough from his previous venture not to have to care. And at least he was keeping his hand in and giving the illusion of progress.

There was some kind of twisted psychology to it.

And a twisted psychology is still an ology.

....

* And, sure enough, as I write these words – months later – they still haven't got the money. But they're having a fucking amazing time not getting it.

8.0

'All the best meetings are taken'

The presentation finally finished, it was time to show it to Angus. Savannah, Karl and I had spent a whole day, and well into an evening, holed up in one of the Feng Shui-ed conference rooms that Peter had built in the office, going through the ten-page slideshow, each taking a different part and each rehearsing and re-rehearsing our parts including our 'tweaked' personal CVs.

Karl in particular was very uncomfortable with the idea of us having to pad out our achievements to make ourselves sound more successful. He had always hated the bullshit of business and was adamant that the best policy was to tell the unvarnished truth at all times. If investors weren't impressed by our CVs, then fuck 'em. He was particularly unhappy about having to pretend that his novel was due to be published.

'It's not true,' he pointed out, with some justification.

'But it might be. Who knows what will happen in 2008?'

'I know what won't happen. My novel won't be published. It's a lie.'

'It's a white lie.'

'What does the colour have to do with it? It's a lie.'

Eventually we came to an agreement that I could leave his soon-to-be-published novel in the PowerPoint, but he wouldn't mention it in the actual spoken presentation. And if anyone asked, he was going to tell them the truth. Karl was a writer – a teller of The Truth – and he was deeply against the weird hype games that being in business seemed to involve. Fortunately, I had no such qualms.

With everything prepared, we set off to the Holly Bush, a gastro pub in north London, a stone's throw from Angus's house, where we were about to give our first ever live presentation to our brand new non-executive chairman. If there was a better metaphor for where we were and where we wanted to be – that train and tube journey from our office in grotty old Battersea to the leafy suburbs of Angus's Hampstead – then I've yet to find it. That was an area where the For Sale signs outside the houses cost more than my entire new flat in East Dulwich.

After our nervous run-through, interrupted every couple of slides by bar staff collecting glasses and drunks asking to borrow spare stools, Angus seemed to think the presentation was pretty okay – good, even – and he agreed to start making some introductions to the great and the good of the angel world. But first, he suggested, we should have a trial run to an actual investor. A practice presentation but with someone who would give us a hard time; to allow us to harden and temper our presentation in a live furnace. To mix more than one metaphor.

And who better to start with than Nic Brisbourne?

8.1

In his mid-thirties and dressed in the new VC uniform of expensive blue shirt tucked into khaki trousers, Nic Brisbourne is young, smart and very, very important. He is a partner at Espirit, the venture capital firm responsible for investing in a host of Internet companies including Lovefilm.com – the online DVD rental site – and WAYN – a social site for young travellers (which is to say gap-year adventurers, not gypsies. Although that's not a bad idea.) Obviously we were at far too early a stage to get venture capital money from Espirit but the company also had a track record of making smaller investments in companies they thought might grow into bigger ones, and, more importantly, Nic would be able to tell us exactly where we were going right – and wrong – with our presentation.

This would be our first opportunity to present the company to a serious investor, and as we walked into his glass-walled meeting room I don't think any of us had been more nervous in our entire lives. If Nic liked the presentation, we could go on to see angel investors safe in the knowledge that the concept of Fridaycities was sound. If he hated it, it might be time to pack up and go home, before we'd even started.

As the closing slide popped into view – a second quote, this time from an obscure blogger who had reviewed Fridaycities, saying the site was more addictive than crack – we held our collective breath and waited for Nic's verdict. It's a horrible cliché but the silence seemed to last for half an hour.

Finally, he took a deep breath and leaned back in his chair.

'I like it.'

He wouldn't invest, of course – we were too 'early stage'. But he liked it. He had listened intently to the presentation – he had asked the right questions about the numbers, he had interrupted when clearly I was talking bollocks (he knew we were stabbing in the dark when it came to figures) and he had made notes; quite a lot of notes. And at the end of the meeting he even asked us to stay in touch after the site launched. Of course, everyone says that – 'stay in touch' is very often the polite man's 'fuck off and never, ever contact me again' – but Nic sounded like he really meant it, even going so far as to join the site the next day and ask a question of his own. Fittingly, instead of uploading a photograph as his profile picture, he chose a cartoon of a man carrying a giant dollar sign on his back.

Quite.

Getting this kind of feedback from a VC before you even begin an angel round is a win-win situation for everyone. The entrepreneur gets feedback for his idea from that harshest of critics, the person who has seen it all before, and the VC gets to see ideas while they're in their earliest stages, before any of their competitors get a look-in.

After Nic, Angus decided we were ready for our first pitch to someone who there was a slim possibility might actually give us some money.

'I'm going to try to get us a meeting with Ricky.'

8.2

Richard 'Ricky' Tahta had become something of a mini-celebrity in the dot com world since he featured as a white knight in the closing chapters of *Boo Hoo*, a book about the rise and enormous fall of online fashion store Boo.com.

If you're looking for a guide to how *not* to start and run an ecommerce business, *Boo Hoo* is the book to read. Written by one of the site's founders, Ernst Malmsten, the book tells how he and his business partner, Kajsa Leander, spent almost £80 million creating what they hoped would be the ultimate online fashion store. Despite being launched in 1998, a time when almost no one had broadband at home, the site utilised the latest web technologies to show off its wares. As a result, the front page of Boo.com took literally minutes to load for some users, assuming it managed to load at all. Meanwhile, behind the scenes, costs spiralled as the company opened dozens of offices around the world, and set up a horrendously over-complicated distribution network with a promise that unwanted goods could be returned free by customers. Their marketing, too, was absolutely mental, with a small fortunate being spent creating what can only be described as the worst cinema advert of all time – a bunch of geeks in sportswear playing basketball.* The effect-iveness of the campaign was further reduced by the fact that the site wasn't even ready when the ads started to appear in cinemas, leading bemused customers to a simple holding page promising that the site would be launching soon.

But the biggest fuck-up of all was staffing, with the book describ-ing in detail a company in which no one took any responsibility for how many people were hired, and what they actually did. Towards the end there's a lovely episode where a consultant was brought in to manage staff layoffs, only to be fired himself and escorted from the building when it turned out he'd faked his CV. Meanwhile, staff who couldn't take holiday days due to their crazy workload were offered free first-class flights and stays in five-star hotels as com-pensation. They weren't so much spending money as haem-orrhaging it.

As the business went from weakness to weakness, the founders started desperately to approach new investors to inject some much-needed cash. One of those they approached was Ricky Tahta, who

---

* Still, at least they were ABC1s.

is presented in the book as an arrogant white knight character, swanning into the Boo headquarters and immediately grilling staff and demanding to see accounts while Malmsten and Leander were away from the office. According to Malmsten, when he called the office to find out what was going on, Tahta swore at him and asked whether he wanted his company to be saved or not. It's a great story. Just a shame it doesn't ring in the slightest bit true.

You see, Ricky is actually one of the most polite and professional people you will ever meet – certainly not one given easily to swanning. And I should know, given how horrendously I'd managed to offend him a year or so before Angus suggested we should approach him for investment.

The incident occurred, like so many did, at Adam Street. I was talking to Angus at the bar about the founding of Moreover when he pointed out Ricky across the room, explaining that he had been one of the early investors in the company. A little later, Ricky came over to say hello. The conversation went a bit like this:

Me: (Drunk) 'So, apparently you're the person who made a ton of money out of Angus' company.'

Ricky: (Smiling politely and walking away) '...'

Of course, at the time I was a newspaper hack and I didn't give a damn. I could offend pretty much anyone I liked and still get paid at the end of the month. It wasn't like I needed anything from these fat cat investors who made their money off other people's success. Same again please, barman!

'I'm going to try to get us a meeting with Ricky.'

'Oh God, is that a good idea? I seem to remember offending him at Adam Street. He was very good about it, though.'

'Yeah. We're going to have to hope he's forgotten about that.'

When Angus called back a few days later to say that Ricky had agreed to meet us, at his office near Bond Street, my nerves got even worse. What if he did remember me? What if he had only agreed to the meeting so he could remind me – in front of everyone – how I'd drunkenly suggested that he had somehow made a wad of cash off the back of one of my friends – and yet here I was now coming cap in hand to him? Perhaps he wouldn't even turn up to the meeting. That'd learn me.

No, I was being ridiculous. It was a whole year ago. It was dark when we met. I'm sure he meets lots of people. There's no way he'll remember me.

But just to be on the safe side, I decided to look as different as I possibly could in the meeting. Out went my usual uniform of jeans and untucked shirt (entrepreneur-casual) and in came a smart suit, tie, combed (combed!) hair and a pair of thick rimmed glasses that I've had for years but normally only wear in the privacy of my own home to watch television. When I met Karl, Savannah and Angus outside Bond Street tube on the morning of the meeting, I noticed my reflection of a newsagent's window. I looked like Mr Magoo, the estate agent.

As we arrived at Ricky's extremely upscale office, I couldn't help but notice that someone had chained a knackered, gaudily painted bike to the railings outside, significantly lowering the tone.

'Nice bike,' I said, sarcastically.

'That's Ricky's bike,' explained Angus. 'If you look carefully at it – it's actually worth a fortune. But he's painted it like that so it won't get stolen.'

Brilliant. Ricky was definitely our kind of guy.

At that, as if by magic, there he was, walking out of the front door to meet us. I immediately stepped back, so that I was standing ever so slightly behind the other three. Perhaps he wouldn't even notice me.

'Hi, I'm Savannah,' said Savannah.

'Hi, I'm Karl,' said Karl.

'Hi . . . Paul.' I said.

Ricky stared at me.

'Yes . . . I know *you*,' he said, with what was either a knowing smirk or one that said 'nice try'. I looked across at Angus. There was no danger of misinterpreting his expression. God Help Us.

We'd come prepared with our presentation on my laptop and all of the various wires required to make it work on whatever big screen Ricky's high-tech office might have. But our host had other ideas. 'Shall we go to Starbucks round the corner?' he suggested.

Definitely our kind of guy.

After buying us all coffee, Ricky joined us at the corner table we'd chosen, as far away as possible from the early morning crowd. 'Okay,' he said, taking a sip of his latte, 'what have you got for me?'

There's something both relaxing and nerve-racking about pitching in a Starbucks. On the one hand, there's none of the formality of a conference room, making it less of a presentation and more of a chat around a PowerPoint. On the other hand, it's hard to be casual when queues of people in suits waiting to buy their morning coffee are eyeing you with a mixture of curiosity and suspicion. I felt like we were trying to organise a bank heist without drawing attention to ourselves.

Before going into the meeting, Angus had warned us that Ricky would almost certainly grasp the concept of the site very quickly and told us not to be fazed if he asked us to skip through some slides, or if he asked unexpected questions. And, sure enough, after the first 'what is Fridaycities?' slide he interrupted with a 'yep, yep, I get that', a clear cue to skip over the next couple of slides.

I was fazed. Surely he couldn't have got the idea of the site that quickly.

'Well, um ... what I was going to say ...' I continued.

'It's okay, I get it.'

And, the thing is, he *did* get it. He didn't need me to walk him through how a question and answer site works. The man wasn't an idiot. He interrupted again a few minutes later, taking us on a ten-minute departure from the script, as he quizzed Savannah on *The Penny* and its revenue and distribution models. It was like being in an exam, where the subject was 'everything that has any relation to anything' and the pass mark was 100 per cent. It was exhilarating and terrifying and great fun. Thank God we were all wired off our tits on our second Americano in half an hour.

After the presentation, Ricky didn't say anything but instead suggested we walk back with him to his office. It was the most nerve-racking walk of our young lives. Had he liked it? Had we fucked up completely? Was this the point where he'd remind me about the Adam Street incident and send me away with a clip round the ear? But, instead, as we reached the door and his chained-up, colourful bike, he started:

'I'll be honest with you ...'

Oh God. Please don't be honest. Anything but honesty.

'Honestly, I didn't think I'd like it. I thought you were going to show me just another social networking site and I didn't think it was going to be different enough ... but ...'

But ...?

'But I like it. I really do. I'm tied up with some other things at the moment, so I couldn't put in the whole amount and I couldn't do anything straight away. But I like it. Yeah ... I'm interested.'

He liked it. And he was interested. The man I'd been so disgracefully rude to a year earlier, who came into the meeting expecting not to like the site – despite those odds, we'd managed to persuade him.

We thanked him for his time, promised to keep in touch and walked away, very, very slowly.

None of us said a word. We just kept walking, the four of us – me, Savannah, Karl, Angus – across the road, round the corner and straight into the pub. Only after we'd ordered four pints of the strongest beer in the house – it was barely past 11.00 a.m. – and sat down, shell-shocked, did one of us finally break the silence. I'm pretty sure it was me, but the whole event is still a daze so it could have been any of us.

'Fucking hell. Did that really just happen?'

'I think it did,' said (probably) Savannah.

'He liked it. He wanted to hate it. But he liked it.'

'And he remembered *you*,' said Angus. 'When he said that I thought it was game over.'

'But it wasn't. He liked it. And he's interested.'

'Fuck.'

'Fuck.'

8.3

Buoyed by Ricky's interest, and using Angus's contacts, we arranged meeting after meeting over the next six weeks. There was Henry Fyson from Creative Capital Partners, a company part funded by the London Development Agency (an agency controlled by the Mayor of London, tasked with 'driving London's sustainable economic growth') which invested public money in London-based businesses. They liked Fridaycities, too, but the terms of their funding meant that they could only invest if another investor had agreed to put money in as well. So they'd have to wait. Also, they hadn't decided whether social networking-type sites were a fad or not.

Then there was the senior partner in the investment firm – he should probably remain nameless – who was utterly obsessed with mobile phones. To the point where, after sitting through our presentation, he announced that he liked the idea of Fridaycities but would only be interested if we got rid of all the silly web stuff and turned the whole thing into a service for mobiles. It felt just like we were in one of those cinema adverts for Orange where the studio executives tell the filmmakers that they love their movie about life in Vichy France . . . but is there any chance that text messaging could be included somehow? Fridaycities relied on people asking very specific questions and receiving very detailed, often quite wordy, answers. We wanted the questioners and the answerers to take time over their contributions and we were employing a team of editors who would further tidy up their spelling and grammar. A bigger gap between that and the short, snappy vowel-less bullshit that passes for mobile phone content there couldn't be – and who did this guy think he was, trying to get us to change our vision to fit his weird idea of what 'the platform of the future' would be?

'Yeah, we'd absolutely consider making it a mobile site,' I said without a moment's hesitation. 'That would be no problem at all.'

Karl sighed audibly. More business bullshit. Across the table Savannah's eyes burrowed into me. Was I a man or a mouse?

A mouse. Definitely a mouse. A greedy mouse who would say *anything* to get that cheese.

'I don't think we'd have a problem . . .'

A sharp heel pressed itself into my leg.

'. . . but having said that, our initial plan is definitely for a web service. I think a mobile site would definitely have to wait until phase two.'

'Definitely,' said Savannah, definitely.

'Okay, well, I think you should give it some serious thought. I think you'll find that web services are definitely going to be super-seded by mobile services very soon.'

And that was that. He was wrong, of course – dramatically so. And Savannah was right to jab in her heel. The fact is that almost everyone who has ever predicted that one media will take over from another – theatre will be destroyed by cinema will be destroyed by video/DVD will be destroyed by the Internet – has been proved spectacularly wrong. Mobile phones are great for accessing certain types of information – short, timely text content and audio, for example – but reading lots of text on a small screen – a screen of any sort – just isn't practical and won't be for a long time. But there's something hypnotic about someone suggesting they'll give you large amounts of money if only you'll surrender your vision and your principles. Something hypnotic and extraordinarily tempting.

Another irresistible draw, particularly for me, was celebrity. And so when one of Angus's contacts suggested that we try to get a meeting with Peter Gabriel – the Genesis front man-turned-humanitarian, now, apparently, turned-Internet company investor – it seemed like a great idea, despite the fact that our pitch had nothing to do with music or saving the earth. Gabriel, Angus's friend explained, had recently invested in a company called We7, which had perfected the technology to insert targeted adverts into audio files. If the technology caught on, it could well prove to be the Holy Grail that musicians and record companies were looking for to combat Internet piracy. Up until now, the record giants had focused on inventing newer and more elaborate ways to prevent music lovers from uploading songs to the Internet and swapping them with their friends. As a result, dozens of complicated 'digital rights management' (DRM) technologies had been created, and an equal number had been cracked by determined hackers.

We7 would turn the situation on its head. The service would work with record companies and musicians to make their music available to download – free and without any DRM restrictions – from the We7 website. The catch was that listeners would be pres-ented with a short advert, embedded at the very beginning of the song, a bit like a radio jingle. And, thanks to the We7 technology, the advert would change depending on who had downloaded the track – a student would hear an advert for a new brand of alcopop, an OAP would get an ad for hearing aids etc etc. The advertising would cover the cost of rewarding the record company and the artist, and the more people shared the tracks, the more advertisements could be 'served'. Suddenly piracy was a legitimate distribution model.

From our point of view, We7 would make the perfect partner for Fridaycities. Our site was city-based and invited users to give us detailed information about their likes and dislikes – exactly the information We7 needed to target its ads.

And then there was the fact that having a celebrity as one of our investors would guarantee us acres and acres of press coverage. So, yes, we would absolutely love to meet Peter Gabriel, although for Karl and me it would actually be the second time we'd met the singer of 'Solsbury Hill' . . .

9.0

'This could be heaven or this could be hell'

It all started with one of those emails that you assume must be the result of an administrative error.

Dear Paul,

I'm writing from Google Europe '06. We're hosting an event later this year called 'Zeitgeist', bringing together some of the top thinkers in the Internet industry to discuss trends . . .

. . . blah blah . . .

. . .Speakers include David Cameron, Peter Gabriel, Martin Sorrell . . . and Google CEO Eric Schmidt. . . .

. . . blah blah . . .

I wondered whether you might be interested in either speaking at the event or joining a panel . . .

. . . blah . . .

. . . hang on . . .

. . . what?

It *must* be a mistake. Why on earth would Google possibly invite me to contribute to an event like that? A former newspaper journalist whose only success to date was bringing together web and print. And they wanted to put me on the same bill as those guys? It just didn't make any sense.

But at the same time, it sort of did.

A few months earlier, Google had launched a bold initiative to scan the world's books and to make them searchable online, in the same way as they make websites searchable now. The plan had caused all kinds of outcry from traditional publishers who claimed that, by scanning books, the search engine giant was breaching their copyrights.

The publishers were right, of course; scanning books in their entirety and storing them on a giant database was a clear breach of the copyrights that publishers have in books, copyrights that only expire seventy years after the author dies. But they were also being short-sighted: when Google's book search returned results from a book, they also linked to various online booksellers where hard copies could be bought. Google's database had always contained a copy (called a 'cache') of the contents of all the websites they indexed, in order to make searching quicker and more efficient. No one ever complained about that. Why should books be different?

There was also the potential for everyone involved to make quite a lot of money out of the scheme, something I'd been trying to encourage publishers to consider – even hosting an online debate on the subject (backed by one of the few forward-thinking publishing CEOs, Richard Charkin from Macmillan, who has since moved to Bloomsbury).

Evidently my experience in the middle of this strange Internet and book publishing Venn diagram qualified me to be a speaker at this super-exclusive conference, hosted by the world's biggest search engine. They were offering to pay my transport costs and to put me up in the country house hotel that was hosting the two-day event. They would even give me a spare ticket for the second day of the event to allow me to bring along a friend. How could I resist?

Annoyingly, a couple of weeks before the event I got a second email. Due to scheduling issues, the email explained, there wasn't going to be any room on the schedule for me to speak after all. Clearly Google had either found someone who was actually qualified to address such an illustrious audience or they'd realised that they'd invited the wrong person in the first place. My money was on the latter, but – the email went on – to make up for it they'd still be delighted to have me as their guest for the event, and I could still stay in a nice hotel. Although, now that I wasn't a speaker, I would have to slum it in the hotel down the road with the other attendees – the CEOs of companies who advertised on Google and various other Internet bosses. That suited me just fine. Five-star or four, a free shower cap is a free shower cap.

The event was to be hosted at the Grove hotel and spa in Hertfordshire, a venue so exclusive that the hotel's website offers instructions for arriving by car, train, helicopter and boat ('by boat: allow eight hours from London's Regent's Park'). I opted for the train and then took a minicab from the station.

'I'll get as close as I can but it's a bloody circus up there,' said the cab driver when I told him where I was going, 'what with all the TV cameras camped out.'

'Really?' I asked. 'TV cameras?' God, this must be an even bigger event than I thought.

'Yeah. They all want pictures of *him*, don't they. David.'
TV cameras camped out? For David Cameron? Christ, it must be a slow news week in Hertfordshire.

'Well, him and *her*, obviously, she's here, too. You know, the missus. I might stick around myself and see if I can see her.'

Now there's no denying that David and Samantha Cameron had a certain glamour, but I was amazed that the cab driver was so impressed. It was only when we got to the hotel that it became obvious there was no way on earth this media scrum was here for the leader of the Conservative Party. Lining the driveway were men with huge cameras slung around their necks and behind them stood gangs of teenage girls holding signs saying 'We Love You Becks!' and 'Posh 4 Eva'.

Fucking hell – it wasn't the Camerons that everyone was excited about. Google had managed to get David and Victoria Beckham to speak at their conference. That was a hell of a coup – and no wonder I'd been bumped. But what the hell could the great and the good of the Internet industry possibly learn from the silent clothes horse out of the Spice Girls and a squeaky gonk whose only real skill was that he could kick a ball into a net better than almost anyone else?

I soon learned that David and Victoria weren't at the hotel to meet Eric Schmidt or to join a panel on the Internet and the environment. Instead, they had come to the spa in Hertfordshire with the rest of the England squad to relax and recover ahead of (or perhaps after) some important game or other.*

David and Victoria Beckham and the entire England squad, sharing a hotel and spa with the A list of geeks and nerds. For two

....
* Football is not my sport.

whole days. This was going to be amazing, I thought. Like *Revenge of the Nerds*, but with roasting.

9.1

Unfortunately, the England management had taken some extreme steps to ensure that the England players weren't disturbed during their stay, closing off large parts of the hotel to stop the press from getting inside, and presumably to avoid David and Victoria accidentally running into any nerds in checked shirts.

The event began with a grand soirée designed to bring together all the guests for mingling and canapés. The hotel's ballroom had been decorated with all manner of technical fripperies, including dozens of elaborate lava lamps (Mathmos was apparently a sponsor) and a giant floor-projected virtual football pitch with animated balls that bounced off your feet as you walked across it. In the corner, a young magician wearing a back-to-front baseball cap made a playing card float in midair, to the envy of the men in suits and the amazement of the much younger and very attractive personal assistants many of the men had for some reason opted to bring with them to the remote spa in the middle of the countryside.

Realising that I literally brought nothing to the party, I decided to perch myself by one of the many free bars and engage in a bit of people watching. And what people there were. CEOs of major companies; hugely successful dot com entrepreneurs from the first and second boom; a purse* of top venture capitalists; I swear an MP or two ... and a flirt† of astonishingly pretty PR girls whose job it was to make sure everyone had a drink in their hand and was having a good time. Naturally, I took my networking responsibilities seriously and shunned the once in a lifetime opportunity to mix with the crème of the crème of the business community in favour of chatting to a ridiculously hot and unconvincingly blonde PR girl called Emma. There's always an Emma.

....

* The collective noun for venture capitalists.

† The collective noun for PR girls.

Emma wasn't allowed to drink alcohol while she was working so between us we hit on a devious plan. I'd order a rum and Coke for myself, a tonic water for her and a straight vodka for my 'friend' who had gone to the loo. When no one from Google was looking, I'd empty the vodka into her tonic and no one would be any the wiser. Whenever one of her bosses came past we'd seamlessly switch from whatever we were really talking about to a heated debate about Google or some other search-engine-related issue. Emma would be able to get slowly drunk while on duty and I would get to enjoy her company while neither of us had to talk to any of the dull men in suits mingling around us.

I'd had about three or four rum and Cokes, and Emma had downed the same number of vodka tonics, when I spotted someone wearing a Google shirt heading towards the bar. It was time to put our fake conversation plan into action, pretending to be deep in discussion about something relevant.

'So, I have a theory about this event . . .' I began, loud enough to ensure that the Google person now standing to our left knew we were talking about work.

'Oh yes?' said Emma, playing along.

'Yes. It occurs to me that Google has hired this big hotel, invited the CEOs of some of its biggest potential rivals: the heads of rival Internet companies, the heads of telecoms companies, MPs who are in charge of competition legislation, that kind of thing.'

Out of the corner of my eye I could see the Google person eyeing us up. He had even stopped talking to his friend. Good, he had obviously heard me. Our cover was safe.

'Well, it's a bit Hotel California, isn't it? How do I know they haven't invited all these people here just to bump us off? What if they've poisoned the canapés to get rid of the competition?'

It seemed like a solid enough conspiracy theory to me; why else would Google invite so many potential competitors to a spa and be so nice to us? But before poor Emma could answer, the man from Google decided to jump in.

'Hey, buddy,' he asked, in a thick Californian drawl, 'did I just hear you say you think we're gonna kill you?'

His companion – a tall Australian fellow in a suit – piped up as well. 'Well that's ridiculous, mate. That's stupid. What kind of faa-kin' ridiculous, stupid thing is that to say?' He was clearly a bit pissed, but then so was I, so I could hardly say anything. (Although I was doing a better job on that front than he was.)

'Well, you have to admit,' I joked, stroking my chin in a sinister fashion. 'It does seem very convenient.'

'That's just ridiculous,' said the Californian. 'Why would we do that? That's just stupid.' The man was clearly taking my allegations very seriously; there had evidently been a huge irony breakdown somewhere. California, probably.

'Ah, yes, but they laughed at Groucho Marx,' I pointed out. 'Anyway, can't stop, got to mingle.' I wandered off, chuckling at my joke, in search of some more canapés.

9.2

The next morning, slightly hung-over and, having forgotten to book myself a wake-up call, ten minutes late for David Cameron's opening speech in which he had promised to lay out his vision for a Britain driven by increasing GWB (General Well Being) rather than GDP, whatever that meant. I ambled up to the reception table to collect my passes to the various events.

'Hello,' I said to the woman at the desk. 'Paul Carr, sorry I'm late. I think you've got some tickets for me.'

'Ah, yes, Mr Carr. Really glad you could make it – sorry about the mix-up with the speaking schedule. Actually, would you mind waiting for a moment, my boss wanted to have a quick word . . .'

'Of course, no problem at all.' She probably just wanted to apologise again for cancelling my talk. How nice. But as the head of PR came round the corner, her face a mask of seriousness, I could tell she had something else on her mind. In fact she looked really cross.

Oh God, what had I done? I cast my mind back to the previous night – had I been really drunk? No, I remember getting back to the hotel. The party was too boring for any of that kind of madness. Had Emma confessed to our booze scam? No, she was a PR. A professional liar.

'Hi ... Paul ... er, can we go round here for a quick word?" she asked, guiding me behind a giant 'Welcome to Google Zeitgeist' board. 'It's just that we've had ... er ... a bit of a complaint from one of our people about you.'

'A complaint? I've only been here twelve hours – what on earth could I have done wrong in that time?'

'Well, apparently there was a bit of a disagreement last night at the party. Did you tell one of our PR people that you thought we were trying to kill you?'

'What?! No, of course I didn't!'

Well, yes, I did.

'But ... oh for goodness sake, are you serious?"

'Apparently one of our guys was at the bar talking to the CEO of ——— and they heard you saying you thought we had some sinister ulterior motive.'

Oh, shit, the tall gobby Australian was only the CEO of ——— a *huge* financial services company and one of Google's biggest clients. Exactly the sort of person you don't want to overhear someone accusing your company of trying to murder. And the Californian with him was clearly the most humourless prick in the history of the world.

If the look on the head of PR's face hadn't been so serious, I'd have laughed out loud. I felt like I was back at school, being hauled up in front of our head of sixth form for sabotaging the headmaster's microphone on speech day. Trying desperately not to crack a smile as I spoke, I explained the entire situation – the Hotel California joke, the fact that her Californian colleague was a humourless dick. The fact that the Australian was bizarrely rude.

'And, anyway, you'd have to be a fucking idiot not to realise I was joking.'

Suddenly I realised she'd been trying not to smile, too. We both failed at the same time. 'Jesus,' she said. 'Well, there does seem to have been a – erm – sense of humour failure. So you don't think we're trying to kill you?'

'Absolutely not,' I said.

'In that case, I suppose I can let you off. And if you have any more trouble from people with no sense of humour, just come and see me. I'm from Ireland – we laugh at everything.'

'Will do,' I said. 'Thanks.'

But as I walked away, I had to admit if I *had* accidentally hit upon a secret plot to kill us all she'd have dealt with it brilliantly. Just to be on the safe side I decided that, at the gala dinner that evening, I'd sit near the door.

9.3

The gala dinner began immediately after the last presentation of the day and if it was designed to impress and overwhelm the guests then it succeeded with knobs on. The weather was abysmal – absolutely pouring with rain – so Google had laid on hundreds of umbrellas (branded, natch) to protect our dinner suits as we snaked behind the hotel and out into the grounds where we were told a marquee had been erected for the dinner. What we saw as we rounded the corner was beyond impressive: it was a marquee in the same way that the Grand Canyon is a pothole – a specially constructed tented village roughly the size of the Millennium Dome. Outside the entrance, protected from the rain inside giant transparent bubbles, were a strange collection of performers – acrobats, contortionists, fire-eaters and the like – laid on to amuse us as we wandered to the first tent where pre-dinner drinks were to be served.

This first tent alone was bigger than the average school playing field and was already packed to the canvas rafters with hundreds of guests, knocking back endless quantities of champagne. Looking around, I wished I'd gone back to my hotel to put on a tie. Even in the new suit and shirt I'd bought specially for the conference, I was easily the most underdressed person in the room. Most of the men were wearing dinner jackets and the women had changed into ball gowns or party dresses.

Across the tent I spotted someone I knew. We had met earlier following David Cameron's speech – he was a senior manager at eBay and it turned out we had a couple of mutual friends back in London. I shared my Hotel California story with him and he admitted that he'd had similar concerns as to why Google was being so generous to everyone. We agreed that, assuming he made it out alive, he'd pitch the idea to eBay for their next corporate event.

Our brief chat was interrupted by a violin fanfare played by two girls, one of whom looked suspiciously like Vanessa-Mae. Dinner was served.

Walking into the second tent, I realised I didn't have to worry about sitting near the exit: the main dining room was so vast that there were about a dozen different entrances and exits. I found the nearest table with an empty place and sat down, introducing myself to my fellow diners.

'I'm sorry,' said one, interrupting me in broken English, 'we are Dutch, we have not the best English. But is nice to meet you.' Apparently they did something to do with marketing. The meal flew by.

After dinner – a four-course feast, punctuated by speeches from various Google luminaries, each of whom was even more delighted than the last to see that so many of us had made it – we were ushered back into the first tent for dancing to the music of Jim Noir, a Manchester-based singer-songwriter who, we were assured, was going to be The Next Big Thing. The fact that his record company was sponsoring the event was entirely coincidental. Apparently one of his songs had featured on an advert for Ginsters' pies earlier in the year. I headed back to the free bar.

'You look as bored as I feel,' came a voice from behind me.

I turned round to see an older lady – perhaps in her late fifties, but dressed as if she was twenty years younger, always a bold decision. She introduced herself and explained that she was in charge of content for a certain giant company's consumer website. This was a huge stroke of luck: the company was one I'd been trying to woo for ages. They had invested a fortune in this amazing site, full of news and entertainment content, but it was – by and large – utter dreck. Finally! I thought: an opportunity for some networking. If I play this right – turn on the old charm, flirt a bit with the old girl – I can swing a bit of moonlighting writing some better stuff for them. The nice thing about writing stuff for big corporations who treat 'content' as a commodity is that they often pay an absolute fortune for fresh words, and it's dead easy work because no one ever actually reads any of it.

'Bored? No I'm having a ball,' I said, sarcastically. 'Apparently this guy used to advertise Ginsters' pies. We're in the presence of greatness. Can I buy you a drink?'

'Isn't it a free bar?'

'Yes,' I admitted, 'but it's the thought that counts, right?'

'I suppose so. So, what brings you here … ?'

I rattled off my CV in an only slightly gilded nutshell and my new friend seemed suitably impressed by what I'd pretended to have achieved. She also nodded enthusiastically at the ideas I threw out for features she should add to the portal, even the one about a fake agony aunt.

'We should definitely chat further,' she said, handing me her card. Being the world's worst networker, I didn't have a card, so I scribbled my email address on a cocktail napkin. Classy.

'Definitely,' I agreed. 'Anyway, I'd better get back to my hotel. Early start tomorrow.' Karl was joining me for the second day and I'd agreed to meet him for breakfast in a few hours.

'Where are you staying?' she asked.

'The hotel up the road. They downgraded me to the one with all the plebs.'

'Oh, I'm staying there, too,' she said.

'Oh. Oops.'

'No problem, let's share a cab back …', Google had laid on a fleet of black people carriers to deliver us safely home, '… then you can buy me a proper drink and tell me more about your ideas for the site.'

'Sounds good to me.'

9.4

Arriving back at the hotel, my new friend went to reception to collect her suitcase which had been delivered during the day. 'You couldn't help me take this up to my room, could you? I've slightly overpacked.'

She wasn't kidding; the bag was bigger than the dinner marquee.

'Sure. Of course.' Extra brownie points, thought I.

Now, had this woman been half the age she was, and were I not a total fucking idiot, I would have sworn I was being chatted up. 'Buy me a drink.' 'Come up to my room.' It couldn't have been more obvious if she'd hit me over the head with a club. But this was a fifty-something-year-old woman in a business suit; in charge of running a huge corporate website. She was also, judging by the ring on her finger, married.

I wheeled the bag into her room (It had wheels! Who needs help with a bag with wheels?) and she closed the door behind her.

'Well,' I said, suddenly very aware of how small her room was, with inches between the door and the bed, and very little space anywhere else. 'I really had better get going. Early start.'

'What about that drink?' she asked.

'Actually, I'm pretty knackered. And I was quite drunk last night. If I show up hung-over for the second morning in a row they're going to think they've accidentally invited Oliver Reed.'

'Okay, well, if not a drink, how about this . . .'

With those words, this fifty-whatever-year-old woman – this fifty-whatever-year-old married woman who I'd spent the evening flirting with trying to convince her to let me write crap for her website – lunged at me. And I mean *lunged*, like a teenager on a park bench.

I should make one thing absolutely clear: I am in no way proud of what I did in response. I sidestepped out of her way. Literally dived to one side; the poor woman almost hit her nose on the wall. At her age, she could easily have broken a hip.

'I'm not sure that's a good idea,' I said, turning on my heel and almost sprinting out of the door. As the lift doors closed I could just make out her last words . . .

'Call me . . .'

Regaling Karl with this story the next morning over breakfast, I could tell he didn't believe me. 'Jesus, she must have been pretty hideous for you to turn her down,' he said, smirking.

'That's a little harsh. I have my standards.'

'No you don't. And you definitely don't when you're drunk'

'I wasn't bloody drunk – and I'll have you know I'm extremely picky. And she was at least thirty years older than me.'

'Oh come on,' he scoffed. 'How old was Nina?'

Nina was a journalist I'd dated briefly when I was twenty-four and, yes, admittedly, she was fifteen years older than me. And, yes, admittedly, she'd written a column about our relationship in a certain woman's magazine in which she referred to me as 'the man cub'.

'But that's not the point. Everyone knows the rule on age gaps is half your age plus seven. Half of thirty-nine is nineteen and a half. Plus seven is . . .'

'Twenty-six and a half,' Karl interrupted. 'And you were twenty-four. So Nina was too old for you as well. And yet . . .'

'Yes, all right. But that was different. I *fancied* Nina. The woman last night was just . . . old . . .'

But Karl wasn't listening to me any more. He'd spotted someone he knew walking behind us.

'Hello!' said Karl, raising his voice in surprise as if he was greeting an old friend.

'Hello,' said the voice I recognised from somewhere, but couldn't place. I turned around to see who it was, but he was already walking away. You could have knocked me down with a feather.

'Wow! I didn't know you knew Peter Gabriel. You're a dark horse.'

But by this point Karl was just looking stunned, and slightly sheepish. And then he burst out laughing.

'I don't,' he said. 'I just looked up and made eye contact and knew I recognised him from somewhere. Before I knew what was happening, I was saying hello.'

'You just accidentally greeted Peter Gabriel, like an old friend.'

'I suppose I did, yes.'

And, of course, Peter Gabriel did what any of us would do in that situation – assumed that he and Karl must have met before and greeted him in kind.

Now *that's* how networking should be done, I thought.

9.5

The last big event of the conference was the real crowd-puller – a 'fireside chat' with Eric Schmidt, the CEO of Google. The fireside chat is a hideous American invention and basically refers to an informal speech, often with a moderator on hand to pitch questions and filter them from the audience. Despite the name, it's very rare for an actual fire to be involved – just a couple of chairs and a couple of microphones – and, in this case, several TV cameras.

The presence of the cameras struck me as odd. The media had largely been banned from the event, with only a few select reporters being allowed in, on the strict understanding that none of the goings-on could be reported. What happens at Zeitgeist stays at Zeitgeist.* There was also a definite buzz in the room, the sense that something was about to happen – a surprise of some kind.

And what a surprise it was.

Just as the last few people were taking their seats, the announcement came: Eric Schmidt would be joined in his fireside chat by none other than Google co-founder and Internet legend Larry Page! The crowd burst into spontaneous applause.

You have to understand that in this room – a room that had for the last couple of days hosted presentations by David Cameron, Peter Gabriel and all manner of multi-millionaire founders of international companies – Larry Page was the nearest thing to a real rockstar they could imagine.

Forget David Beckham and Posh Spice. This guy was A list.

9.6

Larry Page was a student at Stanford in the mid-1990s when he first met his future business partner Sergey Brin. Both were computer science majors and started working together on a research project to demonstrate that the way most search engines rated the websites they searched was fatally flawed – and to find a way to fix them.

....

* Oops.

At that time, most of the popular search tools worked in the same way: by ranking search results by how many times a particular word or phrase being searched for appeared on any given site. So, if a user was searching for 'donkey porn', then the first result shown would be the site that featured the most instances of those words.

For Internet spammers, fooling search sites into showing their site first was a simple matter of including as many popular words and phrases on each page as they could. This was rarely the best way to ensure high-quality content for the end user, but it was the best anyone could think of.

What Page and Brin proposed was a system that supplemented keyword matching with a system that ranked websites by how many other sites linked to them. The more useful or important a site was – they theorised – the more inbound links the site would attract from other sites. But then they went one step further – looking at the sites that linked to the other sites and counting how many inbound links *they* had from still other sites. The key to a top ranking would be to get lots of inbound links from sites that were themselves linked to by other important sites. They developed a demonstration version of their system as part of the Stanford website, christening it 'Backrub'. By 1997, their fledgling search engine was growing at such a rapid pace that they decided to launch it as a stand-alone site, under a brand new name.

The story of the name they ended up choosing is a funny one. One September afternoon, Larry Page sat in his office in the Gates Computer Science Building (named after Bill Gates, who had paid for the facility to be built) at Stanford, brainstorming new names. With him were Sergey Brin and their friend Sean Anderson, another computer science student. The three were each firing out possible names which Larry wrote on a large whiteboard while Sean searched the web to see whether anyone else was already using them. 'How about we call it "Googolplex"?' suggested Anderson. A 'googol' is a number equal to writing '1' with a hundred zeroes after it. An extraordinarily large number, in other words. A 'googolplex' is a 1 with a googol zeroes after it. An extraordinary large number, to the power of extraordinary. Anderson suggested that calling the site 'Googolplex' would show that their new search engine was able to search an almost infinite number of pages. An impressive number for an impressive site. What it also showed was that they were a bunch of nerds.

In the end, Page thought Googolplex was too much of a mouthful and suggested 'Googol'. And so it would have been had Sean been as much of a speller as he was a nerd. What he actually searched for, and the name that was later registered, was spelt 'Google'. And so a legend was born.

In 2001, Google recruited Eric Schmidt, formerly CEO of software company Novell, ostensibly as CEO but really to act as a sensible business head to balance out the youthful exuberance and geekery of Page and Brin. Clearly the plan worked – by 2004 Google was a publicly traded company, valued at $23 billion, and by the start of 2008 it would have grown to over twenty thousand employees, many of whom would be based at the company's main headquarters in Mountainview, California – in a building known as The Googleplex.

9.7

Having a fireside chat with Eric Schmidt to close the conference was more than enough to draw media attention, but scoring Larry Page as well was something else. If Schmidt was Google's Commissioner Gordon, Page was its Batman. No wonder the cameras were jostling for position as the room began to fill to the rafters; standing room only.

The chat got under way with Schmidt and Page talking about the future of Google and fielding questions from the floor. It was all pretty standard stuff – Eric Schmidt made sure of that. What was remarkable was watching how Schmidt abruptly silenced Page when his young charge nearly revealed something commercially sensitive.

One such moment came when an audience member cheekily asked what innovation was coming next from Google. Larry started to answer.

'Well, that's an interesting question! We're . . .'

'Actually, I don't think Larry is going to answer that ...' inter-rupted Schmidt.

The entire room groaned. Page looked suitably chastised and moved on to the next question.

Watching the excitement of Larry Page – constantly innovating and always excited to share his latest plan with the people he regarded as his peers – and the firm hand of Eric Schmidt – all too aware that every utterance from billionaire Page had the potential to rock the share price of this corporate behemoth – you couldn't help but see why the company had grown so big and yet remained so innovative. They were like the ultimate power threesome, with Brin at that moment staying behind in California to look after the kids. All twenty thousand of them.

In fact, Schmidt's role as Google's father figure goes even deeper than chaperoning press conferences. In 2006 a story did the rounds in dot com circles about a row between Page and Brin over which size beds they would have in one of their jets (the same jet, inci-dentally, was also fitted with hammocks for use during parties). When the two couldn't agree, and the row threatened to damage their working relationship, it was Schmidt who had stepped in to resolve things ...

According to reports, he took both Brin and Page into a room and scolded them for their squabbling. 'Sergey, you can have whatever bed you want in your room; Larry, you can have whatever kind of bed you want in your bedroom. Let's move on.' And so they did.

Another telling point during the fireside chat came when the pair were asked about the recent launch of Google in China. The decision had caused huge controversy in the Internet community: China has some of the most aggressive censorship laws in the world, with journalists routinely being jailed for exercising what in the West would be considered basic freedom of speech. In order to get permission to operate in this huge emerging market, Google had agreed to filter its search results to fit in with China's own censorship of the Internet (known to what pass for wags in the web press as 'the great firewall of China'). As a result, if you search for 'Tiananmen' on Google in China you get lots of sites filled with pretty pictures of the Beijing tourist attraction. Do the same in the West and it's tanks and massacres all the way. An audience member asked them how this policy squared with Google's official mission statement: 'Don't be evil'. The answer spoke volumes about how far Google had come from dorm room to boardroom as the two men compared the situation to how German law insisted that Google restrict access to Nazi-related websites. In the same way, they had to abide by the Chinese government's preferences to operate in that country.

'Godwin's Law,' whispered a man behind me to his friend.

'Yeah,' his friend whispered back.

Godwin's Law was first coined in 1990 by the American attorney and author Mike Godwin. It reads: 'As an online discussion grows longer, the probability of a comparison involving Nazis or Hitler approaches one.' Or in other words, eventually in every discussion on the Internet, some idiot makes a comparison to Nazism. The law has spawned a variation which could be more appropriate in this case ... In any Internet argument, the first person to mention the Nazis automatically loses.

It was time to go home.

9.8

Having generously decided not to kill us after all (for this year at least), Google had laid on another fleet of people carriers to take all the Zeitgeist guests back to London.

Each car seated about five or six people, giving passengers one last opportunity for networking on the hour-long journey back to the city. Unfortunately, no one was going the same way as Karl and me so, as we sat waiting for the off, we had an entire cab to ourselves. Until, that is, seconds before the driver slammed the door shut, a smartly dressed woman came running out of the hotel, clearly relieved not to have missed her ride home. She dived in the back of the cab, out of breath, throwing a gigantic handbag on to the seat beside Karl. It was only after she recovered from her sprint that she realised – I realised – that we'd met before.

'Hello,' said Karl. 'I'm Karl ...'

'Hello,' said the woman for the previous night.

I stared out of the window.

It was going to be a very, very long journey home.

10.0

'Nice colour ...
... That's Bone'

A year on from Google Zeitgeist I was certain that Karl's friendship with Peter Gabriel would pay dividends when we met him to talk about We7 and the possibility that he might invest in Fridaycities. Sadly, it was not to be. While Gabriel's 'people' were enthusiastic about the idea of meeting to discuss a partnership or investment in Fridaycities, we would have to wait for a couple of months as he was getting ready to go on tour. 'But do keep in touch,' they said. 'Come down and see us when Peter has finished touring ... we'll definitely have a meeting.'

With Ricky also busy with his other projects, Nic and Espirit not in a position to consider investing until we were at a later stage and Henry Fysom at Creative Capital not able to invest until someone else did (and our mobile phone guy an idiot), our fundraising truck had basically stalled.

But Angus's contact book had one possibility left: Max and Duncan Jennings, two brothers from Newcastle who had made a ton of money from their online marketing business and had spent some of it developing a local reviews site called WeLoveLocal.com. WeLoveLocal was similar in many ways to Fridaycities in that both sites dealt with local people, talking about local things. Angus had heard on the grapevine that the company had some spare money that they were keen to invest in interesting new projects.

Ordinarily the decision to call them would have been a no-brainer – they had money, we needed money – but there was a catch. The brothers were also potential competitors, so if we told them our plans and then they decided not to invest, we'd have basically given away all our secrets for nothing. Frankly, though, at this stage we weren't exactly drowning in investment options so Angus agreed to get in touch with the brothers and set up a meeting.

While Angus went back to the phones, Savannah, Karl and I went back to our whiteboard to examine what we'd learned in the nearly eight months that Fridaycities had been in test mode. In that time, nearly twenty thousand people had signed up to the test site and we'd learned a lot about what they liked about the site and what they didn't; what worked and what didn't. Some users loved almost everything while others hated it all in equal measure. But there was one thing that everyone agreed on: the name 'Fridaycities'. It was awful.

Every single person we spoke to – users, potential investors, friends, family – asked the same question: 'Why the hell did you call the site Fridaycities – what does it mean?' People who didn't know the site assumed it was some kind of bar review site for people going out on the piss at the weekend in cities. Which, judging by the questions that had been posted over the preceding months, was about 50 per cent true.

As we were still in test mode there was time to revise the name before we launched properly to the public. But not much; so if we were going to think of something new, it was essential that we get it right. I decided we needed some more outside advice; this time from someone who knew a lot about branding. Someone, in fact, who had been the first person to tell me – months earlier – that Fridaycities was a crap name. I decided to phone Richard, hoping he was in the country.

10.1

Richard Moross is thirty years old, and a taller, better dressed man you will struggle to meet. There's a scene in the film *Men in Black* where Will Smith is being indoctrinated into the MIB agency. He's taken to a completely white locker room and Rip Torn's character (Chief Zed, the head of the agency) gives him 'the last suit you'll ever wear': black jacket and trousers, white shirt, black shoes.

Now, imagine that look but replace the white shirt with a black one. That's Richard. I've known Richard for nearly three years – been to parties with him, had lunch with him, gone to the pub with him, visited his office, travelled on long-haul flights with him, even been bowling – and I swear I've never seen him dressed in any other outfit. His flat, meanwhile – a bachelor pad in west-central London that he uses on the rare occasions he's in town – is stark white and achingly cool, exactly like the MIB headquarters. I'm assuming it's just a coincidence but if I discovered that the flat once belonged to the film's production designer I wouldn't be at all surprised.

Richard is the polar opposite of me not just in height and dress sense but also in terms of his work ethic. A designer by upbringing, he founded a company called Pleasure Cards in 2004 with cash from venture capitalists The Accelerator Group, the same people who backed Agent Provocateur and also Michael Smith's Mind Candy. The concept was simple (sort of): Pleasure Cards (the second most porny company name in the world, after Cyberbritain) would be *the* hip alternative to boring business cards, for creative and design types. Supplied in packs of one hundred, the front of your Pleasure Card would carry the usual business card information – name, phone number, email address and the like – but on the reverse you could let your imagination run wild. Professional designers were invited to upload designs and images for the cards to Pleasurecards.com, where they could choose the ones they wanted to appear on the back of their personalised cards. Every time a designer's work was used on the back of a customer's card, he or she received a small royalty and the rest of the price of the card would go to Pleasure Cards. As an additional gimmick, each customer would also have their own 'PEP'* number, printed on their cards, which was linked to a personalised page on the Pleasure Cards site where they could add additional information about themselves: updated contact details, favourite music, photos – that kind of stuff.

The really cool thing about the cards was how good they looked. These were really, really nice cards. About the same width of normal business cards, but half the height, they were also identifiable even at a distance as being Pleasure Cards rather than humdrum old business cards. Really, they were stunning

There was just one problem.

....
* I have no idea.

No one wanted to buy them.

While the designs were great and the cards were beautiful, the problem lay with the Pleasure Cards website: it was beyond difficult to navigate, and the PEP numbers were a step of complexity too far for the time-poor, cash-rich hipsters the company was aiming for.

As Richard admitted to the *Guardian* a year or so later, 'it sucked'. Mightily.

So Richard went back to the drawing board. Over the next few months he raised some more money (a *lot* more money) from two more large VCs – Index Ventures (home of Danny Rimer) and Atlas Venture – and began completely to reinvent the business.

The first realisation he had was also the most ground-breaking: users didn't care about choosing thousands of pre-submitted designs from top designers. Someone's business – or pleasure – card is the ultimate statement of who *they* are, and customers wanted the backs of their cards to reflect that. So Pleasure Cards dumped the designers and instead created an ingenious system where customers could upload their own pictures from photo-sharing sites like Flickr or social network sites like Bebo.

The PEP number? Gone. The complex order process? Pared down to an almost Zen-like experience. The cards still looked the same, and they were still as gorgeous as a pre-rehab starlet, but that one change of gimmick – allowing customers to express their personality on the back of the card as well as the front – was all it took to make business explode.

In a little over a month the relaunched site had received orders for over a million cards, each printed on the company's spanking new state-of-the-art printing machines and packaged by hand in their spanking new warehouse conversion offices.

But along with the shift in business model came another, perhaps equally significant, change.

10.2

Shortly before Richard's grand relaunch, I met up with him in New York for the US branch of Michael and Judith's Second Chance

Tuesday. It was a ridiculously hot summer's day and, with a few hours to kill before the event, we went for cocktails on the roof of the Hotel Gansevoort, overlooking Soho House. I felt like a fish out of water, but Richard, with his air of James Bond cool and his *Men in Black* dress code, took the opulent surroundings in his stride, even managing not to gawp at the stunning supermodels parading around the hotel's rooftop pool. He ordered us Perfect Manhattans (the one with both sweet and dry Vermouth – not to be confused with the Dry Manhattan or any of the other million variations on the theme) and I asked him how the relaunch was going.

'It's going really well. We've got the investment in, the new site's almost ready for testing. It's all great, but I wanted to ask you something ... what do you think of the name "Moo"?'

'Moo? Like a cow says?'

'Yes. Moo.com.'

'Is it available? Surely someone already owns Moo.com? Are there really no dairy farmers on the Internet?'

'Yes, someone else has it. But we're going to try to buy it. I reckon if we make the offer in the right way, we can get it for ———.'

'Fucking hell.' The amount was enough to cover Fridaycities' costs so far several times over. This was the difference between a company with venture capital funding and one still hunting for angel investment.

'Yeah – it's a lot of cash, but I think it's worth it.'

'Moo. Mooooooooo. Mooooo dot commmmmm. I like it.'

'Good. So do I.'

Of course, Richard had already decided that he was going to buy Moo and no doubt he'd already made an offer. He was just testing the name out on everyone he knew to see whether anyone totally hated it. But I've always admired people who have confidence in their own decisions but can still make others believe, genuinely, that their opinion matters a damn.

'Okay, my turn – what do you think of Fridaycities for the site we're about to launch?'

'Honestly?'

'No, I'd like you to lie to me. That's why I asked.'

'Well, I mean, it's crap, isn't it? Really bad. It doesn't say anything.

185

Why do you insist on using Friday for everything?'

'Because – you know – there's *The Friday Thing* and The Friday Project, and now this. Like Virgin Trains and Virgin Atlantic and . . .'

'So now you're going to be Richard Branson?'

'I might be.'

'Yes. Okay. You might. But you're not. And even if you were it's still a crap name. You need a name that instantly "positions" the site with the people you're trying to reach. It's just common sense. Fridaycities is separate from the things you've done in the past – it's a new thing – so you need a new brand.'

'Hmmmm. Maybe you're right.'

Of course he wasn't right. Fridaycities was a bloody brilliant name. And, anyway, what did a company name really matter? Take a random example off the high street: The Carphone Warehouse. Wasn't that the most inaccurate brand name in the world? They didn't have warehouses, they had tiny kiosks. And carphones? What the hell is a carphone these days? You're not even allowed to use your phone while driving. They should be called The Streetphone Kiosk. But their weird brand didn't matter because, once a company has been around for a while, customers stop analysing the actual words and they just start recognising the brand. Who actually hears Virgin Megastore now and thinks of a hypermarket full of chaste girls? Who hears Google and thinks just how ridiculous it sounds? It's a typo for God's sake. After a while, people would forget that Fridaycities was a stupid name and they'd just start using it without thinking.

If I'd stopped being so arrogant for one tiny second, I'd have realised that Richard was right and it was me who wasn't thinking. The Carphone Warehouse grew quickly because in the first few years of its existence the name reflected *exactly* what it offered – a vast warehouse full of carphones; the kiosks and phone driving ban came much later – and Virgin got the attention it got in the early days precisely because its name was a bit controversial; a bit sexy. And how many people heard the word Google and forgot it in a hurry?

Richard had realised that Pleasure Cards – with its slightly porny connotations – wasn't right for what he was offering. Moo Cards, on the other hand, was perfect. It was quirky, it was cute, it was easy to remember: just like the cards themselves. And he was right about Fridaycities – it *was* a crap name, one that confused people at exactly the time we most needed them to love and remember it.

10.3

It wasn't going to be easy to go back to Richard, months after our cocktails in New York, and admit that user feedback had proved him right, but I swallowed my pride and sent him a text: 'Are you in London?' When he replied that he was, but was off to San Francisco in a couple of days, I asked whether he fancied a quick beer in a little pub off Charlotte Street later that evening.

Before Richard even had a chance to sit down and take off his (black) jacket, I cut him off.

'Don't say I told you so.'

'I wouldn't dream of it,' he replied, taking a sip of his beer. 'About what?'

'We're going to change the name of Fridaycities. Everyone thinks it's crap'

'I tol—'

'Don't.'

'Okay, but I'm pretty sure I did tell you so, months ago.'

'You may well have done. And, okay, you were right. It is a crap name. But I've got a new one.'

One of the things that had caught us by surprise during the test phase of the site was how popular our reward points system had become. Called 'Kudos' points, users earned them by responding to questions posted by other users, or by inviting their friends to join, or by submitting questions that made it into our weekly newsletter. The more they contributed to the site, the more points they earned. There was a leader board that showed the users with the most Kudos points every week and competition to move up the board had become fierce. The popularity of the points was made even more bizarre by the fact that they were basically worthless.

You couldn't use them for anything; couldn't spend them on anything. They just were.

But the users had started to assign Kudos points with their own value – giving them away to others on the site who answered their questions and even offering actual physical items for sale in exchange for Kudos. Without meaning to, we'd created a currency based entirely on knowledge and we'd decided that the new site would be entirely built around the points.

Richard listened intently while I explained the new focus of the site, and when I was finished he smiled broadly: 'I really like that. It sounds cool.' Which was a huge relief as the designers had been working on the new functionality of the site for weeks.

Then came the big question: 'What do you think of the name "Kudocities"?' I asked. 'Karl came up with it – sticking with the cities idea, but focusing on the Kudos points – I think it really works.'

Richard looked thoughtful. 'So, that's Kudocities to rhyme with atrocities rather than Kudo Cities to rhyme with judo cities?'

'Yeah, Kudocities.'

'Yes. I really like that. That's good.'

'You really think so?'

'Yeah, I really do. And anyway, anything would be better than Fridaycities.'

'Cool, thank you.' Of course, I pretended that his was just one of many opinions I was soliciting; that really we'd already decided to go ahead with Kudocities. In truth, a wave of relief was sweeping over me. I really valued Richard's opinion and if he'd hated the new name I think I'd have gone straight back to the office and started all over again. Or thrown myself under a bus. Either or.

But he liked it.

Kudocities.com it was.

11.0

'MySpace or yours?'

While we were busy settling on a new name for the first proper version of the site – not to mention trying to raise money to fund it, 2007 was fast becoming the year of the 'social networking' site.

'Social networking' was an Internet industry buzzword that described any site that brought people together and allowed them to bond over their shared interests. Fridaycities – sorry, Kudocities – was a social network for people who wanted to bond over the cities they lived in, but there were also social networks for people who were looking to buy houses, social networks for dog lovers,* social networks for book lovers; there were almost certainly social networks for people who loved joining social networks.

But while these niche social network sites were hot, and getting hotter, the real giants of the social networking world – the only ones worth any actual money – were the ones that ignored niches and threw open their doors to the world. And the biggest of these social network giants was MySpace.

Launched in 2003, MySpace was created as a social networking site for young people who wanted to discover new music. Members were able to set up personal profile pages to share their favourite bands, along with all manner of other likes and dislikes. Very quickly, having a cool-looking MySpace page became as important to young people as having the right pair of trainers, or using the correct slang. Yagetmi?

Unfortunately, somewhere down the line, the definition of 'cool' among MySpace users apparently got confused with the definition of 'hideously tacky' and the site's millions of profile pages became a cacophony of flashing images, gaudy background colours and

....

* Dogster – the fourth porniest name on the Internet.

189

photos of underage teens posing in very little clothing indeed. The phenomenon inspired a popular online competition by cult video blogger Ze Frank called 'I knows me some ugly MySpace' with viewers encouraged to send in links to the ugliest profile pages they could find. Meanwhile, the trend for posting misleadingly posed profile photos became the subject of a song: 'You look a lot fitter on your MySpace picture (than you do in real life)' – which became a hit on ... where else ... ? MySpace.

MySpace enjoyed phenomenal growth, thanks in part to favourable press coverage which typically gushed about how the site was a true Internet rags-to-riches story, founded by twentysomethings Chris DeWolfe and Tom Anderson. But behind the media myth, things were not quite what they seemed.

According to the official company line, MySpace was founded in 2003 by Chris DeWolfe and Tom Anderson who worked for a company called eUniverse (later renamed Intermix). eUniverse was founded by an entrepreneur named Brad Greenspan, but Greenspan later left the company, handing over full control of MySpace to DeWolfe and Anderson. As MySpace grew, Tom Anderson, who was twenty-seven when the site launched, became an Internet celebrity thanks to his role as the default first 'friend' that was added to every new MySpace user's profile page. This instant fame led to Anderson being nicknamed 'America's first friend' by various news magazines and inspired one T-shirt entrepreneur to produce a shirt bearing the slogan 'Tom is not my friend'. Hundreds of thousands were sold.

In 2005, with MySpace boasting over 100 million users, the company (and parent company, Intermix) was acquired by Rupert Murdoch's News Corporation for $580 million, making the end of an amazing ride for two plucky young entrepreneurs.

The only slight problem with this history is the fact that it's not true. For a start Tom Anderson had been fibbing to his hundred million friends. He wasn't twenty-seven at all when he started the company. In fact he was thirty-two. Using a younger age was a shrewd marketing move by the founders to help them appeal to the site's target teen demographic. And that's wasn't the worst of the allegations surrounding MySpace. In 2006, the technology site ValleyWag (one of Nick Denton's Gawker portfolio of sites) published a damning investigation by journalist Trent Lapinski,* using information provided by Greenspan who, it had become apparent, hadn't left MySpace voluntarily at all but had been forced out for reasons unknown. Whatever the truth about Greenspan's departure, he was certainly extremely pissed off and launched a site – www.freemyspace.com – to tell his side of the story, giving Lapinski all kinds of juicy details about the real story of MySpace.

For a start, Lapinski's article claimed, MySpace was far from the cute garage start-up that everyone loved. Instead it had begun life as a sinister ploy by hardened marketing execs at eUniverse to persuade young people to opt in to receive targeted advertising from youth brands. The use of Tom – originally hired by the site as a copy editor – as everyone's first friend (with his revised age) was a clever ruse to give some youth appeal, sorely lacking in the other founders.

For his part, Greenspan had a history of being involved in somewhat dodgy advertising schemes, including creating the ad software behind the Kazaa filesharing network which had become popular with music and movie pirates. DeWolfe, too, had previously been the founder of an email marketing firm named ResponseBase – which was acquired in 2002 by none other than eUniverse, but not before building up a database of thirty million email addresses.

The team, with their roots firmly in the world of online advertising, set up MySpace and quickly began to build up the membership base by instructing employees to invite everyone in their email address books to join. Those first contacts invited their friends and so on and so on – and the rest was (somewhat revised) Internet history.

So is Tom really your friend? Or just a marketer's shill? As the man himself put it in an email to all MySpace's staff during the first days of the site: 'I am as anti-social as they come, and I've already got twenty people to sign up.' At the time of writing, anti-social Tom has 217,701,025 friends and analysts predict that MySpace

....

* Who wrote his article at the age of nineteen. Or fourteen in Anderson years.

could be worth as much as $15 billion. The man has clearly got over his shyness.

But while in 2007 MySpace was still the largest of the social networks, its position was by no means secure. In fact, there were two rivals yapping at the giant's heels, including one that had specifically set out to steal the lucrative youth demographic. The fact that this rival had already succeeded in achieving that in several European markets was impressive. The fact that the rival wasn't American but British was astonishing.

11.1

I've got a feeling we're not at Open Coffee any more, Toto.

As I approached the velvet rope that separated the nightclub from the outside world – and vice versa – I was greeted by the imposing form of a Maori warrior in full traditional dress, clutching a guest list. Say what you like about the Maoris, they run a tight ship. A quick scan of the list, a grunt of approval and the rope was lowered, allowing me inside.

I had come to Mahiki – the favourite late-night haunt of Princes William and Harry – for an event called 'Lessons Learnt'. The evening was organised by Robert and it was already encapsulating everything that an Internet People event should be.

I had actually been slightly disappointed that my name was on the Maori's list – it's hard to think of a better anecdote than the one that begins 'What? *These* bruises? Oh, yeah, a Maori threw me out of Prince William's local ...' but maybe next time. Walking downstairs to the basement – which, if I hadn't been told by every tabloid that it was one of London's hottest party venues, I could have easily mistaken for a tacky Hawaiian-themed dive in a chav holiday resort – I edged my way to the bar, wading through crowds of well-dressed entrepreneurs and paid £10 for a bottle of beer. Looks like it's not Marbella either, Toto.

The plan for the evening was to gather together the brightest and the best of the British dot com scene and give each of them a minute with a microphone to share the one piece of advice they wish they'd been given before they'd started in business.

The main attraction of the night – and the reason the event was unmissable for anyone who had even a passing interest in social networking – was Michael Birch, the founder of teenage networking site Bebo: the site that had MySpace running scared, especially in Europe.

Birch may not have the profile of Tom Anderson or Chris DeWolfe but he is a fascinating character, and humble, too, having failed at various businesses before hitting upon the one that was fast becoming Europe's big hope against a Murdoch-owned MySpace.

Birch's first – and least successful – enterprise was a site called Babysitting Circle that allowed local teenagers to arrange baby-sitting appointments among themselves (nobody signed up). Then there was the online will-writing service (nope) and the birthday reminder service, Birthday Alarm. This last one actually did manage to get some 'traction' (a stupid industry term meaning people actually used it in decent, and growing, numbers) before being used as a springboard to launch Bebo.

Bebo was a real winner – co-founded by Birch and his wife, Xochi, with help from his brother, Paul – a social network along similar lines to MySpace, but with a more European flavour and sticking firmly to a youth demographic while MySpace had started to morph into a showcase for musicians and celebrities. The site quickly became the third most popular site of its type in the world, with tens of millions of members creating profile pages. For anyone over the age of twenty a visit to the site is a baffling experience; a world apparently populated by aliens with their own language. Take the following tagline, taken (I swear) from a random user's profile page . . .

'Ім а мσνэмэпτ ьч мчsэif ьτ iм а fσяcэ шэп шэяэ 2gэva ьσч iм gd aι ьч мчsэif ьτ ььч υ, υ мкэ мэ ьэττa'

Which – and please trust me on this – translates as . . .

'I'm a movement by myself but I'm a force when were [sic] together boy I'm good all by myself but baby you, you make me better.'

(It makes more sense, and is actually quite beautiful, when read in the original horseshit.*) The Birches raised $15 million to develop Bebo, a good chunk of which must surely have been spent on special software to remove grammar and punctuation. For sure, Bebo is a site for total fucking idiots – the Jeremy Kyle juniors, if you like – but give a few dozen million of those idiots pocket money and you can see why the company has been valued in the hundreds of millions and had MySpace worried. Hell, give a few dozen million of those idiots typewriters and they could write Shakespeare. Although they'd spell it 'Sчks9эяэ'.

Taking the microphone, and ignoring the one minute rule imposed on everyone else to keep the event moving *allegro*, Michael Birch had two pieces of advice to share with the assembled crowd, who fell totally silent for the first time all night as he cleared his throat to speak. Yeah – screw you, Prince William; to this crowd, Michael Birch is true royalty. I took out my notepad, pen poised, while next to me Jemima Kiss, a blogger from the *Guardian*'s website, cracked open her laptop to report the momentous event live.

'The one piece of advice I wish I'd been given before moving to the US to start Bebo is . . .'

The room held its breath.

'. . . is to look the other way when crossing the road. Turns out they drive on the other side over there.'

Big laugh.

Rich *and* funny.

Wanker.

But seriously folks.

'No, really, the best bit of advice I can give to any entrepreneur is to be a cheap bastard . . . that's a really good tip . . . and if you do manage to fool a VC into giving you lots of money then make it last. We worked from our bedroom for four years before we had enough money to pay for the money we were spending.'

As one, all the entrepreneurs in the room looked down guiltily at their bottles of £10 beer.

With that Birch handed over the microphone and headed back to the bar, as a hundred would-be social network entrepreneurs slowly

---

* And quite how that last comma slipped in is a mystery.

began to edge in his direction, in search of the illusive business card swap.

11.2

Next to the stage came another celebrity – albeit of a more traditional tabloid type – Jamie Murray Wells, the founder of Glasses Direct. In contrast to most people in the room, Jamie was no stranger to Mahiki. The headline in the *Sun* a few weeks earlier had said it all: *'Anyone fancy a Goodtime Girl? (That's cocktail Kate drank on date with Wills' mate)'*. Kate being, in this case, Kate Middleton. Wills' mate, in this case, being twenty-five-year-old Jamie Murray Wells.

Young, quietly spoken and modest in appearance, Murray Wells nonetheless has a remarkable public profile. By night, when he's not dancing with future princesses, he's making tabloid headlines for his other extra-curricular antics. Another story in the *Sun* a few weeks earlier had revealed that Murray Wells had been injured when, along with a friend, he had been caught breaking into a girls' boarding school searching for 'totty' (unfortunately it was the Christmas holidays so no one was there – and Murray Wells later fell off a water tower, breaking his leg).

But by day Jamie makes headlines for something far stranger: driving the optometric industry stark staring mad.

It all began while Murray Wells was studying English at the University of the West of England in Bristol and discovered that he needed reading glasses. Perhaps it was the hours hunched over books. Perhaps it was the fact that he lived with five girls that started to turn him blind. Either way, what follows was one of those classic entrepreneur moments: he was quoted £150 by an optician for what was basically two pieces of plastic and 'less metal than you'd find in a teaspoon'. A bell went off in his head. Surely the mark-up on these things must be astronomical. So Jamie did what born entrepreneurs do when bells go off in their heads: he did some research, speaking to opticians and people who work in optical labs and – basically – anyone who might be able to explain where the £150 goes. And this is what he found out: the real cost of a pair of glasses is about £7. The rest goes on cost of sales – those stark white shops and teams of sales staff don't come cheap – and huge, huge profits.

The second thing he found out was that the way most high street opticians work is, basically, a scam: you turn up, have an eye test for about £20 (barely enough to cover the cost to the optician for carrying it out), you get your prescription and then you get sold a pair of glasses (or two) at a £143 mark-up. But what the high street optician doesn't tell you is that there is absolutely no legal reason why you can't go to the optician, have the cheap eye test, get your prescription and – well – leave. Just walk out. Take the piece of paper with your measurements and get someone else to provide the glasses.

Someone like Jamie Murray Wells.

With those discoveries made and a business plan written, Glasses Direct was born. With just £1,000 from his student loan, Jamie commissioned a web designer to build a prototype of his website and then set about establishing relationships with exactly the same suppliers that provide frames and lenses to the big high street names. At first the suppliers were terrified of pissing off their best customers, but Jamie promised them he'd keep their relationship with Glasses Direct a secret. Money is money is money – and soon Jamie had a website and a supplier who would provide him with pairs of glasses to fit his customers' prescriptions. Prices? From £15 a pair. First year turnover? £1 million.* In 2007, the company received £2.9 million in funding from Saul Klein's Index Ventures and Highland Capital, who also invested money in the successful betting site, Betfair.

And it was with that success, and Murray Wells' growing profile, that the trouble started.

It turns out the major high street opticians don't like it when twenty-five-year-olds start stealing millions of pounds of their business, especially when £1 million turnover for Jamie represents a loss of sales of many times that for his traditional rivals.

Alarmed by Jamie's success, the General Optical Council,† under

----

* The company is projecting turnover to increase to £10 million by the end of 2008.
† There's a General Optical Council – it's the quango that regulates the optometry industry; aren't you glad you now know that?

pressure from Boots, Specsavers, Dolland & Aitchison and Vision Express, decided to consider whether selling prescription glasses online could be 'harmful' to customers. The chairman of the committee holding the debate? Brian Carroll, a consultant for Boots Opticians.

Reading from the top then ...

C

ON

FLI

CTOF

INTEREST

Murray Wells is understandably a little concerned by his rivals' tactics. Until the GOC makes a ruling, the company can't raise any more venture capital money or consider a flotation to raise any more cash. The very survival of his business rests on it. And – surprise – the GOC is taking its sweet time. Jamie even tried to get himself elected on to the committee himself, hoping it might push things through. But the managing director of Specsavers stepped in and nominated his own candidate, encouraging his staff to support his choice, against Murray Wells. Checkmate.

The Specsavers connection is particularly ironic given the brilliant story that Sam Lewis had told when he came back from attending (don't ask) a lunch hosted by the Worshipful Company of Spectacle Makers. Imagine the masons in verifocals.

Sam had been invited to go along to the lunch by a friend whose father had been a high-up figure in the organisation, on the strict instructions that he behave himself and not upset any of the old men in attendance. Which, of course, was like asking a bull not to do anything to upset a red rag. Sam and I had been out at a party the night before so, of course, with the lunch starting at noon, he rolled up still drunk and immediately laid into a bottle of red wine. Soon the other members began to file into the dining room and the sight was one that would disturb even a sober mind: a line of elderly men, all wearing what appeared to be brass gongs around their necks filed in and took their seats. Then one stood and announced the arrival of the most senior member of the company. A slow hand clap began to build, louder and louder, as the entire room rose to its feet. Sam stood up, managing to join in the clapping while still clutching his wine. Clap, clap, clap, louder and louder, until finally the grand master appeared, also wearing a large brass gong, his arrival signalling that the dinner could begin. Jamie Murray Wells had the distinction of being unofficially banned from attending these lunches and Sam's friend had pleaded with him not to mention Jamie or Glasses Direct.

'So what do you make of Glasses Direct?' Sam asked, turning to one of the old men sitting at his table, a senior manager at one of the big optical chains. Sam's face was a mask of innocence.

The manager's face darkened. 'Jamie Murray Wells? A terrible business. Terrible. Just terrible.'

He continued.

'After all, we've *only just recovered from the trauma of Specsavers*.'

So Jamie could be forgiven if he had stood up that night at Mahiki and offered the advice: 'Choose an industry that isn't populated by protectionist old wankers who fear and loathe the Internet – and change in general.' But instead he gave something more practical, learned from his company's recent ill-fated celebrity ad campaign.

'When choosing a spokesmodel to promote your glasses brand, try to choose a celebrity who actually wears glasses, rather than paying an absolute bloody fortune for Nancy Sorrell ... who doesn't.'

Apparently, on comparing the fee paid to Sorrell – who is famous for little more than being Vic Reeves' wife and once appearing on *I'm A Celebrity Get Me Out Of Here* – with the number of extra glasses sold as a result of her advertising campaign, Glasses Direct found that each extra pair had cost them more than £400 in promotional costs.*

Some you win.

---

* Murray Wells' advice evidently fell on deaf ears. Nancy Sorrell was recently revealed to be the new face of Pampers despite, as far as I can tell, not wearing nappies.

11.3

Bringing to an end the formal part of the evening, Robert took back the microphone and announced that he wanted to make a prediction. More of a bet, really, concerning not MySpace or Bebo but the third major social network ...

Facebook.

Facebook was founded in 2004, a year after MySpace, by Mark Zuckerberg, a student at Harvard. After arriving at Harvard, and keen to make new friends, Zuckerberg had become frustrated that the Ivy League university offered no searchable album – or face book – of fellow students. It seemed to Zuckerberg that such an album would be a great way to get to know his fellow students and also to put a name to the many new faces he met wandering around campus. So, at first on his own and then with help from friends, he decided to build one, calling it The Face Book.

The site was an immediate success and by the end of The Face Book's first month of existence more than half of the Harvard undergrad population had signed up. Word soon spread to other Ivy League schools and, by popular demand, the service quickly expanded to cover Stanford and Yale. By April 2004 there were face books for the entire Ivy League.

Buoyed by this rapid growth, and seeing huge potential in The Face Book as a business, Zuckerberg and his friend Dustin Moskovitz quit university at the end of the academic year and moved to Palo Alto, California, to develop the service properly. They quickly closed a round of angel funding with $500k from Peter Thiel, who had previously co-founded the online payment site Paypal. By December, less than a year after The Face Book's launch, the service had over a million users. As the number of users grew, so did the features offered by The Face Book – or just plain Facebook as it was renamed in 2005. Students could send each other messages, organise their social lives and generally keep tabs on what each other was getting up to during their college days.

At the end of 2005, Facebook boasted sites for students in over two thousand colleges and more than 25,000 high schools throughout the US, Canada, Australia, New Zealand, and the UK and

Ireland. With investment money pouring in, including a further $12.8 million in venture capital from VC giants Accel Partners, analysts were suggesting a valuation of up to $2 billion for the company, which at that point was still restricted to registered students – those with recognised academic email addresses. Then, on 11 September 2006, Facebook went global. From that date on anyone with an email address – not just students – could register on Facebook. A new open-to-all social network giant was born.

But the question remained: how much was Facebook really worth? And that was the subject of Robert's bet at Mahiki.

He had been prompted by a comment made earlier in the evening by George Berkowski, then BT's head of Internet strategy but soon to launch his own start-up – a dating site called Woo Me. Berkowski had seen details of a (rejected) offer by Yahoo! to buy Facebook for $1 billion and argued that Zuckerberg had made a huge mistake by turning it down. Robert disagreed. He was convinced that in a few years Facebook would be worth much, much more than 'just' a billion dollars, so much so that he was prepared to risk some money of his own. Standing at the microphone, Robert laid down his challenge: would Berkowski take his bet – that in four years time Facebook would be worth over $4 billion?

The stake: £1,000.

Berkowski, a tall, brash Australian – every bit a match for Robert's confident swaggering – immediately accepted the bet and the two men shook hands, to cheers from around the room.

The evening ended, as so many Internet People parties do, with 'networking and drinks'. Which is, of course, a euphemism for 'getting very drunk indeed'. My last memory of the night is standing at the bar, sucking on an enormous straw – one of half a dozen such straws – jutting out of a giant wooden treasure chest filled with luminous coloured booze. 'This is great,' I half-slurred to the beautiful Brazilian model whose mouth was clamped around the straw next to mine, and who was holding on to the bar with both hands. 'What's in it?'

'Everything.'

'Okey dokey.'

11.4

Facebook's rapid growth was both a blessing and a curse to Kudocities. Our main selling point, the ability to ask and answer questions about your city, had very little to do with social networking, and so wasn't at all threatened by Zuckerberg's continuing success. However, we were planning to make most of our revenue through things like private messaging, quick ticks, stealth dating and the like – all of them social networking-type features. With Facebook getting huge traction in London and offering far superior social features, not to mention millions more users, it was idiotic for us to try to compete on that front. We decided that when we launched the first proper version of the site we'd focus on our strong points – the questions and answers – and tone down the social features, instead making it a doddle for Kudocities' members to invite each other to become friends on Facebook.

Our decision could hardly have turned out to be more prescient. A couple of weeks later, at an event called 'F8', Facebook announced that it was going to launch a feature that would make it easy for sites like ours to build services (known as 'applications', or 'apps') which could integrate with Facebook. For example, we could build an app that would let users actually submit questions to Kudocities from the comfort of their Facebook profiles. Answers would then appear both on Kudocities and on Facebook and we would each take a share of the advertising revenue. Even better, it was a two-way street, making it easy for us to allow Kudocities users to become Facebook friends with each other and for Facebook users to sign up to Kudocities. This was perfect – and we had the advantage of having already decided to go down that route while other social networks had to scramble to figure out their Facebook strategy from scratch to avoid being left behind.

As a final added bonus, Facebook's announcement had got investors all in a lather. Any company that was looking to raise angel or VC money for the next few months better make sure they have a Facebook app somewhere in their business plan. The next day, back in the office, we took out our working blueprint for Kudocities and added a new section ...

Kudocities: The Facebook App.

The investors would surely be putty in our hands; if only we could find some who would actually talk to us. With money fast running out, and only Duncan and Max left to pitch to, it was time to create a bit more hype ...

12.0

'Relationship status: complicated'

As I stood at the back of the converted church hall, waiting to take my place on stage, I looked down and noticed that a small china cup had appeared in my hand. It was half filled with coffee and I had no idea how it had got there, but I took a huge gulp from it anyway, in the hope that it would be strong enough to wake me up.

I am resolutely not a morning person.

The reason for my exhaustion was partly due to the fact that I'd been having trouble sleeping, with the terrifying reality of our fundraising situation and the prospect of Kudocities launching in a couple of months whirling around my head and keeping me awake into the early hours. But mainly it was due to the fact that, the previous night, I'd been on a second date.

Twenty-six years old, blonde, American, smart and funny, Karen had recently arrived in London to read Middle Eastern Studies. Being new in town she'd signed up to the test version of Fridaycities after seeing a link to the site on the popular London blog Londonist.com. She had created a profile in the hope of making new friends and, as was expected for new members, she had also uploaded a photograph.

I had always had a strict policy when it came to meeting women on the Internet: I didn't do it – wouldn't do it – not ever. No matter how many of my friends told me that times had moved on and that 'all kinds of people find partners online now', it still smacked to high heaven of desperation. I mean, honestly, how mentally unstable does a pretty girl have to be that she can't go out into the real world and find a boyfriend? What part of her personality is so hideously off-putting that she would have to hide behind a computer monitor? And it's just as sad for men – if you don't have the confidence to approach a girl in a bar, or at work, or on the train or anywhere else for that matter, how goofy are you going to be when you have to have an actual first date?

Online dating was for losers.

And then Karen signed up to Fridaycities, created her profile and uploaded her picture. And she was fucking stunning. So much so that I sent Matt, who runs Londonist.com, five hundred Kudos to thank him for directing her to the site. I convinced myself that making contact with Karen wouldn't be Internet dating at all: she hadn't signed up to Fridaycities to find a boyfriend, although she had flagged herself as single in her profile; she just wanted to make some new friends in a new city.

The truth was, if she was half as hot in real life as she was in her profile picture, then she was well worth abandoning my golden rule for. If things went well, I could always tell my friends I'd met her in Starbucks. I decided to drop Karen a line, in my guise as a Fridaycities staffer welcoming a new member, using some of the interests she'd listed on her profile to spark a conversation. This plan would turn out to be more difficult than I'd hoped: when I looked at her profile I found that the only interest she had listed was 'coffee', which struck me as slightly narrow-minded. I told her as much in my email and she sent back a funny reply informing me that actually she liked many, many things other than coffee and if I was really interested I should ask her about them.

I was *really* interested.

As we emailed back and forth it soon became clear that we had lots of things in common: our politics, our sense of humour, even our musical tastes. A few weeks earlier I'd been mocked mercilessly on the site for asking whether any of the other users would be going to see Canadian band Barenaked Ladies, who were due to perform a gig in Hammersmith. Karen revealed that she, too, was a fan of the band and that we should definitely go to see them together when they were next in town.

Before I knew it, it was 4.30 the next morning; we'd been emailing back and forth all night and had then moved on to Instant Messaging. Karen was great, and I was slowly becoming fascinated by her. But I couldn't ask her out. Absolutely not. For two reasons . . .

1) I'd met her online. She could be a total freak. I had my golden rule.

2) She was basically a taller, less Anglicised Savannah.

I mean, who was I trying to kid here? Here was this girl – this blonde, American, funny, smart girl – and I'd decided in less than six hours that I wanted to go out with her. Meanwhile, I was spending all day every day with Savannah – the one-time love of my life – before she went home every evening to her live-in boyfriend and I went home to my empty flat. You don't have to be the sharpest tool in the psychological box to work out what was going on in my head.

But, I told myself, Karen wasn't exactly like Savannah. For a start, she was taller. She liked coffee, while I knew for a fact that Savannah preferred tea. She was from Pittsburgh (Go Steelers!), not California.* She was single. God, the two of them were almost polar opposites. And, anyway, there's nothing wrong with having a type.

But I still didn't know anything about this girl. And I'd still met her on the Internet.

And yet. And yet.

Suddenly my Instant Message software pinged, heralding the arrival of another message from Karen.

Karen (4:45 a.m.): So, you should probably ask me out then.

12.1

Our first date was incredible: exactly like they're supposed to be in the movies. We began with dinner in a Polish restaurant near Knightsbridge before going on to her friend's birthday party near Carnaby Street before ending up at the Roxy, an indie club near Tottenham Court Road where we kissed for the first time to the sound of '99 Red Balloons' by Nena. At just after 2.00 a.m., finding myself briefly alone at the bar, I took the opportunity to send Karl a text message. He was the only one who knew where I was (I'd considered telling Savannah, ostensibly to warn her that I might be

....

* I'm aware one is a city and the other is a state.

late to work the next day, but really in the hope it would make her sickeningly jealous). Of course Karl's first reaction when I'd told him about Karen was to roll his eyes: 'Of course you're going out with her; she's *exactly* like Savannah.' But what did he know? The text I sent from the bar simply read,

'Smitten.'

For our second date, we'd gone to the theatre to see a new comedy show based around the international arms trade. What better way, I reasoned, to appeal to her political side (Middle Eastern Studies!) while also introducing her to the British sense of humour? What I hadn't anticipated was the fact that the show would be one joke after another full of obscure British references – references to members of the shadow cabinet, to long-passed storms in Westminster teacups, even to children's television shows of the early 1980s. I had to spend the entire interval and much of the rest of the night explaining to Karen – at enormous length – why Antonia de Sanchez was funny, or what an emu might be doing on a roof with a TV aerial. But, despite the slightly odd topics of conversation, we had a great time, ending up back at her place which is where, after about an hour's sleep, I'd woken up less than forty minutes before I was supposed to be on the other side of town, speaking on a panel about the future of social networking. And to make things worse, I was supposed to be meeting Savannah there.

Oh God. How the hell was I going to make it in time?

And, more importantly, how was I going to stop grinning long enough to actually speak?

12.2

I crashed through the doors at the back of the hall with minutes to spare, to be met by a far from impressed Savannah.

'Good night?' she asked, raising her eyebrows towards the church roof. After my first date with Karen, I'd decided to come clean with Savannah about what I was doing, figuring it was better coming from me than her reading about it on my Fridaycities profile. I'd expected her reaction to be positive – for months I'd been trying to convince her, subtly and not so subtly, that we should get back together. After all, we were spending most of our time with each other and everyone who saw us – cab drivers, people in bars, people in meetings – assumed we were a couple from the way we flirted and bickered. But every time Savannah had rejected me, saying there was no way she and I would ever get back together, especially now we were working together.

But instead of being pleased she actually seemed hurt: 'So all that stuff about us getting back together was just bullshit was it?' she asked.

I protested: 'But you told me there was no way on earth we'd ever get back together.'

'There isn't.'

'Well, okay then.'

'Okay.'

Back in the church hall I knew she knew I'd come straight from Karen's. It was strange, really; a pathetic part of me wanted her to be horrendously jealous that, after almost two years of me hinting that I wanted us to get back together and being rebuffed every time, I was finally moving on. But an equally pathetic part of me wanted exactly the opposite: for her to think that my dates with Karen didn't mean a damn and that she only had to say the word . . .

I'd seen this kind of behaviour before, of course, and I realised to my horror what I was doing. I was acting like every ex-girlfriend I'd ever complained about – convincing myself that I was falling for someone new just to compensate for not having what I really wanted.

'Yeah, it was okay,' I lied. 'I didn't get home till late and then forgot to set my alarm.'

'Sure.'

'No, really.'

'Drink your coffee. You're on in two minutes. You slut.'

The event was the New Media Knowledge Forum, an annual conference to discuss the hottest trends in new media, which of course this year could only mean one thing: social networking. Throughout the day a whole host of panels and presentations had been scheduled. There was a debate on how the mainstream media should use social networking, featuring representatives from the BBC, Channel 4, the *Guardian*, Yahoo! among others. There was a keynote speech by Nic Brisbourne about how actually to make money out of the social media, all ending with a free-wheeling, wine-fuelled panel on 'future gazing' where the audience would get a chance to grill a selection of the day's speakers on what the future held for social media. The highlight of the day, though, was the early morning keynote speech by Jason McCabe Calacanis, the founder of a new search site called Mahalo.

Calacanis had gained fame – infamy is perhaps a better word – during the first boom as the publisher of the *Silicon Alley Reporter*, a must-read trade publication covering the Manhattan new media community (the so-called Silicon Alley, a sort of homage to northern California's Silicon Valley). Calacanis was a famed party animal and the *Silicon Alley Reporter* would often feature reports from glitzy new media gatherings, leading one New York magazine to describe him as the 'yearbook editor of Silicon High'. Calacanis rode out the dot com boom by selling the *Silicon Alley Reporter* and founding a pure Internet media company called Weblogs, Inc. Much like Nick Denton's Gawker empire, Weblogs, Inc. specialised in publishing ultra-targeted blogs for various niche groups (gadget freaks, film nuts etc . . .) in the hope that advertising dollars would follow closely behind. The difference between Gawker and Weblogs, Inc. was that Gawker chose to roll out a relatively small number of sites and concentrate on building them each into major brands, while Weblogs, Inc., created dozens and dozens of sites – fifty in its first year of operation – in the hope that a few would be successful. Between Calacanis and Denton, similarity had bred contempt and it wasn't long before the two men became mortal foes, with Calacanis poaching blogger Peter Rojas from Gawker's gadget site, Gizmodo, to join his own, Engadget.

One of Calacanis' closest friends was once quoted as saying: 'Jason would never stab you in the back. He might stab you in the face, though.' It's not clear if the friend was speaking meta-phorically: Calacanis holds a black belt in Taekwando.

Watching the situation from this side of the Atlantic, Robert Loch's view on the Calacanis/Denton debate, and their constant sniping at each other, was slightly more to the point: 'I just wish Jason and Nick Denton would stop whining and sleep together so the rest of us can get some peace.'

I had never met Calacanis but knowing that he was a sworn enemy of Angus's old pal Nick meant I was keen to see his keynote. But, sadly, by the time I rushed in, he'd already left the stage. Ah well, I would have to catch up with him at the after-party which, befitting his status as visiting foreign dignitary, was being held in Calacanis' honour back at Adam Street.

But first I had business to attend to . . .

12.3

'The next panel is called "The Upstarts": Does Social Media Have Long Legs to Match its Long Tail?'

The event's organiser, Mike Butcher, took to the stage and introduced our panel. Mike was a famously outspoken dot com journalist and he and I hadn't always seen eye-to-eye. A couple of years earlier we'd had a very public spat after he wrote an article accusing me of using my *Guardian* column for blatant self-promotion (he was absolutely right, of course, but there was no need to draw attention to it). Given our history, I was quite surprised to be invited to take part at all, but since the spat we'd run into each other a couple of times and had made up. He'd (sort of) taken back some of his nastier comments and I'd called him a wanker. All was well again.

His introduction continued as I took my seat behind a long table containing a row of microphones and lots of little bottles of water. I poured the contents of one into a glass and drained it in one gulp. God, I was exhausted.

'The panel will talk about whether or not the entities being created at the moment – sites like Trustedplaces.com* and Fridaycities, whatever Fridaycities is . . .'

He couldn't resist. Wanker.

Aside from Mike, the only person on the panel I'd met before

---

* Another local review site, and a competitor to WeLoveLocal.com

was Walid Al Saqqaf, the Parisian co-founder of Trusted Places. Although, like WeLoveLocal, Trusted Places was technically a competitor, we'd decided to restrict our competitive urges to regular Mojito-fuelled games of table football in Walid's favourite French bar, Café Kick. Walid would beat me to a pulp every time. It was embarrassing, but I was honing my skills and one day I'd beat him. Or at least he'd surrender – he was French, after all. The other panellists included Phil Wilkinson whose site, Crowdstorm, aimed to bring people together to share information and reviews about products they want to buy either online or on the high street. Next to him were the Internet consultant Jemima Gibbons and Justin Davies from Buddy Ping, which was a mobile social network for people on the move. I immediately thought back to our mobile-obsessed VC; maybe I should introduce him to Justin.

With all the panellists introduced, Mike took a deep breath and asked his first question, directed at Walid.

'Walid, you've recently raised money. How much was that?'

It's *always* the first question.

Walid happily explained how Trusted Places had raised half a million pounds in angel funding (which was true: they had, the bastards), and that they were using it to develop Trusted Places' personalisation features and also to develop a mobile version of the site.

In my head I edited our Word document, adding the line

Kudocities: the mobile version.

Gulping down my second glass of water, I braced for Mike's first question aimed at me. I was sure he'd be unable to resist either pitting Walid and me against each other, or somehow making me defend Fridaycities.

'I have two questions ...'

Or maybe he'd do both.

'First, how do you differ from Trusted Places? Are you basically the same?'

He obviously wanted me to say Fridaycities was far, far better than this two-bit (well-funded) pretender, but I wasn't going to play his game. Instead I took exactly the opposite tack, pouring praise on my friend Walid and explaining how we each offered a different spin on a similar idea to users. In fact, I went on, we expected many users to be members of both Fridaycities and Trusted Places.

Take that, you cocky little git.

But, of course, I couldn't resist adding: 'It's worth pointing out, though, that Fridaycities is about asking about anything at all, not just about restaurants and bars.'

And then came Mike's follow up.

'And how do you react to people who say that there's an element of flash in the pan to all of this social networking business?'

'Oh, that's simple . . .'

Pause.

'I ignore them.'

The audience laughed, and so did the panel. I'd dodged a bullet. But in reality, every single person in the room was, like me, laughing more out of nervousness than anything else. We were all in a constant state of terror about that very question. What if social networking *was* just a flash in the pan? What if, despite the hundreds of millions of people flooding to MySpace and Bebo and Facebook and the gazillion niche social network sites, it was all just a fad – like the hula hoop or Tab Clear? What if, while we were all rewriting our business plans to become social networks, Internet users found some other kind of site to get excited about. None of us had any way of knowing – given that none of us knew anything at all. All we could do was laugh about it – and cross our fingers tightly behind our backs.

One thing that the whole panel could agree on was that local social networks – that is, networks based around the users' physical location – were the future. People were hardwired to be more interested in people on their doorstep than people halfway around the world. And if the Internet really was all about sex, then statistically it's much more likely that you'll be able to have sex with someone in the same town or city as you than halfway across the world. I found all of this hugely comforting; yes, there was still a huge chance that what we were doing would turn out to be a flash in the pan, but at least we'd be one of the brightest flashes. For a few seconds, I felt what I thought was a flash of confidence. It might just have been the coffee finally kicking in.

By the time the floor was opened up to questions, I was surprised at how amicable the proceedings had remained – particularly as several of us on the panel were competitors. All that changed when a stocky American in the audience stood up, not to ask a question but to make an observation:

'I just want to say, as an entrepreneur from the US ...'

Uh-oh, I thought to myself. He sounds like an activist at a TUC conference. 'As a Marxist single father, I just want to say ...'

He went on: 'People in our industry are delusional. Instead of saying "why can't something happen?" we say "why might it happen?" and I think that's an asset.'

Ah, the old 'entrepreneurs should be dreamers first, pessimists last' argument. It was a stereotypically American viewpoint, and apparently we in the UK were letting the side down. He explained.

'You guys need to listen to me. Last night I went to a networking dinner over here and I was surprised and depressed at how quick everyone is to kick each other and be cynical. And the press is so cynical about stuff. I wouldn't want to be an entrepreneur here, because you'd get your ass kicked. I'd want to go to the US.'

Well, fuck off back to the US then, you smug Yankie cunt, I thought, suddenly feeling the same overwhelming urge to defend our national honour that I felt every time Walid put another little plastic baby football past my defender and into the back of the net. How dare he come over here and lecture on being positive?

'Wait a minute ...' I interrupted, incensed. 'I really have to defend British cynicism here. That cynicism is what makes Britain such a wonderful place to live in.'

'Yeah!' The audience – 99 per cent cynical Brits – were with me, too.

But the American was having none of it. 'Yeah, but there are parents who use that attitude towards their kids and they turn out neurotic.'

I really couldn't help myself; he'd left himself wide open.

'I think you'll find we have fewer therapists over here than you do in America.'

Big laugh, even a smattering of applause this time. And then, as the other panellists weighed in, too, I swear I could hear the first swells of 'Land Of Hope And Glory' in the background. Sensing a full-scale diplomatic incident was about to erupt, Mike stepped in to move things along. 'There'll be a fight later on in the car park,' he joked.

At least, I think he was joking.

I felt pretty good about my performance on the panel. I might have damaged the special relationship ever so slightly, but, given that I could barely keep my eyes open, I was pretty damned pleased with myself for putting the lippy little fucker in his place. Hopefully it would get a mention in the press coverage of the event, giving Fridaycities a much-needed publicity boost. What with that and the news that local social networks were the future, I could go home and get some sleep before the party.

With Jason Calacanis in attendance, I had some serious schmoozing to do later. I only hoped he wouldn't hold the fact that I'd bitch-slapped one of his countrymen against me. Nah, he'd probably find it funny – judging by his spat with Nick Denton, Calacanis was as cynical as they came.

Savannah was less than impressed by my new-found national pride.

'You really get off on stuff like that, don't you?'

'What? I was just fighting Britain's corner.'

'No you weren't. You were playing to the gallery and you know it. You're such a bloody child sometimes.'

She was clearly still jealous about my date with Karen. That was the only explanation.

12.4

The after-party began at eight o'clock the following evening at Adam Street, although describing it as a party isn't entirely accurate. Mike had restricted the invitations to just the speakers and panellists and a smattering of other web luminaries. The aim was to give everyone the maximum opportunity to mingle with each other and to meet the guest of honour – which suited me down to the ground. By a total coincidence, Robert was hosting a networking dinner in an adjoining room so I knew the soirée would get a lot more crowded later on. Savannah and I had an hour at most to track down Calacanis, sell him on the idea of Fridaycities and convince him to introduce us to his wealthy Silicon Alley mates so they could invest in us. Hell, if we did a good enough job, maybe he'd invest himself. What was it that idiot American had said at the conference? 'Dream more'? Okey dokey.

But first I had to work out which of the dozen or so people in the room was Jason Calacanis. I cursed myself quietly for missing his keynote speech, but fortunately Angus was on hand to help me out.

'Which one's Calacanis?' I whispered.

'He's around here somewhere,' he said. 'Come on, I'll introduce you. But then you're on your own. Remember: be nice to him; be impressive. He's very important.'

'10-4, chief!'

'Jason, have you met Paul and Savannah from Fridaycities?'

Jason McCabe Calacanis turned round and smiled.

Oh. Shit. Of all the arrogant, stocky Americans, in all the audiences in all the fucking world, why did I have to bitch-slap the important one? Shit, shit, shit. Un-be-shitting-lievable. There was only one grown-up way to deal with a situation like this: suck up like a vacuum cleaner ...

'Hi, Jason, nice to meet you! I just wanted to say I really, really enjoyed your keynote speech yesterday – you made some really interesting points,' I lied, praying that he wouldn't ask me any questions about a keynote speech I hadn't even heard.

'Thanks very much,' he said, 'I think it went pretty well. So, where are you guys from? Fridaycities? What's that?'

Oh thank God, he hadn't remembered me. No, wait a damn minute here! He hadn't remembered me! He hadn't remembered a single word I'd said about Fridaycities or presumably anything else I'd said on the panel. And I know for a fact he *was* in the same room because I'd spent five minutes arguing with him. But not a flicker of recognition.

The bloody smug Yankee cu ... But Angus's words were ringing in my ears. Be nice. Be nice. Be nice.

'Let me buy you a drink. Savannah will tell you all about what we're doing.' He graciously agreed to let me buy him a double whisky – 'Scaatch on the rocks' – and I ran off to the bar, leaving Savannah to begin the pitch.

'Hey, buddy, what can I get you?' asked Andreas, Adam Street's head barman.

'A double Scotch on the rocks for my new friend, a beer for Savannah and I'll take a rum and Coke. Actually make it a double.'

'Tough day?' asked Andreas.

'Ask me again in an hour.'

The main bar at Adam Street is, I swear, one of the wonders of the modern world. Andreas is a walking, talking encyclopaedia of cocktails and the menu is packed with his inventions, including the most recent addition: the Bobby Loch.

Late one evening Robert – who practically lived at Adam Street before he moved into Mr Rong's – had convinced Andreas that, as he spent so much money at the bar, it was only right that he had his own cocktail on the menu. He saw himself like a member of the Rat Pack who would insist that the pianist played their signature song whenever they walked into their favourite bar. Adam Street didn't have a pianist, but it did have Andreas.

The next time Robert came in, he was served the very first Bobby Loch – a variation on the Zombie, but even more potent with at least two extra types of rum thrown in for good measure. To give you an idea of how strong that is, you need to know that the Zombie is one of the strongest cocktails there is. Invented in the 1930s by a restaurateur called Donn Beach, it's served in a tall glass containing fruit juice, various liqueurs and a whole lot of different types of rum. Beach invented it for a friend of his who was about to go to San Francisco on a short business trip. His friend drank three of the things before leaving and on his return complained that the drink had turned him into a zombie for the entire trip. Which is perhaps not surprising, given that it has the same alcoholic strength as seven normal cocktails.

And, incredibly, the Bobby Loch was even more potent than the Zombie. In fact, so potent was it that Robert and I would order them whenever we were with friends who weren't heavy drinkers. He and I had developed a pretty good tolerance for them over time, but even we couldn't drink more than two without the room starting to spin. Three, especially after wine with dinner, and it was Goodnight Vienna.

Having already insulted the guest of honour, the night was starting to look like it might yet turn into a Bobby Loch night. But that would have to wait – I only had about forty-five minutes of schmoozing time left.

I wandered back to Jason and Savannah and, although Jason was talking animatedly, I could tell the schmoozing wasn't exactly going according to plan. Calacanis didn't seem really all that interested in hearing about Fridaycities, but, on the other hand, he was clearly absolutely fascinated by Savannah. In fact, he was busy telling her about his summer house. This, it should be noted, is the man who told the *New York Observer* in 2000: 'I can't tell you how many propositions I get, it's absolutely insane ... My life is surreal. I'm not used to women liking me ... it's depressing to think they like me for my Rolodex, or for what I can do for their dot com.' The article was entitled 'They're Single, Ambitious, Worth Millions, But Can New York Women Download Their Megabyte Egos?'

I caught the tail end of their conversation: 'You really should come over to visit some time. You can stay in my summer house. And of course you can bring your boyfriend. Do you have a boyfriend ... ?' I plonked down his drink and sat on the stool that was between them. It was the only grown-up course of action.

'One double whisky on the rocks,' I smiled sweetly, through gritted teeth. I couldn't really blame him, of course – Savannah was looking particularly hot that evening and, anyway, he was a married man. There was no reason for me to dislike him over some harmless flirting.

'He's a bit ... *much*,' said Savannah as Calacanis disappeared to make a phone call.

'Do you think?' I replied. 'I hadn't noticed.'

'Oh, for God's sake, you can't possibly be jealous.'

'Jealous! Don't be stupid. Why on earth would I be jealous of a multi-millionaire describing his fucking summer house to ...' Before I knew it I was raising my voice.

'To what? Your business partner?' She silenced me with a raised eyebrow. Busted.

'Well, I just think we should be trying a bit harder to network.'

'Actually, I've got his business card and I told him I'd send over some information about Fridaycities.'

'Well ... uh ... that's good ...'

One Bobby Loch, please, Andreas.

Not long after, Robert's dinner spilt out into the main bar. Suddenly the room was packed. It had been one of the better attended Internet People dining events and I recognised at least a couple of the angel investors and VCs who had suddenly appeared. At a stroke, the combined net worth of the room had increased considerably, which could only mean one thing – we were about to witness a subtle, but definite, dick-swinging competition.

'Who wants a drink?' shouted Calacanis over the hubbub. 'My round. Paul?'

I ordered a dark rum on the rocks; Savannah the same, but with Coke.

'Are you sure you don't want a man's drink, Paul?'

Oh yes, I thought, rum, the drink of choice for Hunter S. Thompson, Ernest Hemingway, pirates ... and girls.

'Double Scaatches for everyone,' he shouted, to no one in particular. 'Hey, Paul, you don't mind getting them in do you?' He threw his Amex card across the table at me; it landed on my lap.

Be nice. Be nice.

'Sure, no problem,' I replied, hissing under my breath at Savannah, who was smirking away: 'You're really enjoying this aren't you?'

'I don't know what you mean.'

Evidently revenge for my second date with Karen was a dish best served on the rocks. I scooped up the red Amex and stomped over to the bar. 'Fifteen double whiskies,' I said, before suddenly realising what I was holding in my hand. A multi-millionaire's Amex card. How often does that happen? For a glorious moment, an image flitted across my mind: a press release, headed: 'Fridaycities secures first round funding from Jason Calacanis' credit card:

City-based social networking site today announced the closure of its angel round, with an undisclosed six-figure investment from Jason Cal-acanis' American Express card. The deal was announced to industry journalists today, and will be announced to Calacanis in about thirty days.

Heh. But, no, that would be slightly too much revenge for some harmless flirting and a bit of macho grandstanding. Instead I shouted back over to Andreas who was lining up the whiskies. 'Actually, can you stick a couple of rum and Cokes on that order as well and two – no – make it four Bobby Lochs? Just leave them in the bottle for now – I'll get them later when we've finished these.' The least the cheeky fucker could do was pay for Savannah's and my drinks for the rest of my night.

Later on, after Calacanis had left to go back to his hotel, Angus asked me how the networking had gone. I rolled my eyes. 'He's a dick.'

'Really? I thought he seemed decent enough. Why do you say that?'

I explained about the flirting, which carried on even after I'd told him Savannah and I had once been a couple (at which point, incidentally, he'd smirked at Savannah and expressed surprise that she'd dated below her league. Which may or may not be a fair point); then there was the stunt with the drink; and just the fucking arrogance of the man.

'So, you don't like him because he does exactly the same kind of things as you do, but with fifteen million times better credit?'

Yeah, that was about the size of it.

But at least the free drinks took some of the sting out of that particular unpalatable truth.

12.5

My encounter with Jason Calacanis gave me good reason to stop and take another look around at where my life had taken me, or perhaps where I'd taken my life. I'd had my first book published at twenty, been a 'latter-day Jonathan Swift' at twenty-two, a *Guardian* columnist at twenty-three, the Managing Director of a book pub-lishing house at twenty-five, and now ... and now ... having given it all up in search of YouTube-founder levels of fame and fortune I was ... essentially nowhere. Speaking on panels at the pleasure of former adversaries, dating a girl I wasn't in love with and in love with a girl I wasn't dating and spending all my time schmoozing and pretending to like people in the hope they'd give me some money. I couldn't have been more depressed at what I saw in the mirror of my career – I was succeeding backwards.

I had spent the last two years trying to be a big-shot business person and it had so far come to nothing. Jesus, I couldn't even get arrested in this town.

Things couldn't be any more depressing.

And then I got arrested in this town.

13.0

'Banged up'

This couldn't be happening to me.

It was two o'clock in the afternoon and I was still wearing the same clothes I'd put on the day before. All except my belt and my shoes. I was in agony having spent seven hours lying on my back on a thin rubber mattress, laid on top of a concrete shelf. I didn't even have a blanket so I was also freezing cold. Above me on the ceiling were the stencilled words: 'Have information about a crime or people involved in criminal activity? Speak to us in confidence and you could reduce your sentence.' I wondered whether, if I told them that a friend of mine at secondary school had once stolen a copy of *Schindler's List* from WH Smith in Dartford, they'd at least give me something to keep me warm.

As anyone who knows me will testify, there are many – many – occasions on which I should have been arrested. Occasions on which my being bundled into the back of a Black Maria would be entirely justifiable, if not on grounds of public safety, certainly those of my own. But this really wasn't one of them.

It was totally and utterly ludicrous. I hadn't even been drunk: it even said so on my arrest record ... 'Showed no signs of drunkenness. Pupils not dilated, speech not slurred.' There it was in black and white. Neither drunk nor disorderly. And yet here I was, very much under arrest. Locked in a tiny concrete box, where I'd spent the previous night, the entire morning and, now, much of the afternoon.

It was all Savannah's fault, of course. For months after launching the pilot version of Fridaycities, she had been suggesting that we organise a semi-formal 'meet up' for the users who had been helping us test the site. A few beers in a pub to get to know our punters and then perhaps on to a club, depending on how terrifying they turned out to be in person. Now, with Kudocities in the planning stage, time was running out before we threw the doors open to the masses, so she'd chosen a pub, put an open invitation on the events section of the site and the first Fridaycities London 'meet up' had been confirmed.

The evening was a huge success – the users turned out to be a pretty normal bunch, all told; even the nutcases. There was a UK Independence Party supporter called 'devilskitchen' (they all insisted on using their online identities as that was the only way most of them knew each other) – we'd had a heated debate about whether UKIP was a joke party with a joke of a leader who could only communicate through shouting (yes) or whether it was a legit-imate force of political opposition (no). Then there was 'Brave-NewMalden' and 'Mamfer' and 'MonkeysAhoy!' and 'Pottytime' and a couple of dozen others – all of them great fun, and big fans of Fridaycities.

It was a long night, and by 2.00 a.m., buoyed by the success of the evening, Savannah and I had ended up, along with a five or six of the more hardy users, partying away in a nightclub off a back-street near Oxford Circus. I was rather hoping the fun wouldn't end but Savannah, being far more sensible than me, decided it was time to call it a night. She came over and shouted into my ear, over the deafening music, that she was going to get the night bus home.

Now, I am nothing if not a gentleman. Particularly at 2.00 a.m., after a pub crawl, and for reasons somewhere between chivalry and a faint hope that she'd be so grateful that she'd realise I was the only man for her and would immediately decide to go out with me again, I insisted that she would under no circumstances get the night bus. Instead I would pay for her to get a proper black cab home.

You hear such terrible stories, don't you? As my mum would say.

The only slight snag was that I didn't actually have any cash left, just the company debit card that I'd been using to ply the users with drink, and my own credit card. No problem, I thought, and I forced the company card into Savannah's hand along with my pin number that I had scrawled on a piece of paper. She protested that there were better uses for the card – getting the users drunk so they'd say nice things about the site for one – but I wouldn't take no for an answer. Very reluctantly, and reminding me sternly that I wasn't responsible for her safety any more, Savannah took the card and left. I later found out she took the night bus anyway, empowered woman that she is. She's so cute when she's empowered.

Two hours later – the specifics are a little hazy by this point – and I'm in the back of a black cab parked outside my house, being yelled at by a cab driver. And I do mean yelled at.

13.1

'WHAT DO YOU MEAN YOU DON'T HAVE ANOTHER FUCKING CARD?'

I suddenly snapped sober. After walking up and down Tottenham Court Road for the best part of an hour on leaving the club, I'd managed to find a cab that accepted credit cards. It was only at the end of the thirty-minute journey home that I realised my credit card – the only one I had – had expired the previous week. And the bank hadn't sent me a replacement.

Just my luck, I thought. This is what happens when you don't open envelopes from the bank.

'Look, I'm really sorry, mate,' I pleaded as he opened the little plastic window separating him and me – presumably in case I'd been unable to hear how loud he was yelling with it closed. 'I've got my wallet here with a business card in it – my house is here, right here. If you phone me tomorrow, mate, I'll make sure you get paid. It was a genuine mistake, mate.'

Apparently I thought that by calling him mate, repeatedly, I would in some way endear myself to him. To make doubly sure, I'd also adopted a fake cockney accent that was even worse than the one used by Dick Van Dyke in *Mary Poppins*.

No dice.

'I DON'T FUCKING WANT YOUR BUSINESS CARD; WHAT FUCKING USE IS A BUSINESS CARD? I CAN'T FEED MY KIDS WITH A BUSINESS CARD ...'

He was right, of course, but was also misunderstanding the

subtleties of my business card plan. I wasn't suggesting that he should take the card and attempt to feed it to his young, but rather that he should use it to contact me the following day to arrange payment. Payment that he could then use to buy a KFC Bargain Bucket or whatever it was that idiot cab drivers feed to their children. I tried again, more slowly this time, even going to the effort of showing him how the name on the business card matched the name on the credit card I'd given him moments ago. I was clearly who I said I was – we could easily resolve this if he'd just wait until the next day.

'ARE YOU FICK OR SOMETHING, MATE? I NEED TO BE PAID, OR YOU'RE NOT GETTING OUT OF THE CAB.'

It was a stalemate, and no mistake. Getting desperate now – and wanting nothing more than to get into my house and go to bed, I made what was in hindsight quite a facile suggestion.

'Well, if you take me back to my friends in town, I'm sure one of them will lend me the money.'

'I'M NOT TAKING YOU ALL THE WAY BACK INTO TOWN. IF YOU WON'T PAY, THEN THE ONLY PLACE WE'RE GOING IS THE POLICE STATION.'

'It's not that I *won't* pay ... I ...'

This was getting ludicrous but, actually, thinking about it, his police idea wasn't so bad. At least I would be able to explain the situation to someone who wasn't shouting and they could ensure I paid up the next day.

'Okay,' I said, finally, 'let's do that.'

'DO WHAT?'

'Let's go to the police station.'

'SUIT YOURSELF, MATE.'

And off we went.

On arrival at the police station, the desk sergeant came up with a foolproof way to verify I was who I said I was. If I could give him the number of someone who he could phone to confirm my identity and my address, then he would make a note of those details and ensure I sent the cab driver the money the next day. If I didn't, I'd be committing fraud and would go to jail. Which I didn't want to do.

It was a sound plan – with only one snag. Who the hell could I phone from a police station at 4.00 a.m. who:

(a) wasn't one of my parents. That would be hideous

(b) wasn't a friend who would immediately tell all of my other friends, thus condemning me to a lifetime of ribbing about my 'criminal record'

(c) wouldn't ignore a phone call from a strange police station phone number at four in the morning

... ?

There really was only one person who fitted the bill. Savannah.

'You can phone my friend Savannah. She'll confirm I'm me. Her number is 07 . . .'

The desk sergeant started to dial. The cab driver glared at me, still convinced I was pulling a fast one.

Then the sergeant put the phone down and sighed loudly. What the hell was going on?

'That number's no good,' he said, sternly.

'What do you mean no good?!'

'I mean it's not a valid number.'

'Look, try it again, please – 07 . . .'

He tried again. Still nothing.

Oh God, what the hell was going on? Where was Savannah? And why wasn't her phone working? She was my only hope. Things were suddenly not good at all.

'I swear that's the right number – it's the only phone number I know off the top of my head. If I was making it up, I'd hardly be able to give you exactly the same number twice, would I?'

'Be quiet. Sit down. I've tried it twice.'

'Oh don't be so stupid,' I said, to the police officer, stupidly. 'You've got my details, I've given you my friend's phone number. Fuck's sake, I haven't even committed a proper crime. Tell you what, why don't you call the number on the business card I've given you? The mobile phone in my pocket will ring. Then you'll know that's my business card – with my office address on it – and I can go home to bed and sort this out tomorrow.'

Given that (to the best of my knowledge) I was the only one of the three of us who had been drinking that night, it still amazes me that I was the only one who saw the crystal-clear logic in that solution.

'You can't verify your own identity, sir.'

'Well, I seem to be doing a better job than you are, officer.'

Big mistake.

'Just sit down.'

Meekly, miles from home and absolutely shattered, I sat down.

An hour – a pointless hour – passed.

5.30 a.m.

I tried one last time to be reasonable: 'Look, this is stupid. It was an honest mistake. I've done all I can do this morning. You've got my card and my details. Are you going to arrest me for something or can I just go and come back tomorrow?'

The desk sergeant looked up from his forms and sighed.

'You are currently being detained.'

'What does that mean?'

'It means you're being detained.'

He looked at me like I was a simpleton. It was a simple enough concept, and yet one I'd shown myself unable to grasp – being detained meant I was being detained. Duh.

'So what happens if I try to leave?'

'You can't.'

'So, I have been arrested then?'

'No, you're being detained.'

And on and on and on we went, back and forth. I literally had no idea what he was planning to do. And that's when the horrible realisation hit me: neither did he. He was just waiting out the clock. In another hour or so the day shift would start. He'd go home to bed and I'd be someone else's problem.

'Well, if you're not going to arrest me or tell me what you mean by "you're being detained" then I'm going to leave.' I felt a surge of rebellion. I knew my rights.* And I was taking them home with me, to bed.

'I wouldn't recommend that, sir.'

'Because I'm being detained.'

....

* I had no idea what my rights were.

225

'Because you're being detained.'

'But you won't tell me what that means.'

'It means you're being detained.'

'Oh for goodness' sake.'

I stood up, calmly, and took a step towards the door. You have never seen someone get out from behind a desk quicker. I hadn't made it more than four steps before the desk sergeant was in front of me, slapping on a pair of handcuffs.

'I'm now arresting you for making off without payment. You do not have to say anything . . .'

13.2

There then followed the most boring experience of my life, an experience I can relive at any time in the comfort of my own home – because from the moment they slapped on the handcuffs, I have a word-for-word transcript of everything that happened. It's all written in neat block capitals and photocopied from a custody record, beginning with the fact that I wasn't drunk. Which is handy because no one would believe that when I told them.

Highlights include:

– my first ride in the back of a police van, locked inside a metal cage. A useful tip if you find yourself in a similar situation: they really hate it if you mess with the handcuffs. Twirling them round and round your wrists, say. Apparently some people deliberately move their wrists around like that and then claim the resulting marks were the result of police brutality. 'He's messing with the handcuffs, Sarge,' said one of the policemen who had come to pick me up. 'Stop messing with the handcuffs,' his colleague warned me. Or what? I thought. You'll take them off me?

– the inside of a second police station. This one in Peckham. Another long hour passes as I sit, waiting to be checked in.

– having my photograph and fingerprints taken. I asked if I could pull a funny face for the photos. I was told I could. I did. There's a famous mugshot from when a very young Bill Gates was arrested in New Mexico for speeding in 1977. The fact that he simply smiled for the camera always struck me as a missed opportunity; even a lack of ambition. If there was a chance you'd become rich and famous and that some journalist would dig out your old police records, then you wanted your mugshot to at least look amusing. Mine will definitely add a bit of light relief to my appearance on *This Is Your Life*.

– a DNA swab. This I refused. There was no way on earth I was going on a DNA database with all the rapists and murderers. For what? For an expired credit card? At this point I learned something I didn't know before: you're not allowed to refuse to give DNA. Fingerprints you can refuse, but not DNA. And even if you're acquitted or released without charge, they got to keep the DNA. For ever. Even worse, I was told by the very stern custody sergeant that if I refused to give a mouth swab voluntarily they'd have to put on special gloves and it would be more difficult and uncomfortable for me. And they'd assume I had something to hide. Just for shits and giggles I made them put on the special gloves before reluctantly allowing them to take the swab. They looked just like ordinary gloves to me

– just before being bundled off to my cell, I noticed a sign that said one of the cells was closed due to 'ligature points'. I asked whether I could have that cell as it provided the only possible escape from the tedium of the arrest process.

Before going to the cell, I was asked, like in the films, if I'd like to make my one phone call. Yes, I bloody well would. I dialled Savannah. She had some 'splainin' to do.

It was at that exact moment – as I dialled the number and heard the 'number not in service' tone – that I realised what had happened and why they'd thought I'd given a fake number for Savannah. You see, Savannah – the only person who could have prevented me from being arrested – had had her phone stolen from outside a restaurant two nights earlier. This fact I had known. I'd know it because it was me who had called up the phone company on her behalf to have it cancelled. This fact I'd forgotten.

'This number is not in service. Beep-beep-beeb.'

Until that exact moment.

I explained everything to the custody sergeant – the stolen

phone, the fact that I'd totally forgotten about it but that it was easy to solve: if he would just give me my mobile back and let me make another call, I could swallow my pride and call a different friend.

But he refused. I'd had my chance to make a phone call and I'd blown it. And with that it was off to the cells, where, after sleeping through breakfast and lunch, I'd woken up, starving hungry and freezing cold, several hours later.

13.3

Lying on that thin rubber mattress, staring at the ceiling, I'd had plenty of time to think. With no interruptions, no ringing mobile, no choice but just to lie and think – about what I'd achieved, and about where my life was heading. And what I saw made me depressed. Three years earlier I'd been bringing in a few hundred pounds a month, if I was lucky; I had little or no prospect of striking it rich or ending up on the front pages of the papers (unless it was because I'd written the article) – but I was happier than I'd ever been. I was getting paid for something I loved doing; I was picking my hours and I didn't have to answer to anyone.

A year later, at The Friday Project, I was earning a lot more money, and my name was appearing semi-regularly somewhere towards the back of the papers and there was a moderate chance that I could end up striking it moderately rich. But I was actually less happy; I'd had to force myself into an office routine, I had to answer to shareholders and I was getting paid to edit other people's words, rather than write my own.

And now what was I doing – apart from languishing in a police station cell? I was trying to make myself ludicrously rich and ridiculously famous; the next Steve Chen or Chad Hurley. And to achieve that I was whoring myself to venture capitalists and the only things I was writing were PowerPoint presentations and business plans. The further up the ladder of 'success' I'd tried to climb, the less happy and content I'd become. In fact, it occurred to me that, were it not for the fact that I got to sit opposite Savannah every day, I'd actually be pretty fucking depressed.

I got up from my freezing 'bed' and pressed the buzzer on the wall. It didn't make a sound. I pressed it again. And again. Nothing. Just silence. I pressed it again, keeping my finger on it for a good thirty seconds.

Nothing. I started banging on the door.

'Hey! Is anyone there? I've been in here for hours!'

Footsteps. Clump, clump, clump. A little metal window in the door was pulled open.

'Can I help you?' asked a gruff sounding pair of eyes on the other side of the door.

'Yes, I hope so. I've been locked in this concrete box for hours. When are you going to let me out?'

'There's a solicitor on the way to see you. She'll be here soon.'

The window snapped shut.

'But no one knows I'm here,' I protested through the door. 'People will be worried.'

But that was the problem. No one *would* be worried. It was the weekend. Anyone trying to get hold of me would just assume I was lying in bed at home, hung-over and ignoring my phone. Hell, they'd be hung-over, too – they probably wouldn't even phone. I could be rotting here until Monday afternoon before anyone even got curious, and even then Savannah would just assume I'd gone round to Karen's house and refuse to call me on principle. I was going to die in this concrete box; a miserable failure, with only a stencilled entreaty to grass up my mates for company. I lay back on my shelf, consigned to my fate.

An hour or so later (I had no way of knowing), the footsteps returned. But this time they were accompanied by a second sound: the clip of high heels. The little metal window opened again.

'Mr Carr?' said a soft sounding, faintly condescending female voice. 'I'm Jacqui – and I'm a legal representative. Would you like to talk to me?' At that point she could have been Jacqui the Jehovah's Witness and I'd still have invited her in for a chat.

13.4

Jacqui's first victory was to convince the custody sergeant to allow me to get my phone back so that I could find the number for the office. I knew that Savannah had planned to head into work that afternoon to post a report about the party on the site. I prayed to God that she would be there when I rang. I dialled the number and it rang. And then it rang some more. And rang. Until, just as tears had started to well up in my eyes ...

* Click *

'Hello?'

'Oh thank God you're there,' I said, trying not to sound too pathetic. It was all I could do not to sob with relief on hearing her voice. After ten hours in a cell. I was pathetic.

'Are you okay?' she said. 'Where are you?'

I told her everything and, to her credit, she gave me all the sympathy I deserved.

'It's not bloody funny,' I said.

But it was, really.

'I'll be right there,' she said. 'Just try not to get yourself into any more trouble before I get there.'

I was finally interviewed at four o'clock by two women police officers. It was exactly like it happens on TV with the big tape machine on the table and people announcing themselves when they enter and leave the room. There was even a good cop and a bad cop, although the bad cop clearly hadn't been doing the job very long as her badness was limited to laughing at what an idiot I'd been to get myself arrested for something so bloody stupid.

'So, you gave one of your cards to your friend without checking that the other was valid?'

'Yes.'

'And then you tried to phone her even though she'd had her phone stolen.'

'Yes.'

'Even though it was you who'd reported it stolen?'

'Yes.'

'And she's on her way now to verify that?'

'Yes. Actually, she's probably been sitting outside for the last hour.'

'Is she a blonde lady? Funny accent. Dutch or something?'

'Yes. That's her.'

'She's very pretty. Your girlfriend is she?'

'Look, is this going to take long?'

In the end, the three of us – me, the good cop and the bad cop – came to an agreement. Assuming Savannah would verify who I was and lend me the thirty quid for the cab, which the police would then forward to the driver, the matter would be closed. No charge, no record, just an innocent mistake and a night in a cell to remind me to be more careful next time.

'*In vino stupitas*,'* I said.

'What?' asked the good cop.

'Nothing. I just want to go home and get some sleep.'

As I sat waiting in the interview room, the good and bad cops went outside to explain to the custody sergeant what we'd agreed, and that they were going to recommend 'NFA' – no further action.

But he had other ideas.

'I dunno,' he said, sucking air in through his teeth. 'He seems like a good candidate for a caution. I think I should ask the CPS whether they want to press charges.'

'What?' said Jacqui.

'What?' I said.

'Sorry,' said the good cop. Apparently no matter what we'd agreed, what the custody sergeant says, goes. And with that I was marched back to my cell. Another hour passed, all the time with Savannah still – presumably – sitting outside, waiting, prettily. And then footsteps again.

'Please tell me it's good news. They're letting me go, right?'

By this stage I'd been locked up for fourteen – maybe fifteen – hours. I had no idea of time. I didn't even know what day it was any more.

Jacqui frowned. 'They're – I can't believe this – they're going to charge you under Section 2 of the Fraud Act.'

....

* Literally: '*I'm a snotty nosed little prick who did Latin at school. Please lock me back in my cell officer, but not before you've given me the hiding I so richly deserve.*'

'You're fucking kidding me.'

Fraud?! I was in the middle of trying to raise money for a new company – money I'd have to be credit- and police-checked before I could get – and now I was being charged with fraud!

Section 2 of the Fraud Act ('fraud by false representation') reads:

'(1) A person is in breach of this section if he —
   (a) dishonestly makes a false representation, and
   (b) intends, by making the representation —
     (i) to make a gain for himself or another, or
     (ii) to cause loss to another or to expose another to a risk of loss.

(2) A representation is false if —
   (a) it is untrue or misleading, and
   (b) the person making it knows that it is, or might be, untrue or misleading.

(3) "Representation" means any representation as to fact or law, including a representation as to the state of mind of —
   (a) the person making the representation, or
   (b) any other person.

(4) A representation may be express or implied.'

Or, to put it another way, if you get into a cab and you *know* that you don't have the money to pay, then you're committing fraud. The fact that I didn't know I didn't have the money and that it was a total accident was something I'd now have to prove in court, in front of a magistrate – or, if I preferred, a jury of my peers. And if I was found guilty, the Fraud Act allowed me to be sent to jail for anything up to ten years.

'What the hell is going on?' I asked Jacqui. 'Why did the custody sergeant ignore what the other two suggested?'

'I have no idea. Did you do anything to annoy him?'

'Well, I did make a joke about hanging myself. And I pulled a funny face in my mugshots. Oh, and I told them they'd have to pry my DNA out of my cold dead cheeks.'

'Yeah, that would probably have been it.'

And with that I was charged, bailed and released to appear in court a month later. I was given back my shoes, my belt, my phone and my wallet and led out of the custody suite. Savannah was sitting outside the station on the front steps, reading a magazine. She looked radiant. I looked like I'd been raped by a hedge.

'Hey,' I said, quietly.

'Hey,' she replied. 'You okay?'

'Not really. I haven't eaten for God knows how long, I slept in a concrete cage last night and most of today – oh, and instead of allowing me to pay them the £30, they're sending me to court on fraud charges. But, God . . . It's good to see you.'

'I wish I could say the same but you look like crap,' she smiled. 'But come on, let's use some of that £30 to go buy you a Happy Meal.'

'Thank you.'

What I really wanted to say was 'I love you'.

14.0

'Running on fumes'

As the summer of 2007 drew to a close and the number of daylight hours began to dwindle, so did the pounds in our bank account. Within the space of three weeks we received invoices from our graphic designer, our web developer and our web-hosting company. Things were, if not desperate, then certainly pathetically, terrifyingly, *unbelievably* desperate.

So desperate in fact that to raise a bit of extra cash we'd bribed Adam Kay – everyone's favourite singing, swearing doctor – to re-form with his old singing partner, Dr Suman Biswas, for two comeback gigs at the New Players Theatre in Charing Cross. Given that their band – the Amateur Transplants – had split shortly after the release of 'London Underground', this had been no easy task. But, as the promoters, we stood to make almost ten grand from the shows, and the spin-off DVD sales. Money that would tide us over for another month or so.

Given that none of us had any experience of putting on a proper show, the gigs went remarkably well, with only half a dozen or so audience members storming out and demanding their money back each night. To be fair, the walkouts had little to do with the content of the shows and a lot to do with the title – it was called *The Black and White Menstrual Show* – and the fact that we'd decided it was best not to vet Adam and Suman's playlist before opening night. As a result, it included a song to the tune of James Blunt's song 'You're Beautiful', which began:

> *My life is brilliant, my name is James*
> *I'm only seven, and that explains*
> *Why I've never had a best friend*
> *Until you came along*

> *But people stop and they look at us*
> *And they say that it's wrong*
> *They say ...*
> *... you're a paedophile*
> *you're a paedophile*
> *they say*
>
> *Your name is Clive, and you're forty-five*
> *But you don't let that come between us*
> *And you make me hold your ...*
>
> *... hand.*

'You're A Paedophile', as the song was called, was followed by another crowd-pleaser, to the tune of Nina Simone's 'My Baby', about the dangers of having children beyond the age of forty-five ...

> *Your baby's got a flattened nose*
> *A widened gap between his toes ...*

The extra income from the shows – the first actual revenue that had come into the company since we launched – would allow the development of the new Kudocities site to continue for the time being, but there was no getting away from the fact that our upcoming meeting with Max and Duncan from WeLoveLocal could be the difference between the company surviving and us losing everything.

14.1

With so much riding on closing our angel round it wouldn't be helpful if too many people found out that a Managing Director of the company was awaiting trial on fraud charges; things like that tend to spook potential investors. So I decided, for the first time in my life, to use what I'd learned in my law degree. I wrote a letter to the Crown Prosecution Service.

The CPS publishes a list of guidelines to help their solicitors determine when a prosecution is in the public interest and, more importantly, when it's not. The idea of the guidelines is to avoid completely pointless cases going to trial just because, say, a custody sergeant is having a bad day. Reading through the guidelines, the fact that they'd decided to push ahead with the trial seemed even more bizarre: mine was a first time 'offence', it had been the result of a mistake, no one had been hurt, and I'd offered to make amends by paying the cab driver.

I wrote a long letter explaining all of this and reiterating that I'd be happy to pay the thirty quid to the cab driver and save the many times more that it would cost the taxpayer to drag me through the courts. It was a very, very long shot – normally submissions to the CPS would be made by a lawyer, but I was damned if I was going to pay legal fees for something so stupid.

I spell-checked the letter – noticing just at the last minute that at one point I'd misspelt fraud as freud* – and then popped it in the post, with a first-class stamp to show I meant business. And then I waited. There were two weeks before my court date.

14.2

The day of our make or break meeting with Duncan and Max Jennings arrived and, as arranged, we met Angus outside the We-LoveLocal offices. When he arrived, he looked – for the first time – as nervous as we did. If these guys didn't want to invest we were out of options and would have to reconsider completely how we were going to fund Kudocities – if it could be funded at all.

On the dot of ten we were buzzed into the building and made our way up the narrow stairs that led to the offices of WeLoveLocal and the brothers' parent company, eMomentum. A staffer welcomed us in and offered us a drink. 'Water, please,' we all said in near-perfect unison. I busied myself setting up the presentation while the others sat and stared nervously around the room, waiting

....

* I'm sure there's a name for that kind of error.

for Max and Duncan to arrive. We were sitting in what seemed to be the company's conference room; yet another stark, white room with very little furniture, just a few bookshelves and cool corporate toys. A mini-fridge hummed away in a corner even though in the opposite one there was a perfectly good fitted kitchen.

There's an unwritten rule, I'm pretty certain, that every successful Internet business must have a mini-fridge in a corner. We'd had one at The Friday Project – even though it remained empty for the entire time I was there as it was too mini to hold even a single upright bottle of beer – and there had been a similar fridge at most of the offices we'd visited. And yet the Fridaycities offices didn't have one. Maybe that's where we were going wrong. I made a mental note to log on to Firebox.com when I got back to the office. Surely, a tiny fridge was the least Michael owed me.

A few minutes later, Max strode in, bringing with him apologies from Duncan who had been caught up at another meeting and wouldn't be able to make it. We all breathed a collective sigh of relief – pitching to one person is always easier than pitching to two – partly for reasons of strength in numbers, but also because, unless the one person is a total despot, it's unlikely they'll make a negative decision there and then. There will be at least one other person they'll need to go away and speak to before saying no, which at least gives you another bite of the cherry.

I fired up my laptop and we began the pitch. With Max we had the distinct advantage that he was the same age as us – or, more specifically, the same age as Savannah and me. This was, of course, totally sickening, but it also boosted our confidence a million times as it was the first time we'd felt like we were discussing the business with a peer, rather than sucking up to a grown-up. It also helped that Max had been a member of Fridaycities since it had been the *London by London* newsletter. He was an actual, *bona fide*, fan of the site and of the business, before we'd even opened our mouths. This was good – very good – and it got even better when he was joined later in the meeting by Dan Bower, WeLoveLocal's technical genius. Turned out Dan, too, was a fan of Fridaycities and was really enthusiastic to hear about our plans for developing the new site.

An extra bonus came when Max said that, while they were weighing up the investment potential of the company, they'd like to buy some advertising space on the site to promote WeLoveLocal. The money they were willing to pay for the space wasn't great – less than £1,000, in fact – but it was a financial commitment, which was more than any other possible angel since Angus had give us. And God knows, at that stage beggars could ill afford to be choosers.

'That was a *great* meeting,' said Savannah as we left, once we were out of earshot of the office. Even Karl appeared for once to have enjoyed the experience of whoring himself for the promise of money. Angus headed back to his proper job and Karl set off to the office to finish off the day's editorial, leaving Savannah and me to consider the morning's events. We headed to a pub around the corner for some lunch.

'I think we're going to be okay, you know,' she said. The meeting had been really positive and, barring some huge objection by Duncan, it really looked like WeLoveLocal might invest.

'Yeah, I think we are,' I agreed.

'Unless you end up in jail. That would probably fuck us a bit.'

'Yeah.'

Jail prospect aside, I did have a good feeling. There was just something about talking to Max that had given me a buzz that the other meetings hadn't. It took me a few days to work out what it was: while all the other potential investors had been very enthusiastic about the business and the site, their enthusiasm centred on the fact that it was a good idea, with a solid business model behind it. That is, it provided a good investment opportunity.

I remembered feeling a similar kind of frustration when Clare and I had raised money for The Friday Project. One afternoon we were invited to the RAC Club* to do a presentation for a group of elderly angel investors. There were about twenty of them – all men, mean age about seventy – sitting around an enormous conference table. Between them they'd been on the boards of a dozen blue-chip companies and they had all heard of the Internet but knew very little about it. All they did know was that it represented an opportunity.

....

* A member's club of the oldest school, where ties were compulsory and undertakers were on speed-dial.

Before beginning our presentation, Clare and I handed around some copies of the books we were publishing so that they could see the kind of thing we did and we watched in fascination as they picked up the books, glanced inside and then closed them almost straight away. One of them summed up the attitude perfectly: 'Okay, we believe you know about books – now tell us about the business.'

Most of the people we'd presented Fridaycities to had felt the same way. Okay, you guys know content – we get that – now tell us about the business. Prior to the WeLoveLocal meeting, only Nic Brisbourne, who took away and read a copy of the *London by London* book we gave him as a gift, had actually given a shit about what Fridaycities was *saying* to visitors. One of the investors we'd met had actually slid the book back across the table without opening it, explaining with no sense of apology: 'Thanks but I really won't read it.' How could he not care what this business – and he'd already said he liked the business and was interested in investing – was saying to the world? Did he really see the journalistic and editorial side of it as just another feature? It was both nutty and phenomenally frustrating given the effort we put into giving Fridaycities a distinct voice: making it informative, entertaining and – and funny, dammit.

But Max hadn't been like that. He was a long-time fan of the content of the site; the questions and answers, the editorial, the *voice*. He read it, he subscribed to the weekly email newsletter; he understood it. Any schmuck can look at a website, or a magazine, or a book, or a movie and see pound signs. But if they don't bother to listen to what it's actually *saying*, how can they possibly know if it's any good?

As expected, Max contacted us a couple of weeks later and told us that Duncan was keen to meet us to talk through some specifics of the business. The meeting, back at their offices, couldn't have gone better, especially when it turned out that a few days before, by a strange coincidence, Karl had published a photo of one of Duncan's friends on the site to illustrate an article he'd written. It was a review of an event that Karl had attended and he'd simply pointed his camera at a group of attendees and taken the picture.

Of all the millions of people in London, he'd accidentally snapped one of our potential investors' friends.

'That's just one of the many personalisation features we're developing,' I responded without missing a beat. 'Eventually we hope to allow you to keep track of where all your friends are through Kudocities.'

14.3

With Max and Duncan now very much on board with the concept of Kudocities, and with a promise that they'd get back to us in a couple of weeks with their answer about investment, Savannah and Karl turned their attentions back to the forthcoming launch of Kudocities – with Savannah focusing on getting the community features right while Karl worked on the editorial. I, on the other hand, turned my attention back to the Crown Prosecution Service and the fact that, with three days to go until my court date, they still hadn't responded to my letter. I decided to phone the enquiries number they gave on their website.

'Hello,' I said, not really sure of the tone to adopt when you're calling the CPS (I opted for posh but apologetic), 'I wonder if you can help me. I'm calling about a letter I sent you about my court appearance.'

'Please hold,' said the voice on the other end.

As I sat on hold, I noted that they didn't have any hold music at the CPS – and found myself scribbling a list in my notepad, in the hope that I might be able to use it as a cheap gag somewhere. The list was entitled 'Top five hold music tracks at the CPS'. It read:

1) Please release me

2) Jailhouse rock

3) He ain't guilty (he's my brother)

4) Addicted to love (/crystal meth)

5) When you say nothing at all (but it may harm your defence if you do not mention when questioned something you later rely on in court).

It was a silly list, and not very funny, but it was the first thing I'd written in almost a year that wasn't a business plan or a pitch document. Finally:

'Hello, can I help you?'

After giving my reference number, my scheduled court date and a whole host of other details I was put through to the CPS lawyer who would be able to tell me whether my letter had done the trick. Or at least she would have done if . . .

'I'm sorry, we don't have any record of a letter from you. When did you send it?'

Panic! 'Um, weeks ago – you should definitely have it. Are you sure? Can you double check?'

'If we'd received anything from you we'd have it on the computer under your reference number. When's your court date again?'

'It's in three days.'

'Oh dear, you're cutting it very fine.'

No kidding.

'Can you fax it over to us again?'

Well, yes, I could if we had a bloody fax machine in the office. Come to think of it, does *anyone* use faxes any more?

'Yes, no problem, what's your number there . . . ?'

Seriously panicking now, I clicked open the file on my laptop and sent another copy of the letter across our office network to the printer, getting ready to dash out in search of a fax. It was almost five o'clock and I knew that even if I could find a newsagent's with a fax service, there was very little chance the CPS would receive it before close of business. That would give them exactly one day to make their decision and one more day to inform the court of their decision if I was going to avoid having to attend. Shit. Shit. Shit.

And then, at that exact moment, as I stood over the printer, willing the damn thing to just print a little bit faster, my mobile rang. It was a withheld number. Maybe it was the CPS phoning to tell me that they've found my letter, I thought. I answered with my posh voice just in case.

It wasn't the CPS but I was glad to have used my posh voice anyway as on the other end of the phone was our bank manager at Lloyds TSB. A couple of weeks earlier, realising that we might possibly need a financing Plan B, I'd decided to ask the bank for a loan under the government's Small Firms Loan Guarantee Scheme (SFLGS). These brilliant loans were designed to help new businesses where the founder(s) didn't have any assets to secure a traditional loan against – people like me, for example, who didn't own their own house and had bugger all other assets. Under the terms of the SFLGS, a high street bank would provide you with a loan, backed by the Department of Trade and Industry. If you defaulted on the loan, the DTI would cover the shortfall to make sure the bank wasn't out of pocket. They weren't easy loans to get, but we'd managed to get one for The Friday Project and I was relatively confident that we satisfied all the criteria (Starting a business? Check. Almost skint? Check. No house? Check). The downside was the sheer volume of paperwork that needed to be completed before we could be assessed for the loan – and the endless meetings with the bank manager to go over that paperwork. The longer the gap between the meetings, the longer it took for everything to be approved, and the more chance we'd run out of cash before the faceless civil servant at the DTI who approves the loans agreed that we should get the money.

'Hi, Paul, it's Douglas from Lloyds TSB here. Do you have time to talk?'

I wedged the phone under my chin and grabbed the letter out of the printer, knocking over a half-empty (definitely half-*empty*) cup of coffee in the process. The coffee ran across the desk and poured into the top drawer where I kept the company cheque book and my spare tie in case I suddenly had to go to an event with a dress code. 'Fuck. FUCK.'

'Sorry? Is this a bad time?'

'Nothing – sorry – it's a bad line, what can I do for you, Douglas?'

'Well, I just wanted to give you the good news that we've got the first lot of paperwork back from head office and there are some forms you need to get filled in so we can move the loan forward.'

'Okay, no problem. When do you want me to come in?'

'How's Friday?'

'Um ... Friday as in this Friday?'

Three days' time.

'That's right. It's just that I'm off on holiday for two weeks on

242

Saturday so we really need to get the forms sorted before then or they'll have to wait until I get back.'

Was it possible that I'd killed an angel in a previous life? Raped a sacred swan? Who up there was doing this to me?

'Yep, Friday will be fine. What time?'

'Twelve thirty? I've got meetings all day apart from then.'

My court appearance was scheduled for 10.30 which, assuming it lasted no longer than half an hour, would give me exactly an hour and a half to get from Tower Bridge Magistrates' Court to the Kingston upon Thames branch of Lloyds TSB. Assuming, of course, that they didn't send me to prison or – a more likely scenario – the case preceding mine didn't run a single minute over time. It was mission impossible.

'Twelve thirty sounds good to me. See you then!'

I ran out of the office and into the street. I had absolutely no idea where I was going to find somewhere with a fax machine. And now, with a £100k loan riding on me not having to spend a morning in court, not to mention being keen to avoid a fraud conviction, it was absolutely vital that the letter made it to the CPS. I knew that within running distance of our office there were at least three newsagents. I decided to start with the nearest one and keep working down the road until I found one, fell down in an exhausted heap or ended up in Clapham, whichever came first.

The first newsagents – no dice.

The second – yes, they had a fax machine – no, it wasn't for public use, the newsagent explained; just for sending their daily newspaper order. Could I use it if I paid them for the cost of the call? No. They'd had fraudsters come in and ask to use their phone to dial premium numbers so they didn't lend their phones any more. I was just about to ask – outraged – whether I looked like a fucking fraudster, and then I remembered what I was asking him to fax. I thanked him for his time.

The third – no, they didn't have a fax machine, but had I tried the pub next door?

I tried the pub next door. Yes! They had a fax in the office! But the barmaid was the only member of staff in the building and she wasn't sure how it worked.

'Pleeease ...' I pleaded. 'It would get me out of a huge jam.' Throwing caution to the wind, I blurted out an explanation of the whole sorry situation, trying my best to end with a kind of little-boy-lost face that I figured a barmaid couldn't possibly resist. I just hoped she didn't hear the word 'fraud' and chuck me out.

She arched an eyebrow. 'So, if I send this fax you could get a hundred grand and you won't have to go to jail?'

'Something like that, yes.'

'Okay, but if I try to send it, you'll need to give me, like, 50p for the cost of the call so my boss doesn't go mad.'

Only 50p? I wondered whether I should warn her about the fraudsters. Probably not the right time.

'Tell you what. If you help me out with this, I'll give you a pound for your boss and I'll buy you a drink as well.'

'Deal. But I can't promise anything. I'm not really sure how it works.'

She disappeared up the 'staff only' staircase, clutching my letter. Five minutes passed. Ten. A line of disgruntled drinkers was slowly building around the bar, craning their necks to see where the service was hiding. Finally, she returned, still clutching my letter and looking utterly traumatised by her run-in with 1970s technology.

'I think it went through okay,' she said.

'Did it give you any kind of confirmation message?' I asked – this was bloody important. 'I mean, did it say 'OK' or 'SENT' or anything?'

'I don't know. It beeped after I dialled the number, then the paper went through. Then it beeped again. I didn't see a message.'

That would have to do. It was well past 5.30 – too late to check with the CPS if they'd received the fax. But I'd find out soon enough whether my last-minute appeal had been successful or whether I was going to the entrepreneurial gallows. In about twenty-four hours to be exact.

In fact, I didn't have to wait that long. I got back to the office, wiped up the spilt coffee and headed home for the night. As I was on my way to the station, my phone rang. Withheld number again – I nearly didn't answer it. Whoever it was could wait.

But I did answer, just in case, and it was the lawyer from the CPS.

'Mr Carr? We spoke earlier – I'm ringing from the CPS. I just wanted to let you know I received your fax just as I was leaving the office and thought I'd better deal with it now as it was so urgent.'

I was stunned. The entire process had been so boring and traumatic that I'd assumed no one in the British justice system was even human, let alone capable of an actual act of kindness.

'Gosh, that's very decent of you. Thank you. And what's your verdict?'

'Well, I've spoken to my colleague here and we agree with your interpretation of the guidelines. It's our view that a prosecution wouldn't be in the public interest.'

'That's great news. Can I ask on what grounds you decided that, exactly? Just out of curiosity.'

'Well, in short, because there's almost no realistic possibility that you would be found guilty. We're sorry it went this far.'

'That's fine,' I lied. She was so very nice about the whole thing and I'm so terribly British in these kinds of circumstances. Locked me in a cell for a day? No problem at all. Decided you were going to prosecute me for fraud even though you'd already told me you were going to drop any charges? Don't mention it. Lose my letter and make me panic right up until the wire? Probably my fault, come to think about it.

'There's just one more thing, Mr Carr. The matter of costs.'

Ah yes, of course. Even if the CPS dropped their charges, I'd still have to pay the costs of getting this far.

'Will it be very much? It's just that I'm a bit skint at the moment,' I explained.

'No, sorry, I meant *your* costs. You're entitled to claim costs incurred for the time you spent dealing with this.'

'Really?'

This was nuts. An hour ago I'd been a criminal awaiting trial for fraud, over a £30 taxi fare. And now, thanks to a sternly worded letter and a helpful barmaid who had more than earned that drink, the tables were well and truly turned. Now the CPS wanted to give *me* money to make up for my lost time – and, hell, I could use it right now. All I had to do was go into the court and collect the forms.

'Er ... no, that's okay, thanks. I think I've had enough of courts for one year. And, anyway, I've just spilt coffee on my court tie.'

'Oh dear. Well, at least you've got Friday morning free to buy a new one now.'

14.4

As a postscript to the episode, a few days later a bulky envelope arrived at the office. Inside was a transcript of my arrest and the two tapes from my interview. Apart from the fact that my DNA would forever be sharing a hard drive with that of Fred West and Jeffrey Archer, all the remaining evidence was mine to do with as I pleased. The bulk of it went straight into the bin but I couldn't resist pinning up the first page of the arrest record behind my desk, and highlighting the words 'showed no signs of drunkenness – pupils not dilated, speech not slurred' with a thick yellow marker. Savannah hadn't believed me before that I'd been sober when I was arrested – but now it was official. Right next to that page I pinned the final page of the transcript of my tape-recorded interview, this time with the very last line highlighted. Apparently my lame '*in vino stupitas*' joke had been lost on whoever had the unfortunate task of transcribing it.

The official record shows me explaining my behaviour as a case of '*in deano jupidas*'.

14.5

With the loan forms filled out, our bank manager off on holiday and DVD sales still providing all of our income, everything was still riding on the decision from WeLoveLocal.com. I was still hugely confident that the answer would be a resounding yes, but as the days ticked past with no answer, Savannah and Karl began to have their doubts: how long did it take to make a decision? Especially considering how enthusiastic they were during the meetings. Partly through ego – how could they have been fans of *London by London* and not want to invest in Fridaycities! – and partly through panic at what we'd do if they weren't interested, I dismissed their doubts, almost out of hand. 'They're just looking over the numbers we gave them – we'll get their answer in a few days, you'll see!'

And so they did see. The answer arrived while I was out of the office interviewing someone who we hoped might become our new chief technical officer, assuming we ever got the funding to pay him. I could feel the weird buzz in the air the moment I walked back into the office. Something big had definitely happened while I'd been out.

'What? What is it,' I asked.

'Something's happened,' said Karl, his face utterly without emotion.

'What? Something good? Or something bad?"

'Just read your email,' said Savannah.

And there it was ...

Hi Guys,

In terms of the investment opportunity discussed at our last meeting, we have taken the decision not to move forward with this. We think the site and concept is excellent and I know the partnership activity is moving forward extremely well.

From an investment point of view there are two things holding us back. The first is that we already have quite a considerable investment in the local space through the welovelocal project. Whilst the sites are certainly very different we feel as though we'd like to get more exposure outside of the local space. The other issue is that a large part of the expansion is based on the model working in a number of international cities.

I appreciate that this is counter-intuitive to the current exercise of raising the funding, however, as an investor we'd have far greater confidence with similar traction in another city too.

I really appreciate you taking the time to prepare the stats I requested and as the business develops and shows traction in other countries we certainly wouldn't rule out getting involved in a later funding round.

On a side note I'm looking forward to paying out lots of Kudos to Fridaycities members for their great reviews.

Thanks
Duncan.

Oh.

I slumped down at my desk.

We couldn't have wished for a nicer, more professional email – straight to the chase, honest, positive, decent. But no matter which way you cut it, it was still the worst possible news. Our angel investment round hadn't so much hit a wall as ploughed into it before bursting into flames and killing everyone inside.

'Fuck.'

I didn't know what else to say.

There was nothing we could say, and there was nothing else we could do that day. We shut down our computers and went home.

'Don't worry,' I said to Savannah as we walked to the station. 'I know we put a lot of faith in Max and Duncan – but WeLoveLocal was always just one possible investor. There are loads more out there. We'll just have to come in tomorrow and decide who to call next.'

'You don't even believe that though, do you?' she asked. 'If there were others we'd have already called them. We're just too early stage for everyone. And yet how can we get traction – FUCKING TRACTION, I HATE THAT FUCKING STUPID WORD – without the money to launch the site? It's just a ridiculous catch-22.'

She was right, of course – about everything. And I was bullshitting; just trying to make her feel better when the truth was I had no idea what to do next, who to call. But I really did believe we'd think of something. We'd have to, otherwise everything we'd achieved up until then – the twenty thousand users, the test site, the rebranded and relaunched Kudocities that was nearing completion – would all be for nothing. We'd be just another fatal crash on the information superhighway.

14.6

I may not have had the first idea what to do about our fundraising woes, but I had at least made one sensible decision that week. I'd been seeing Karen more and more since our first dates and I was spending an increasing amount of time at her house. The only problem was that I had developed the rather unpleasant habit of only turning up very late at night, after spending the entire evening with Savannah, either working late in the office or going to some networking event or other. When Savannah left to go home, I'd head back to Karen's – at whatever the hour – and, saint that she was, she'd let me in and make me something to eat before we'd both crash into bed. The next day I'd disappear back to work and start the cycle again. I was treating her more as a guesthouse than as a girlfriend.

Unsurprisingly, this routine had started to wear a bit thin with Karen who pointed out that I only ever seemed to end up back at her house when I'd been out late with Savannah. And she was right: the intensity of the investment process had brought Savannah and I closer than we'd been for years and I much preferred to spend time with her after work than see anyone else. Of course we'd agreed there was no way that she and I could possibly get back together while we were trying to raise money for Fridaycities – we didn't need any more stress or weirdness – but the truth was that, even so, I didn't want to be with anyone else. I decided to stop acting like a dick and end things with Karen.

The next night, I went around to Karen's house, as promised. She'd made a traditional Polish chicken dish for dinner (much of her family was Polish), and she looked absolutely stunning. It was as if she knew what I was going to say and wanted to present one last sartorial 'fuck you'. Like the scumbag I am, I kissed her – I couldn't help it – and then told her there was something I needed to tell her.

14.7

Karen took things remarkably well, considering the ham-fisted way I broke up with her: telling her that I still had feelings for Savannah and that I couldn't carry on seeing her. She sent me a long email a few days later – her birthday – telling me that she never wanted to see me again, and I could hardly blame her. But what was important was that I wasn't living parallel realities any more – telling Savannah that Karen didn't mean a thing, while telling Karen that Savannah and I were ancient history. It was unfair and mean, but most of all it was fucking exhausting. I'd finally done the right thing. It was over. And in a couple of week's time, Karen was off back home to Pittsburgh for a month. Out of town, out of mind.

'So let me get this straight,' said Sam, as we sipped our beers and compared our lot, 'you've dumped Karen – who was hot as hell, who put up with far more shit than you had any right to expect her to, who *cooked* for you and who for reasons I can't fathom seemed to think you were some kind of a *catch* in order to ... sorry, what exactly?'

'... in order that I don't have to lie to Savannah about it any more.'

'Savannah, who you work with and who has a boyfriend and who doesn't want to go out with you?'

'Yes.'

'Okay.'

And that about summed it up. I had no girlfriend, no money, no idea how we were going to raise money for Fridaycities – but at least I had the satisfaction of knowing I'd done the right thing for once.

Great.

14.8

Following the news that WeLoveLocal didn't want to invest, there was an obvious question we needed to ask ourselves. Did we definitely need to raise angel funding in order to launch Kudocities or could we at least get the site up and running without it?

There was no doubt that with the new site under way and revenue coming in, we'd stand a much better chance of getting other investors to the table. But could we afford to do without angel funding until then? Putting the question was a bit like being shipwrecked and asking whether food and shelter were simply bourgeois affectations. Exactly what choice did we have?

Even with the DVD and the bank loan (Lloyds permitting), we would still be sailing extremely close to the wind and it would put enormous strain on the business and on all of us. We agreed to plough on but also agreed that self-sufficiency would only be a temporary measure and that we'd continue to push hard to find other possible angel investors. It was really the only decision we could make, apart from simply packing up and going home.

I didn't say anything to the others, but at the same time I was asking myself an even bigger question: was I cut out to be an Internet entrepreneur? Even assuming the bank gave us the loan and things turned around, I had to admit I'd been a pretty crap Managing Director. Fridaycities and Kudocities had been running for nearly a year and I'd failed in my most important job: raising money to keep the company alive. I'd learned about PowerPoint and I'd created a decent presentation and I'd produced a blueprint for Kudocities, but without any investment none of that meant a thing. All my insecurities and memories of how much simpler things had been when I was a journalist came flooding back. Savannah and Karl had left for the evening and the office was deserted: I got up from my desk, closed the door and sat down on the floor with my head in my hands and sobbed.

I was exhausted.

15.0

'Denial'

While I was sitting on the dusty office floor, feeling more sorry for myself than I probably had the right to, the wider Internet industry was having a crisis of confidence of its own.

America had been hit by a credit crunch following an over-eagerness by lenders to loan money to what were called 'sub-prime' borrowers. Think Ocean Finance customers in pick-up trucks. Amazingly, many of these 'sub prime' borrowers had defaulted on their loans and the American financial industry had gone into meltdown. It's a pretty solid rule that when America catches bird flu, the rest of the world stops eating Chicken McNuggets and so there were real concerns among financial experts that we might be heading for a global recession.

For Internet investors, this uncertainty had started to affect their own confidence. What if the companies they were investing in were part of a second Internet bubble? And what would happen if a global downturn made that bubble burst?

Pop!

A clear sign of this new level of uncertainty was the number of discussions being held on Internet panels with subjects like 'Bubble 2.0?' and 'Are we heading for another dot bomb?' and 'Do you want to consolidate all of your debts into one manageable monthly payment?' An even clearer sign came when Robert changed the final question at his Internet People networking dinners.

15.1

Robert's Internet People dinners are an opportunity for people in the same sector to get together with their peers to discuss the important issues affecting their industry. Most industries have these kinds of events, to a degree, but entrepreneurs seem disproportionately keen on them. Adam Street alone plays host to at least three industry-leading ones; there's the Mandrake Club, founded by Channel 4 chairman (and former head of Pizza Express) Luke Johnson and The Carphone Warehouse's David Ross; there's the Supper Club, Duncan Cheatle's dinner club for successful entrepreneurs whose businesses turn over at least £1 million a year; and, of course, there's Robert's Internet People dinners, where influential members of the Internet sector gather around a table over a three-course meal and excellent wines to thrash out the future of new media.

Some wag once said that the secret to organising a good networking dinner is to seat each guest between someone they'll want to work with and someone they'll want to sleep with. They clearly had never been to an Internet dinner: the industry remains a sausage fest and, despite Robert's best efforts, it's rare that there's more than one female face among the ten guests at each dinner.

It's the calibre of these guests that makes an Internet People dinner either a roaring success or a total washout. The *beau idéal* is to get a good mix of people, representing different areas of the industry. Too many media types and the topics of conversation tend to focus around whether content or commerce is king and whether advertising or paid subscription is the way forward. Too many tech people and the questions are all centred around whether the latest Facebook or Google feature will make it easier or harder to share data between social network platforms – or whether 'Ruby on Rails'* is a better platform for web development than some other sodding thing. Too many marketing people and after ten minutes you're clutching your bread knife ready to kill everyone in the whole room. (Although, to be fair, you do leave with a bigger penis and a foolproof investment in the Democratic Republic of Congo.)

A few days after we'd made our decision to go it alone without angel funding for the time being, I was invited to attend a dinner with what might just be the perfect storm of attendees. Nic

---

* The programming language that many next generation web sites are built with.

Brisbourne was there, as was Martin Brennan from First Capital (another VC firm). Also, Bebo's Paul Birch; Tom Hughes from Milk Round, a job site for recent graduates; Andy Evans from online ad company Net Communities; and Ien Cheng, a former journalist and now the managing editor of the online version of the *FT*. The female face at the table belonged to Julia Chalet from WeeWorld which, (despite having the *third* most porny name after Cyberbritain and Pleasure Cards, is actually a site where you can create little cartoon representations of yourself – 'Wee Mees' – which can then be used as your online identity or, as it happens, be printed on the back of your Moo Cards). Finally, there was a really drunk guy who claimed to work for a big merchant bank. I'm a great believer in every dinner having its own drunk guy from the start – someone who is absolutely trashed before the wine has even been uncorked. That way no matter how drunk anyone else gets, they can always feel ever so slightly superior when they wake up in a ditch the next morning without their laptop or their shoes. At least they weren't as bad as the drunk guy!

My reason for attending was simple: if anything was going to make me remember why I wanted to be an entrepreneur, it was going to be this dinner, with this crowd.

Every dinner begins the same way, with everyone around the table introducing themselves and suggesting a topic for discussion. The topics are all written in a notepad and worked through one by one, in order. There is then one compulsory question – added by Robert – at the end that has to be answered by all attendees. These questions act as a fascinating bellwether for how the industry is doing.

For the first year and a half of the dinners, the question remained constant: 'In one minute, tell the rest of the group what you believe the future of the Internet will be.' This became something of a running gag as most of the regulars trotted out the same answer every time, to the amusement of the other regulars and the bemusement of newcomers. My own theory was that the Internet would one day become as ubiquitous and unremarkable as electricity. Whereas today we think of businesses being 'Internet businesses' or 'traditional businesses', the future would see the distinction removed. Every business would be an Internet business and every piece of technology, from phones to alarm clocks, would be connected in some way to the huge global network, allowing everyone and everything to talk to the other. Like electricity, everything will in some way be powered by the Internet and we'll only notice it when, for some reason, we're cut off.

It's actually a relatively dull answer, but the fact that I repeated it *every single time* made it a source of rich amusement for my fellow diners, to the extent that whenever Angus overheard anyone talking about something that was going to be 'the future' of anything – he'd say 'just like electricity, Paul', simply to wind me up.

One day, after a year and a half, the question changed to something new: 'In one minute, tell the rest of the room which web services you use every day.' This change reflected the fact that future gazing had – ironically – had its day. The Internet was no longer just a load of exciting possibilities – it was now a load of exciting realities. The future was now (albeit we were still waiting for our hoverboards and self-drying trainers)!

But tonight Robert had a surprise for us all. A new final question. Only the third in two years.

'Going round the table ... "Is the Internet industry about to experience a boom, a crash or will it stay the same?"'

Around the table we had venture capitalists, a former financial journalist, several entrepreneurs and even a drunk banker. If anyone could answer that question, then they were probably sitting in this room. It fell silent as everyone was forced to confront the question that, really, none of them wanted to answer. The drunk banker tried to top up his glass from the empty bottle in front of him and decided that he would answer first. Internet People events, like most similar dinners, are strictly off the record, so how everyone voted is a secret. But the results were split like this. Of the ten people around the table:

– six of us believed things would carry on the way they were for a few months, with few big investments or acquisitions, and then when everyone realised it wasn't a bubble there would be a sharp upward spike

– three of us believed that there would be a dip, and then, after a few months, a spike

– one of us didn't really understand the question, but wanted to make it absolutely clear that he considered us all his best mates.

The confidence in the room was heartening, but perhaps not surprising. I mean, who around that table was going to say, 'I predict that in two months I'll be living in a cardboard box, eating cat food?' That might have been exactly what I was *thinking* but who would be stupid enough to actually to *say* it? These things tend to become self-fulfilling prophesies.

But it was more than just confidence, as one diner explained.

'The thing is we're at a point now – towards the end of 2007 – where lots of companies are going to run out of their first funding round very soon.' He rattled off a list of companies we were all familiar with and whose funding was about to run out, to nods from around the table. 'So what's going to happen then?'

Another diner chipped in. 'They're either going to have to find an exit or they're going to die.'

By exit he meant they'd have to go public or sell to a bigger company. Essentially, the argument was that companies were about to run out of money, therefore they were going to have to go public – leading to a big spike in dot com companies going public or getting sold for millions (or billions), and thus creating a boom. The possibility that, by the same logic, the exact opposite could happen didn't seem to have occurred to any of them. Rather, it had occurred to them but they had all blocked it out. The only way was up.

15.2

Self-confidence is a powerful weapon for the entrepreneur but there's a danger it can turn into denial. Back at the office, I was very aware that we were tiptoeing a fine line between the two. By waiting a bit longer before we paid non-essential invoices and pushing hard for the bank loan we could just about stay in the black, but we were playing it really close to the wire – a fact that I was trying my best to keep from the outside word. If raising money when you *want* it is hard, then raising it when people know you *need* it is impossible.

And there's no denying that the stress was taking its toll on our personal relationships, too. Karl, in particular, had never been a fan of business and had started talking openly about wanting to leave Britain with his girlfriend to sit on a beach and write. Savannah – a full ten years younger than Karl – was more concerned that she had to pay her rent and was sitting on a law degree that could be earning her much more than the meagre sum that Kudocities was paying. But she believed strongly in the business, and had become close to the users, so – despite the odd wobble when someone posted something negative on the site – she was determined to plough on.

I still didn't know how to feel. I was still spending all my social time with winners – entrepreneurs whose businesses were getting bigger and better; who still had angel money in the bank and, if my dining companions had been right, were heading towards this huge liquidity payday. And fame! And fortune! I'd be a fool to walk away from the possibility of joining them, and Savannah was right – there was so much potential in Kudocities. It really was an awesome site.

And yet every night I was heading back to my flat in East Dulwich. Worried about the money my parents and my uncle had put into the business; worried about Savannah and Karl; worried about the company and what I'd do if it didn't make it as far as the relaunch.

On paper I was an Internet entrepreneur like my friends, but in reality the gap between my life and the people I spent my time with was wider than ever.

But whatever insecurities I might have had, none of them excuses the absolutely stupid thing I did next.

15.3

It wasn't my fault, of course. I had arrived home to my empty flat and run myself a deep bath to try to drown everything that was on my mind – just for half an hour while my laptop was busy downloading a day's worth of personal emails that I hadn't had a chance to deal with in the office. Walking over to my desk in the corner of my living room, wrapped in a towel, I noticed an icon I hadn't seen for a long time.

It was a picture of a blonde girl, and next to it the word 'Hey'.

I should have ignored it. I should have checked my email and turned off the computer. I had enough crap to deal with; I really didn't need this.

'Hey,' I replied.

'You never replied to my email.'

'I didn't think you ever wanted to hear from me again.'

'I didn't. Were you in the bath?'

'How did you know that?'

'I know everything. So – I'm off to Pittsburgh tomorrow for a month, but I wanted to see you before I go.'

'Is that a good idea?'

'Probably not.'

'Okay. Shall I come round to yours after work?'

'No, let's go somewhere else. I'm going to be in Holborn: shall we meet there? Seven?'

'Okay.'

I was an absolute fucking idiot. I'd promised Savannah that I wasn't going to see Karen again. Hell, I promised myself. But why not? Why did Savannah care anyway? And why shouldn't I see her one last time? I had missed her.

Karen left for Pittsburgh the next day and I left her house, grabbed a coffee from Starbucks and headed for the office, just in time for a meeting. I scraped in with minutes to spare, meeting Savannah at the door as I did.

'Good night last night?' she asked, with those eyes.

'Yep – bit dull really.'

'Oh, really, I tried to call you about midnight to ask you to bring some stuff for the meeting.'

'Oh, sorry, did you leave a message?'

'No.'

Phew.

'Oh, maybe I was in the shower or something.'

'I tried to call you this morning, too. About an hour and a half ago. I guess you must have already left the house?'

I shrugged.

'I guess.'

I felt as guilty as an adulterous husband. Why the hell didn't I just tell her the truth? 'Yeah – I saw Karen last night, what of it?' But I couldn't. Wouldn't. Not when we had so many more important things to worry about. Or at least, that's what I told myself.

Over the next few weeks, Karen phoned me every night from Pittsburgh. The time difference meaning she would be heading out for dinner just as I was stumbling home after whatever networking event or dinner or booze-up I'd been to that night. Before I knew it, we were making plans – when she got back we'd give things another go, I missed her too (I really did), no – Savannah and I were still just business partners – she wouldn't care . . .

In deano jupidas.

15.4

The email was waiting for me when I arrived in the office.

To: Paul Carr
From: Lloyds TSB

Dear Mr Carr,

Having given full consideration to your request for finance under the Small Firms Loan Guarantee Scheme, it is with regret that I have to advise that the Bank are unable to help you at this time. Unfortunately at this stage the request is too speculative with no proven income stream and you are in principle looking for the Bank to be a Business Angel. I feel that the concept has a lot of merit & I would be very interested in re looking at this proposal three months after launch with the benefit of 3 months 'live' management figures. I wish you the best for launch.

Best regards

Douglas Smith

15.5

'Everything's totally fucked.'

'Oh, come on, it can't be that bad.'

'It's that bad. It's worse than that bad. The bank have turned us down for the loan – the fucking SFLGS loan that is designed for people who can't get bloody loans – Savannah and Karl are working their arses off and I can't even promise them that they'll be able to pay rent until Christmas and the developers are taking their sweet time finishing Kudocities which means either telling them to stop work, or letting them carry on, knowing we can't pay them.'

Sam listened patiently as I gabbled on; listing problem after problem after problem. He finished his pint and stood up to go and get another round – but he'd thought of something to cheer me up . . .

'Still, at least Karen's back in a week . . .'

Thud.

The sound of my head hitting the heavy wooden pub table caused the old man at the table next to us to turn round. 'Don't worry, old chief,' he said, 'at your age I was fighting a war.'

Where do I sign?

15.6

Things were starting to get messy again and I knew that if there was any chance of the Karen situation being resolved, allowing me to focus on bringing Kudocities back from the abyss, then drastic action would be required. I would need to do the grown-up thing: to be honest with both her and Savannah and to make my mind up what the hell it was I wanted. Karen was suspicious about my relationship with Savannah and Savannah claimed not to care about Karen, as long as I was honest about what was going on. This was an easy situation to solve.

Easy, that is, unless I was to get absolutely steaming drunk and decide it would be a good idea to introduce them to each other.

I'm not entirely sure what possessed me to make the call or exactly what I'd said, but I do know that last orders had just been called when Karen walked into the pub that Savannah and I had been drinking in since we'd left the office.

In the sober light of day, Savannah and Karen meeting was never part of my brilliant plan to solve all my personal problems. My brilliant plan was that I'd sit down with them both independently. I'd explain to Savannah that I was really sorry that I'd used Karen to try to make her jealous, and to admit that I'd started seeing her again, but that I didn't know whether it would go anywhere. Be honest. Then I'd explain to Karen that, yes, I still loved Savannah but that she and I weren't getting back together – certainly not now – and that I wanted to give things a try. It was the only adult course of action.

But then evidently I'd decided, after another stressful day in the office and another evening of drinking with Savannah, that I could kill the two birds of my brilliant plan with one stone by inviting Karen to join Savannah and me in the pub, while at least two of us were plastered.

And that's the last thing I remember about the evening.

16.0

'Two girls, one fuck-up'

I woke up the next morning in my own flat. A good sign, I thought. In my own bed. A great sign. I was still wearing my shoes. Not quite so good, but still okay. I even had my phone and my laptop bag with me. Everything was fine.

I remembered, vaguely, speaking to Savannah on the phone the night before when I got back to my flat: I couldn't remember the access code for my front door and she was good at things like that, so I'd called her and she'd helped me get in. Good old Savannah.

It was the weekend so we didn't have to be in work, but I thought I'd better call her anyway to check that I hadn't done anything stupid. I picked up my phone from beside my bed and scrolled to the last calls list to redial her number. But, oddly, Savannah's number wasn't the last number I'd dialled – Karen's was. As was the second to last call. And the third. And the fourth. This was very weird – I didn't remember phoning Karen, but in fact all the last calls I'd made the previous night were to her. I hadn't called Savannah at all. What the hell? I was *sure* I'd spoken to her.

It was at that point that I suddenly started to remember things. Oh God – Karen was at the pub, too. I'd phoned her up and invited her to join us because there was something important I needed to tell her. I was going to sort things out.

Oh Jesus. What the hell had I said?

And even if Karen was at the pub that still didn't explain how I'd spoken to Savannah when I'd only dialled Karen's number.

Unless.

Oh God.

No, it can't be.

With fear in my heart and panic in my fingers, I dialled Savannah's number. An American voice answered.

'Hey.'

'Hey. I'm not sure I want to know the answer to this question but why do you have Savannah's phone? And why did she have yours when I phoned last night?'

'Why don't you ask her yourself? She's right here, making a cup of tea.'

OH. MY. FUCKING. GOD.

16.1

As it turned out, the whole sorting things out with Karen and Savannah like a grown-up thing hadn't gone entirely to plan. Apparently Karen had arrived at the pub to find me with my hand on Savannah's leg, flirting wildly. Quite reasonably, a loud argument had ensued and, in an act of sisterly solidarity, Savannah had taken Karen to one side to calm her down and have a chat. Evidently I'd been quite happy for this to carry on and had headed home, oblivious to the damage I'd done.

With Karen incredibly and understandably upset, Savannah had offered to let her sleep on her couch, but not before they spent half the night comparing notes on what a complete and utter bastard I was – including things I'd told each of them about the other, and places I said I'd been, and where I'd actually been. And now the two of them were having breakfast. This was my worst nightmare.

Savannah came to the phone.

'Well, I guess that probably solves the question of us getting back together, and what I should do about Karen.' Keep it light, I thought.

'Yeah – I think that pretty much nails it,' she replied, with characteristic understatement.

*Click *

16.2

Over the next few days I thought about Karen a lot. She wasn't answering my calls and her face had disappeared from the contacts list on my instant message software. In a way I was glad that, no matter how badly I'd handled things, at least things were definitely over now. I didn't have to make the decision on what to do – it had been made for me. But I still wondered whether Karen was okay; what she was thinking, what she was doing.

I wouldn't have to wait long to find out.

16.3

'HAHAHAHAHAHA!'

The uncontrollable laughter on the other end of the phone belonged to Sam. Seven days had passed since the incident with Karen and Savannah, and I was trying to forget about all my troubles by deep-cleaning my flat.

'What? What *now*?'

'Nothing. Just reading Karen's blog.'

'Karen's *what*?'

'Her blog. Her blog about you. It's really good.'

'Please tell me you're joking.'

'You haven't seen it? Brilliant ... go to ...'

'You had better be kidding me. She wouldn't set up a blog about me, she's not even talking to me.'

'Oh, but she is.'

Click. Click.

Oh Jesus.

And there it was. An entire website dedicated to me – created by Karen and full of details of our relationship, stories about how much of a crap boyfriend I had been in every single way. How her friends had always hated me. How I was a worthless 'douchebag' (her favourite word). But it was worse than that. Much worse.

She'd been recruiting.

Not satisfied with telling her own stories about me, Karen had gone to the effort of tracking down everyone she knew I'd fallen out with in my entire life and encouraged them to add comments to the blog. Ex-girlfriends I'd mentioned casually while we were together, including a girl I'd dated for a couple of weeks before she'd got so clingy my brother took to calling her 'mental Kate' (how can you track someone down using only that information? It was like *CSI: London*). She'd even got in touch with a guy who had written some reviews for a magazine I co-founded years ago and that had folded after three issues over some pretty dramatic 'artistic differences'. He still held me responsible and would occasionally post some malicious nonsense about me on his own blog. But now there they all were, almost everyone I'd ever fallen out with, united at last in their hatred for me. It was the most terrifying thing I'd ever seen in my life. This was more than a Google bomb – this was full-blown character genocide.

Sam couldn't stop laughing – the bastard.

'This is without doubt my new favourite site. I've bookmarked it, and be assured I'm sending the link to everyone we know.'

The *utter* bastard.

I laughed about it, too, of course; it's all I could do. But the truth was it was deeply embarrassing – and hurtful. Which was exactly the point, of course: I'd spent ten years of my life using the Internet for self-publicity and now she was using it against me – embarrassing me like I'd embarrassed her by using my ego and vanity against me.

Now when anyone searched for my name online, among all the stuff I wanted people to see – the Wikipedia page saying that I'd been described as a 'latter-day Jonathan Swift' by the Christian Scientists; five years of Friday Thing archives; the books and articles I'd written – there'd be this extra little nugget. This blog telling the world how I'd broken the heart of a girl who had been nothing but nice to me, just because I wanted to have it all.

17.0

'Taking stock'

When Stooky Bill made his first appearance on TV, and Gutenberg printed his first Bible, and Marconi invented radio – they were all creating the same thing: a new one-way medium. TV, books, radio, recorded music, film – these were all new and interesting ways of broadcasting information in one direction; from the brains of publishers and broadcasters to the ears and eyes of many. The method of distribution was controllable and was controlled.

The Internet changed all that. It allowed someone like me – an arrogant punk who wanted to become famous – to create a website that could be accessed by anyone in the world. And on the back of that website, it allowed him to get book deals, and a job on a newspaper, and to write jokes about terrorist attacks and make a ton of money in the process. He could create his own legend, and no one could stop him.

But the Internet also made him more accountable than ever before for what he did – just like the author reviews on Amazon.com penned by real customers held authors to account, or the feedback ratings on eBay held sellers to account, or millions of blogs held politicians and business leaders and – gasp – even journalists to account.

When Jennifer Ringley started posting every detail of her life online, she had to accept the reality that there would be plenty of people – teenage boys mainly – who would attack her appearance, call her names, even threaten her from behind a veil of anonymity. For every company or politician with an official website there's a disgruntled former employee, or a political opponent with their own site, or their own attack campaign. For every Nicholas Hellen there's a Zoe Margolis with a Google bomb. For every Million Dollar Homepage there's a Russian Mafioso waiting to strike under cover of anonymity. That's the price of freedom. The trade-off of the Internet.

And just as I could create my own legend, so could someone else tell their version of my story, for good or ill. That ten years of carefully managed image could be destroyed with the click of a mouse, by one determined ex-girlfriend with a lot of time on her hands, brought home everything I loved and everything I hated about the Internet.

A few days after Karen's blog appeared, more strange things started to happen. The listings of my books on Amazon started to receive negative reviews, complete with mentions of me spending time in a cell for fraud. My Wikipedia entry that boasted of all the things I'd achieved suddenly sprouted links to Karen's blog. Even a group I'd created on Facebook was spammed with stories about what a rat I was. Mutual friends who had spoken to Karen said that, while she obviously admitted being responsible for the blog, she swore the other attacks had nothing to do with her.

Weirdly, I believed them – she'd taken responsibility for the blog and there would be no point in her lying about the other stuff. More likely someone had stumbled across the blog and decided to help out a damsel in distress. Perhaps it was someone I knew and who I'd upset in the past – the disgruntled reviewer? Another ex-girlfriend? Perhaps it was just some loser who wanted to impress a pretty American girl who had been wronged. I had no idea. That was the beauty of the Internet: nobody knows if you're a dog.

Nobody knows anything.

17.1

Karen's blog made me realise a lot of things: that it was finally time for me to let Savannah get on with her life with a boyfriend who wasn't such a fuck-up; that almost all farces begin with a well-intentioned lie that snowballs and ends up causing chaos and destruction; that in future it's probably not the best idea to give a girlfriend a list of people you've pissed off in the past. But most of all it made me realise the person I'd become over the previous two years.

Twenty-four months ago I'd only had myself to worry about – had Karen's blog appeared back then it would still have been pretty embarrassing but it wouldn't have hurt anybody but me. In fact I'd probably have used it as the subject of a newspaper column or to provide a moral lesson towards the end of a book. But now I was trying to raise money for a company and having something like this showing up on Google under my name risked damaging not just my livelihood, but that of everyone I worked with.

And it wasn't just Karen. I looked back at all of the scrapes I'd got myself into during the preceding few years: the arrest, possible fraud conviction, the Hotel California incident with Google; offending Ricky at Adam Street, bitch-slapping Jason Calacanis, getting drunk at the Nibbies, nearly getting jailed for contempt of court, being named and shamed by the *Evening Standard* – the list went on and on. For a journalist they were all brilliant stories and could provide inspiration for a hundred columns, but for an entrepreneur any one of these events had the potential to come back to bite me on the arse and potentially drag others down with me.

Karen was just the straw that broke the camel's back.

Enough was finally enough.

17.2

December 2007 was exactly a year since I'd left The Friday Project to start Fridaycities. It also marked the five-year anniversary of me moving to London and starting to go out with Maggie. Despite the fact that the two of us found it hilarious that we'd ever fancied each other, we'd remained extremely close friends

Maggie had recently trained to be a life counsellor, and was someone I knew I could phone up whenever I was feeling sorry for myself and needed to be slapped around the head and reminded how positive things really were. But this time I didn't need to phone. She'd seen Karen's site and she invited me round for homemade soup, a DVD and a chat.

Over dinner she asked me how things were going with Kudocities and how I was feeling about Karen. I started giving her just the edited highlights, not really in the mood for any life coaching, no matter how well intentioned. But before I knew it, I was on my feet, pacing backwards and forwards in her kitchen, telling her the whole ridiculous story. All my uncertainties about whether I could cut it as a dot com entrepreneur, how I was worried that Karen's site was going to reflect badly on the company at the worst possible time – fuck it, how bloody miserable I was about everything.

I went on for a good half-hour, barely pausing for breath. Maggie listened in silence, her eyes following me up and down the room. Only when I'd finished did she say anything.

'What I don't understand,' she started, 'is why you ever thought you wanted to be an entrepreneur in the first place.'

'I don't know. I guess I wanted the fame, and maybe the money.'

'But you've just said yourself, the way you live your life makes that impossible. If you had to give it all up: the adventures, the parties, the being your own boss, the working your own hours, the ability to tell that Calacanis guy to stop flirting with your ex-girlfriend and that you'll drink whatever damn drink you want. If becoming a rich and famous Internet mogul meant you had to give all that up, would you do it? And would it make you happy?'

We both knew the answer.

'Well then. Why force yourself to be something you're not? It'll just make you miserable. You're not cut out to be responsible for other people's futures – you're barely able to manage your own. So stop trying. Do what you're good at. If you're meant to be famous and rich you will be, whatever your day job.'

And she was right. It was time to stop trying to be something I knew I couldn't be. Time to leave the entrepreneuring to people like Richard Moross and Michael Smith and Alex Tew and Michael Birch and Angus Bankes and Nic Brisbourne and Mark Zuckerberg and – yes – to Chad Hurley and Stephen Chen. I might envy all of them, in different ways, but I would never – *could* never – be like them.

What I could do, though – and what they would never be able to do – was stand at the back of the room, sipping their imported Spanish beer from their free bars, watching them. And then I could go back to my desk late at night and write about what I'd seen, without worrying how it would affect my share price, or whether it would upset my investors.

17.3

Larry Page is worth nearly $20 billion, making him one of the top thirty richest men in the world. He has a private jet with a king-size bed and a row of hammocks for parties. Alongside Sergey Brin he regularly appears on the cover of newspapers and magazines around the world. And yet every time he stands on a stage or picks up a pen to write, there's someone standing over his shoulder, watching him. Someone whose job it is to make sure he doesn't upset the stock market by saying anything too candid, or by being honest with his peers about the things that interest and excite him.

That's the real life of a rich and famous Internet entrepreneur.

And, Larry, you're welcome to it.

18.0

'The End Game'

Fridaycities Limited moved out of its offices a few days before Christmas 2007. Savannah was the last to leave, locking the door behind her and carrying a plastic box containing the last of the company's files. Karl had already left the company to follow his writer's life, away from the bullshit-ridden realities of business.

The site remained live, but the only new questions posted during December were from long-time users wondering why everything was so quiet, and why there had been so little news about the much-anticipated relaunch. Things were so quiet in fact that one user even created a sweepstake for when Fridaycities.com would vanish for good.

On 27 December 2007, he got his answer. At the stroke of 10.00 p.m. Fridaycities vanished from the Internet forever.

18.1

At 10.01 p.m. anyone typing in the Fridaycities.com web address would be greeted with a 'page not found' error message.

18.2

At 10.05 p.m. on 27 December 2007, a brand new site called Kudo-cities was launched on an unsuspecting world.

With its new bright red logo and bold new design, it was almost unrecognisable from the Fridaycities site it replaced. Even more unrecognisable, though, was the business behind it. Forced to decide between office rent and paying the development team,

Fridaycities Ltd had moved out of its offices and taken up new premises in Savannah's living room.

Using a small amount of additional investment from Angus, it had been Savannah who for most of December had been liaising with the developers to get Kudocities ready for launch; Savannah who had ensured that she had followed up with all the advertisers who had expressed an interest in advertising on Kudocities ahead of the launch. And it had been Savannah who a few moments earlier had been sitting next to the lead developer when he pressed the button to make the site live.

I remained a shareholder in the company – with shares held in trust for my uncle and my parents in exchange for their original seed funding – and Angus remained non-executive chairman. But the new head of the company – the CEO – was Savannah; the one person who hadn't gone into the business to become famous and wealthy; the person who didn't mind swallowing the business bullshit if it got the right result, but who wouldn't suffer fools gladly. The person who just wanted to help city dwellers share information about their city.

Against all odds, Kudocities was alive. Within hours feedback would start coming in from users. It would be, by and large, excellent. A few days later, the first revenues would start to come in and, all being well, the site would soon secure the angel investment it needed to expand globally. If anyone could make it happen, Savannah could.

EPILOGUE

December 2007 and I'm back in the bowels of the Adam Street private members' club in London. Once again a very special group of people is crammed into a private room, supping imported Spanish beer from a free bar.

The value of the companies owned by the people squeezed into this tiny room is anyone's guess. The Internet industry continues to grow steadily but there is a growing level of chatter about what 2008 has in store. Will the industry continue to grow or will there be a second correction? No one is using the word bubble tonight.

I'm standing at the back, again, getting slowly drunk with the event's organiser, Robert Loch. He's in his element: just over a month earlier, Microsoft invested $240 million for a 1.6 per cent stake in Facebook. The deal valued Facebook at around $15 billion. He's won his bet with George Berkowski and will soon be £1,000 richer. He plans to use the money to install a stripper pole at Mr Rong's.

Standing next to us is Michael Smith. Michael is celebrating, too. The Receda Cube was eventually found, buried in woodland a hundred miles north of London, by amateur archaeologist Andy Darley. By the time Mr Darley came to the Mind Candy offices in Battersea to collect his prize money, more than fifty thousand players in ninety-two countries had joined in the search. The success of Perplex City has spurred Michael and Mind Candy to launch their next venture: a site called Moshi Monsters, which combines puzzles and virtual pets. It is already gearing up to be the interactive phenomenon of the 2008.

Alex Tew couldn't make it tonight. Instead he's at home, making arrangements for the Pixelotto prize draw. Standing at a little over $300,000, the prize fund is slightly lower than the two million dollars that Alex was hoping to split between himself and the winner, but sales of pixels have slowed to a crawl and Alex has decided it's time to make the draw, close the site and move on to his next idea. When the draw is eventually made a few weeks later, the winner will be one 'K. Moguche' from Kenya.

For probably the first time in history, someone in Africa will receive an email, sent from the UK, with instructions on how to claim a huge international lottery win.

Meanwhile, 5,370 miles away in San Francisco, Richard Moross is in a business meeting, hoping to convince another social networking site to allow its users to create personalised Moo products. Products that now include stickers, note cards, postcards and greetings cards. Business is good, and it just keeps getting better.

Also doing some international networking, is Ruth 'Mimi' Fowler who has moved to London to buy a house with the proceeds of her book. She'll be off back to New York in January though – to Sixth Avenue to be precise – for a meeting with Alison Benson at Pretty Matches who is taking a very careful first look at her recently completed screenplay.

As always, a microphone is being passed around and we're watching and listening as a succession of young – mostly under forty – men – mostly men – rattle off their CVs and their future plans. Suddenly the microphone is thrust into my hand. I knock back the last of my beer and introduce myself.

'My name's Paul Carr and I'm writing a book about the dot com industry. So, be warned, if things get too messy later and we end up at the Gardening Club, there's a very real chance you'll all be in it.'

Big laugh.

Excellent.

Nothing to see here.

ACKNOWLEDGEMENTS

Before I get into the business of thanks, a quick disclaimer. Everything you've read – or are about to read – in this book is true. More or less. A couple of names (no more than a couple) have been changed at the request of those with reputations more valuable than mine to protect. When faced with either keeping them out of the book or giving them a pseudonym, the decision was a no-brainer. Also, for reasons of space, I've had to leave out a number of people who have been enormously influential on me and my adventures. I hope they'll forgive me.

As far as possible I've relied on the many Moleskine notebooks I've carried with me over the last eight years or so to make sure that events are described exactly as they happened. Emails and press cuttings have helped a lot, too. Inevitably, though, I've had to rely on my memory to reconstruct some of the conversations and the chains that connected various events.

Given the amount of alcohol consumed at Internet events, there's a possibility that my memory has let me down in places. If I've quoted you inaccurately, then I apologise, sincerely. Feel free to email me with any corrections – paul@bringingnothing.com – and I'll them put on my blog, www.bringingnothing.com (which also contains bonus content and all that good stuff).

Alternatively, perhaps try to say something more memorable next time.

. . .

And so to the thank-yous. If I know the entrepreneurs featured in this book – and I do – then this will be the first page they turn to, before even starting to read the rest of the book. I don't blame them; that's exactly what I'd do, too.

Thanks firstly to the London Internet community, without whom there would be no story to tell. Particularly Robert Loch, Angus Bankes, Michael Smith, Tom Boardman, Richard Moross, Emily Dubberley, Oli Barrett, Zoe Margolis and Alex Tew. Alex: sorry about the trainers. And Michael: feel free to copy and paste any part of the book for your next business card. What's mine is yours, you cheeky bastard.

Thanks to Clare Christian for being a great friend and an amazing business partner and for giving me more opportunities than a lazy law student ever deserved. Thanks to Heather Smith and Clare Weber for all of your hard work during my time at The Friday Project – your professionalism saved my arse on more occasions than I can count.

Thanks to Maggie Richards for constantly reminding me that we're all responsible for the paths we take and to Michelle Acton-Bond, Anna Melville-James, Eddie Crozier, Paul Walsh, Scott Ruth-erford, Sarah Bee, Elizabeth Varley, Ruth 'Mimi' Fowler and the rest of the members of Mr Rong's for always trying to convince me to take the path marked 'Warning: danger of death'.

Thanks to my parents for patiently rolling their eyes as their eldest son flits from job to job. I owe them everything. Thanks to my agent, Robert Kirby, and my editor, Alan Samson, for being a dozen kinds of brilliant and for batting back the bores. Thanks to Bea Hemming for taking care of all those things that people in publishing houses rarely get credit for but, if left undone, books would never get published – and a special thank you to Rebecca Gray for being the best publicity manager a book could wish for, and for still talking to me, despite what I did to 'those poor women'.

Thanks to Karl Webster for all the years of brilliant writing and exciting adventures. May you enjoy success and happiness in all that you do.

And finally to Savannah Rose Christensen: thank you for sticking around through the best of times and the worst of times. Without you lots of things would still have been possible, but none of them would have meant a damn thing. This book is dedicated to you.